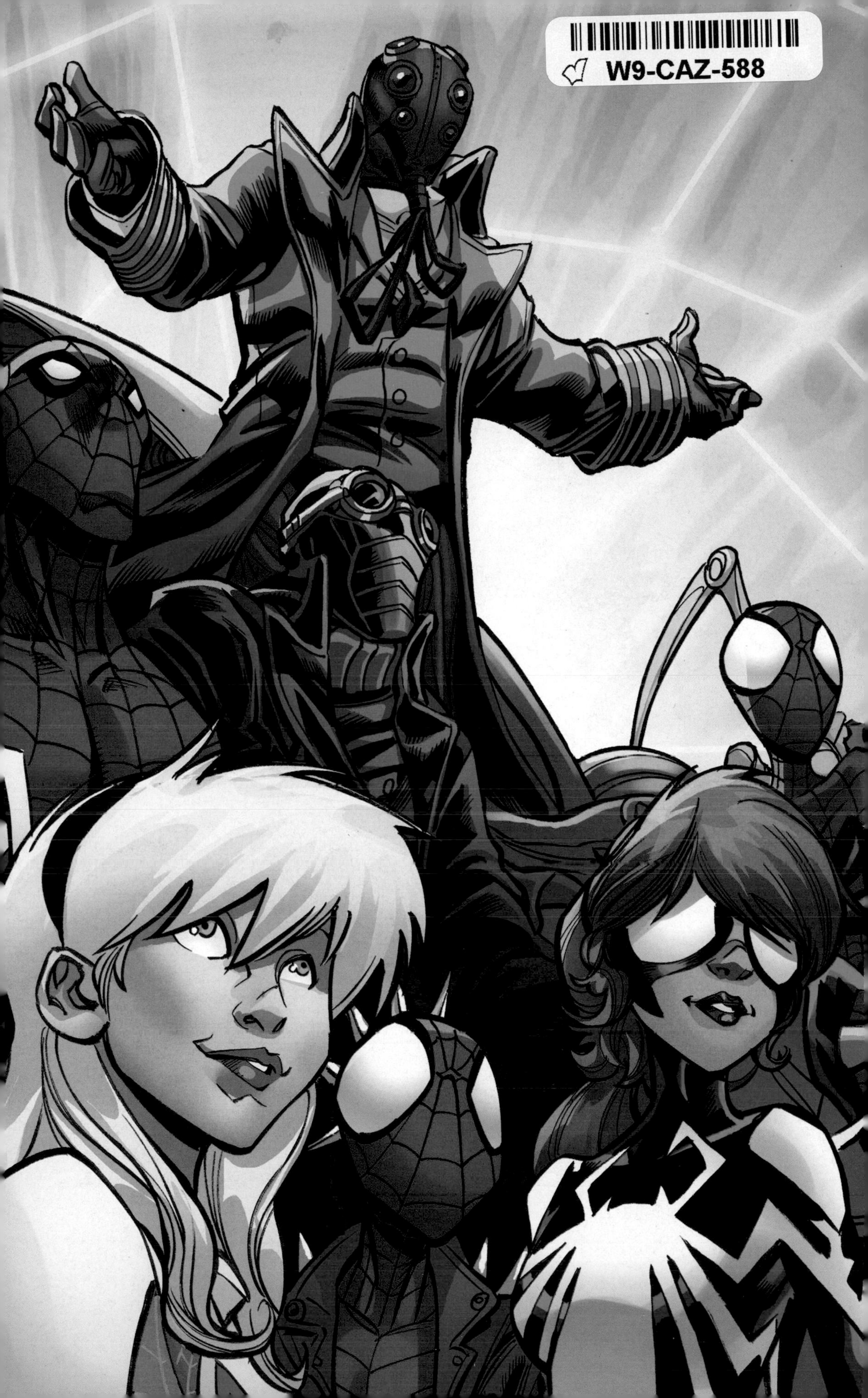

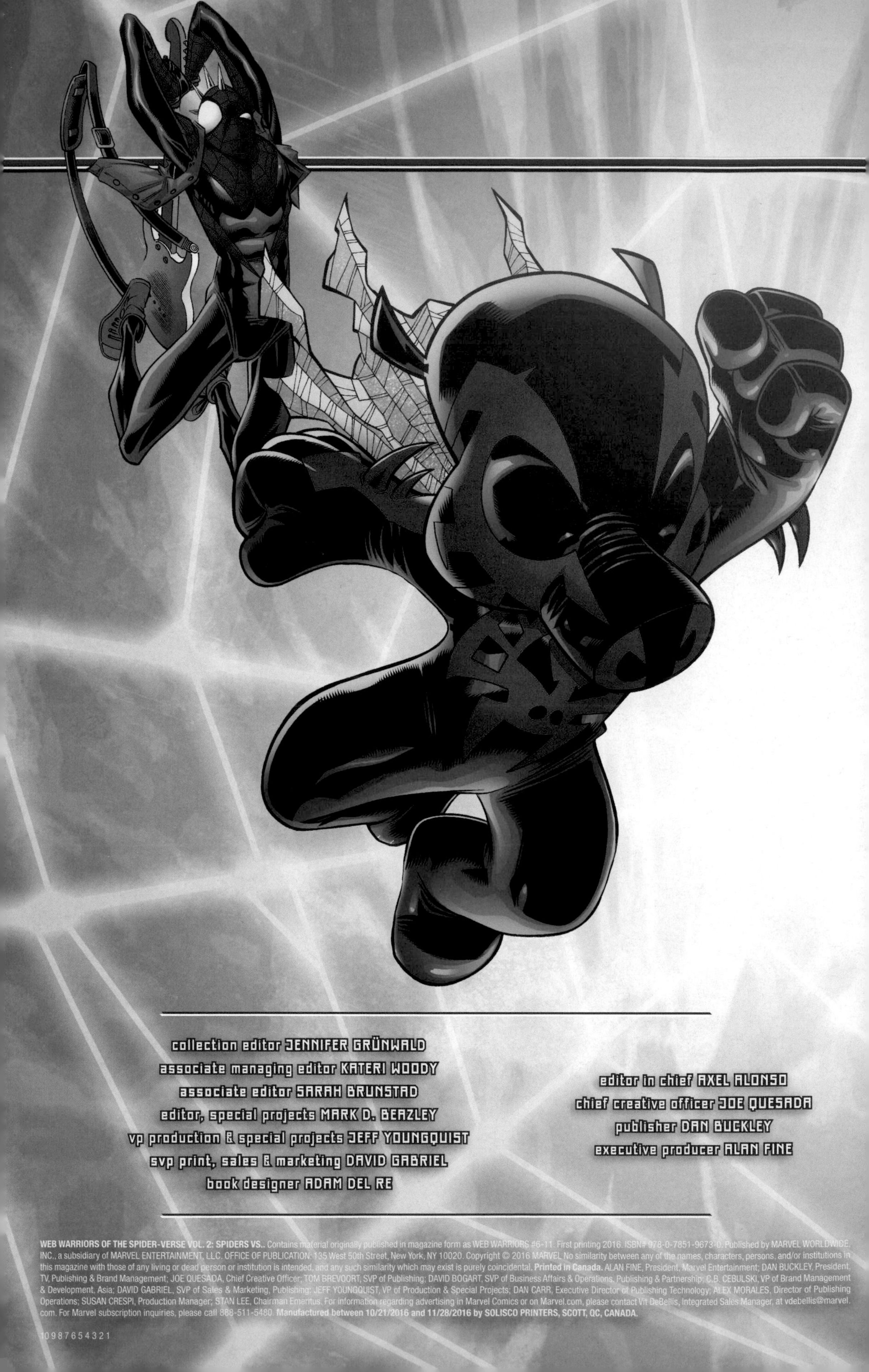

collection editor JENNIFER GRÜNWALD
associate managing editor KATERI WOODY
associate editor SARAH BRUNSTAD
editor, special projects MARK D. BEAZLEY
vp production & special projects JEFF YOUNGQUIST
svp print, sales & marketing DAVID GABRIEL
book designer ADAM DEL RE

editor in chief AXEL ALONSO
chief creative officer JOE QUESADA
publisher DAN BUCKLEY
executive producer ALAN FINE

WEB WARRIORS OF THE SPIDER-VERSE VOL. 2: SPIDERS VS.. Contains material originally published in magazine form as WEB WARRIORS #6-11. First printing 2016. ISBN# 978-0-7851-9673-0. Published by MARVEL WORLDWIDE, INC., a subsidiary of MARVEL ENTERTAINMENT, LLC. OFFICE OF PUBLICATION: 135 West 50th Street, New York, NY 10020. **Printed in Canada.** ALAN FINE, President, Marvel Entertainment; DAN BUCKLEY, President, TV, Publishing & Brand Management; JOE QUESADA, Chief Creative Officer; TOM BREVOORT, SVP of Publishing; DAVID BOGART, SVP of Business Affairs & Operations, Publishing & Partnership; C.B. CEBULSKI, VP of Brand Management & Development, Asia; DAVID GABRIEL, SVP of Sales & Marketing, Publishing; JEFF YOUNGQUIST, VP of Production & Special Projects; DAN CARR, Executive Director of Publishing Technology; ALEX MORALES, Director of Publishing Operations; SUSAN CRESPI, Production Manager; STAN LEE, Chairman Emeritus. For information regarding advertising in Marvel Comics or on Marvel.com, please contact Vit DeBellis, Integrated Sales Manager, at vdebellis@marvel.com. For Marvel subscription inquiries, please call 888-511-5480. **Manufactured between 10/21/2016 and 11/28/2016 by SOLISCO PRINTERS, SCOTT, QC, CANADA.**

10 9 8 7 6 5 4 3 2 1

WHEN A DANGEROUS FAMILY OF INTERDIMENSIONAL VAMPIRES STARTED HUNTING SPIDERS, THE SPIDER-MEN AND WOMEN FROM ACROSS THE MULTIVERSE HAD TO BAND TOGETHER FOR THEIR OWN SURVIVAL. MANY FELL IN THE CONFLICT, AND NOW A SMALL TEAM OF THOSE WHO SURVIVED USE THEIR POWERS TO SHOULDER THE RESPONSIBILITIES OF THE FALLEN AS THE...

PROTECTORS OF THE SPIDER-VERSE
WEB-WARRIORS

SPIDERS VS.

writer
MIKE COSTA

penciler
DAVID BALDEON
with JAY FOSGITT (#10)

inkers

WALDEN WONG (#6-8, #10-11), **TERRY PALLOT** (#6, #11),
SCOTT HANNA (#6, #11), **RICK MAGYAR** (#7, #9),
ROBERTO POGGI (#8), **MARC DEERING** (#9),
JOHN DELL (#10-11), **JAY FOSGITT** (#10) &
LORENZO RUGGIERO (#11)

colorists

MATT YACKEY with **RACHELLE ROSENBERG** (#6, #8, #11),
ANDREW CROSSLEY (#10) & **ANDRES MOSSA** (#11)

letterer
VC's JOE CARAMAGNA

cover art
JULIAN TOTINO TEDESCO

editor
DEVIN LEWIS

senior editor
NICK LOWE

THE WEB-WARRIORS HAVE SWORN TO PROTECT THE
WEB OF LIFE AND DESTINY — A TREMENDOUS WEB ON
EARTH-001 THAT LINKS ALL OF REALITY TOGETHER —
FROM THE FORCES OF EVIL.

MADE UP OF THE SPIDER-MEN AND WOMEN (AND A PIG)
OF VARIOUS WORLDS, THEY TRAVEL THE WEB IN
ORDER TO SAFEGUARD WORLDS THAT HAVE BEEN
LEFT WITHOUT THEIR SPIDERS.

LED BY ANYA CORAZON (SPIDER-GIRL OF EARTH-616),
THE TEAM HAS SUFFERED LOSSES — INCLUDING THE APPARENT
DEATHS OF BILLY BRADDOCK (SPIDER-UK OF THE
CAPTAIN BRITAIN CORPS. OF EARTH-833) AND
MAYDAY PARKER (SPIDER-WOMAN OF EARTH-982).

DESPITE THE DANGER, THE WEB-WARRIORS CONTINUE TO TRAVEL
THE WEB AND PROTECT REALITY, ONE WORLD AT A TIME.

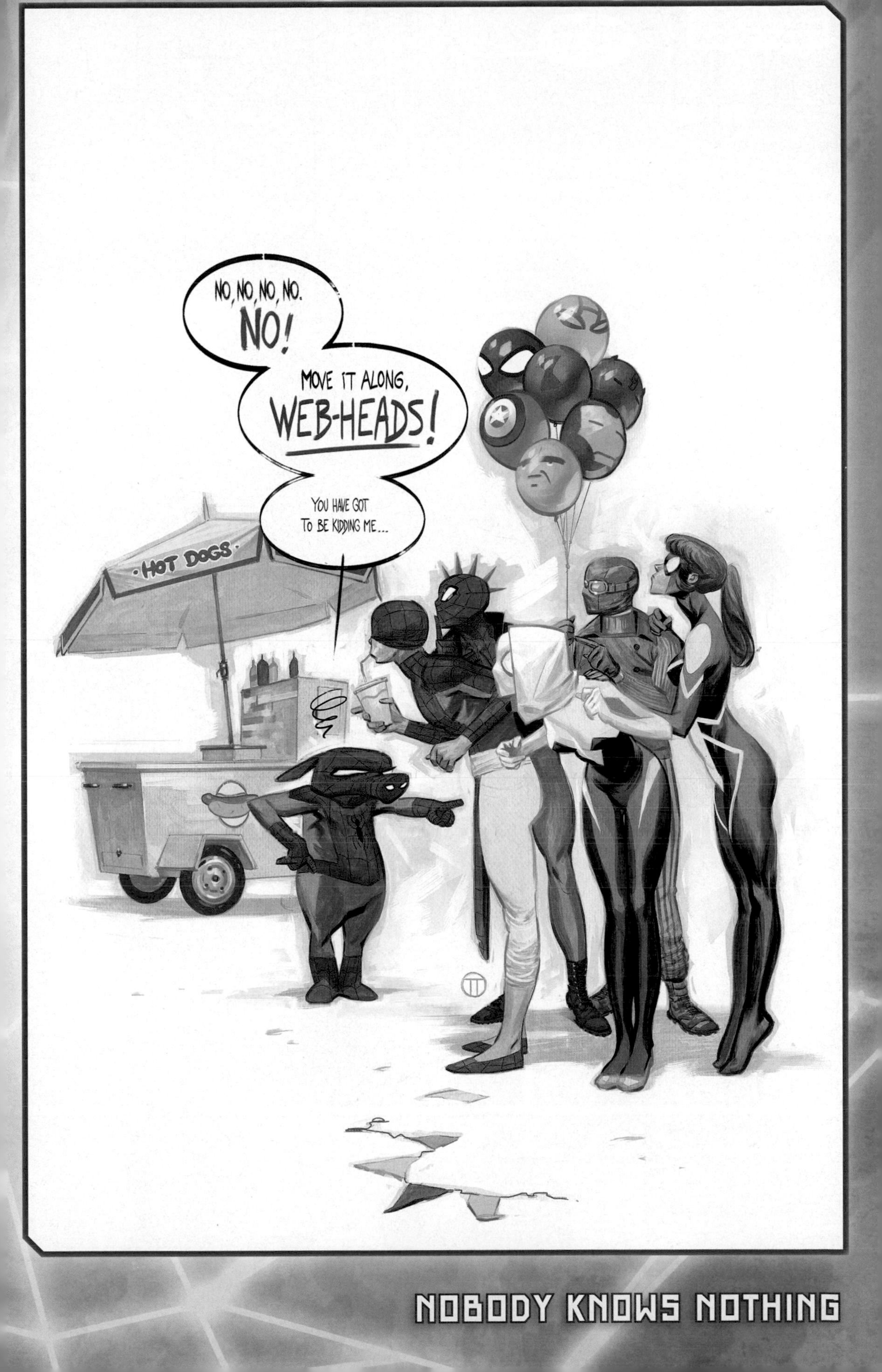
NO, NO, NO, NO. NO!
MOVE IT ALONG, WEB-HEADS!
YOU HAVE GOT TO BE KIDDING ME...
HOT DOGS

NOBODY KNOWS NOTHING

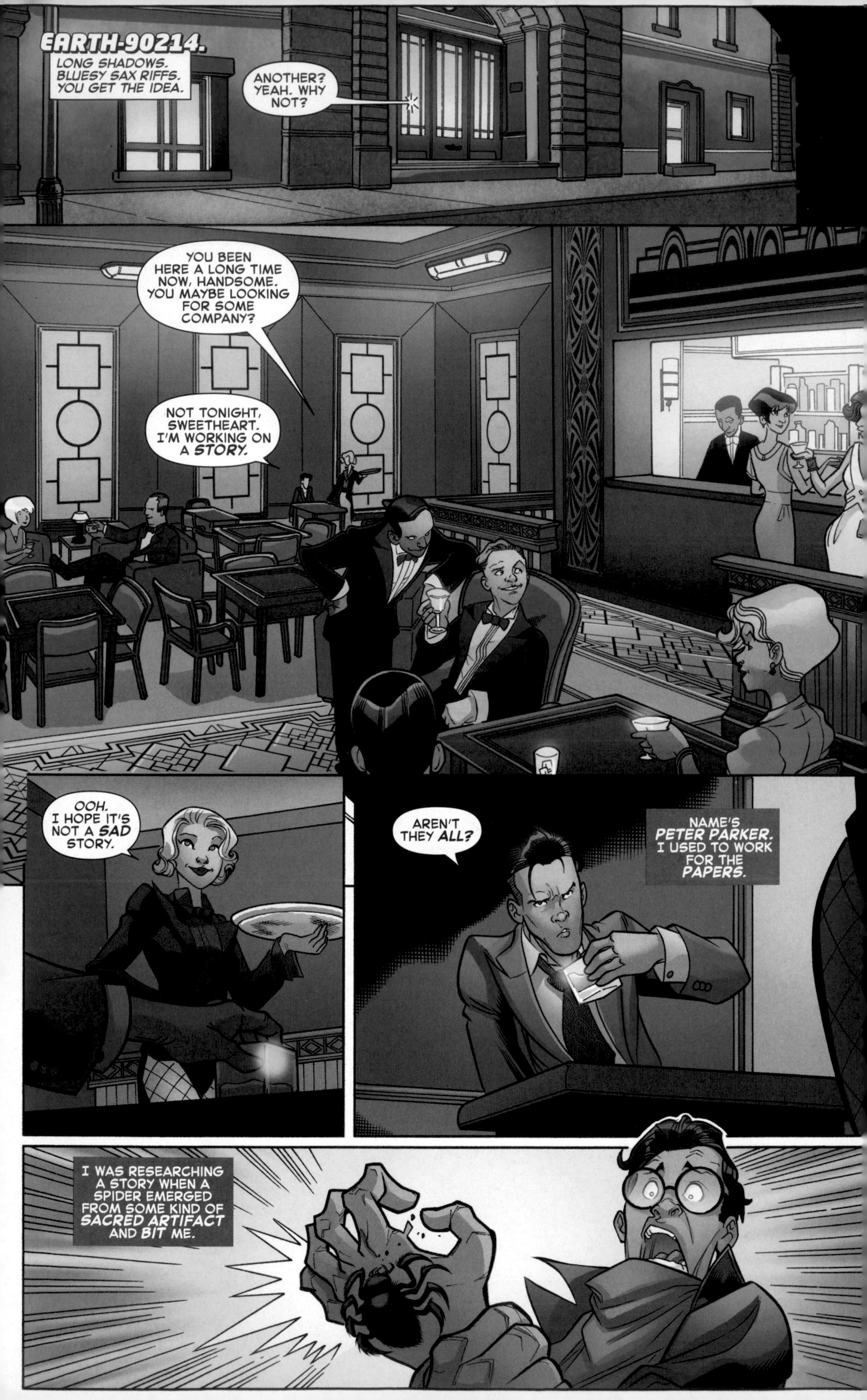
EARTH-90214.
LONG SHADOWS. BLUESY SAX RIFFS. YOU GET THE IDEA.
ANOTHER? YEAH. WHY NOT?
YOU BEEN HERE A LONG TIME NOW, HANDSOME. YOU MAYBE LOOKING FOR SOME COMPANY?
NOT TONIGHT, SWEETHEART. I'M WORKING ON A STORY.
OOH. I HOPE IT'S NOT A SAD STORY.
AREN'T THEY ALL?
NAME'S PETER PARKER. I USED TO WORK FOR THE PAPERS.
I WAS RESEARCHING A STORY WHEN A SPIDER EMERGED FROM SOME KIND OF SACRED ARTIFACT AND BIT ME.

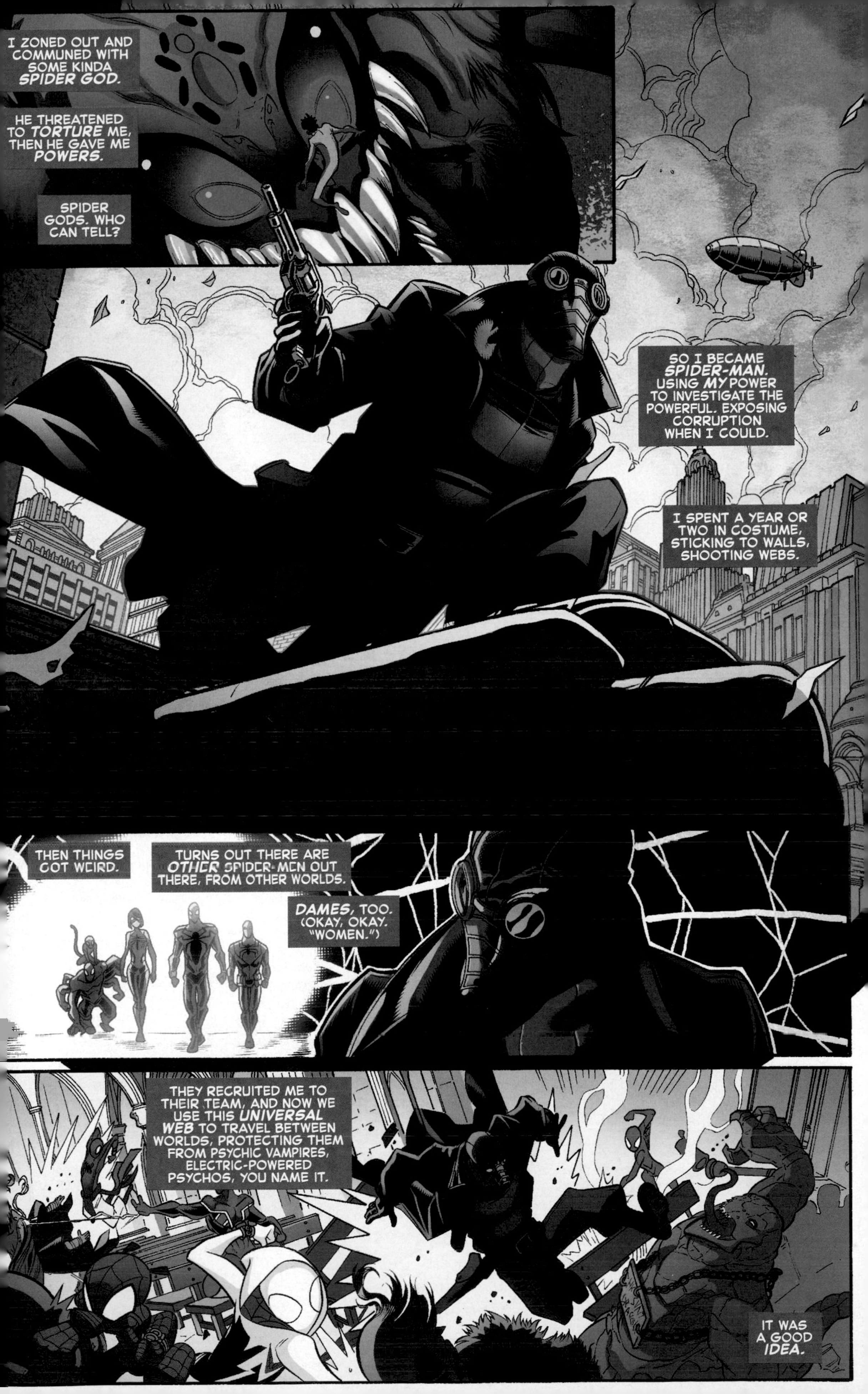
I ZONED OUT AND COMMUNED WITH SOME KINDA SPIDER GOD.
HE THREATENED TO TORTURE ME, THEN HE GAVE ME POWERS.
SPIDER GODS. WHO CAN TELL?
SO I BECAME SPIDER-MAN. USING MY POWER TO INVESTIGATE THE POWERFUL. EXPOSING CORRUPTION WHEN I COULD.
I SPENT A YEAR OR TWO IN COSTUME, STICKING TO WALLS, SHOOTING WEBS.
THEN THINGS GOT WEIRD.
TURNS OUT THERE ARE OTHER SPIDER-MEN OUT THERE, FROM OTHER WORLDS.
DAMES, TOO. (OKAY, OKAY. "WOMEN.")
THEY RECRUITED ME TO THEIR TEAM, AND NOW WE USE THIS UNIVERSAL WEB TO TRAVEL BETWEEN WORLDS, PROTECTING THEM FROM PSYCHIC VAMPIRES, ELECTRIC-POWERED PSYCHOS, YOU NAME IT.
IT WAS A GOOD IDEA.

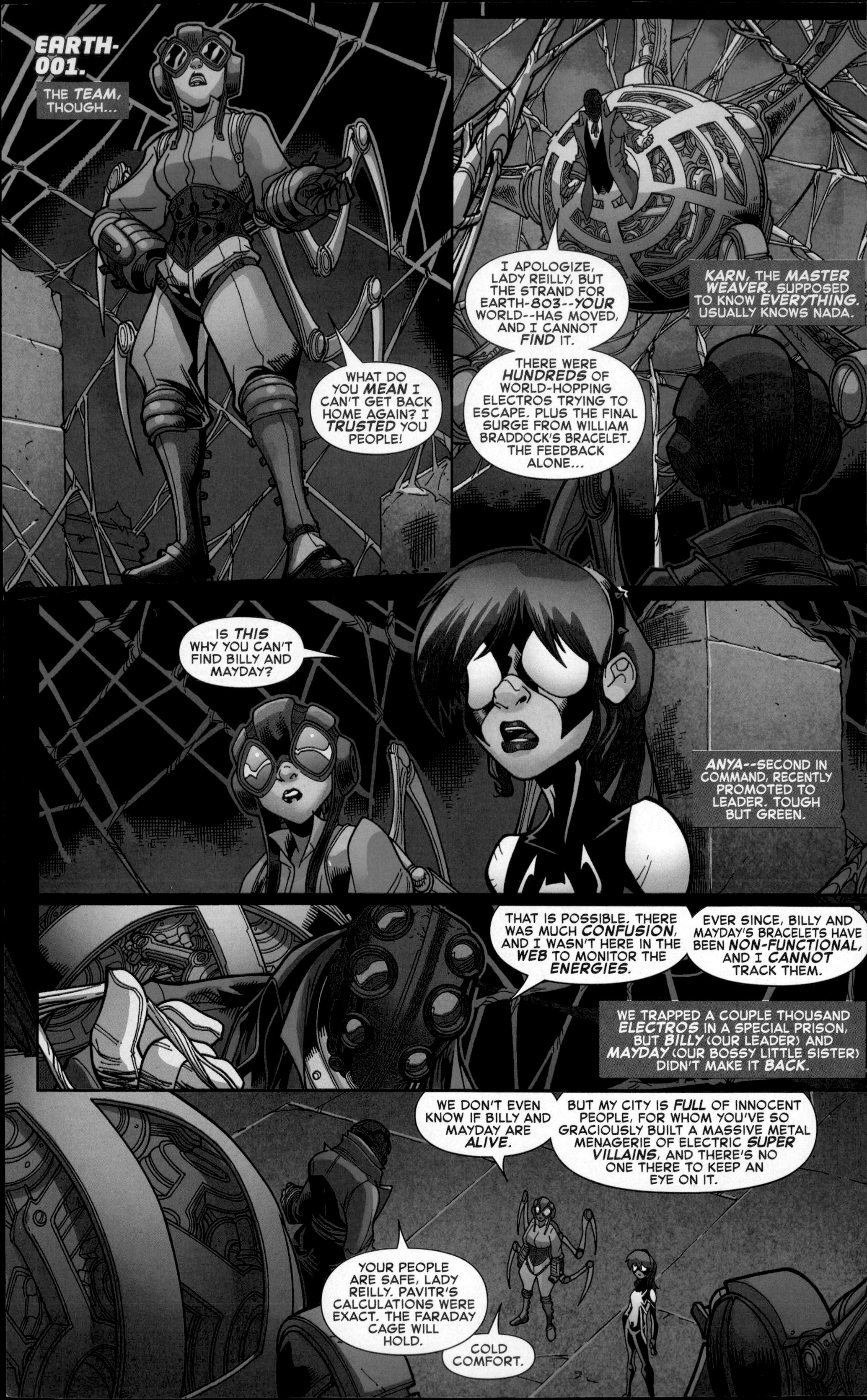
EARTH-001.
THE TEAM, THOUGH...
WHAT DO YOU MEAN I CAN'T GET BACK HOME AGAIN? I TRUSTED YOU PEOPLE!
I APOLOGIZE, LADY REILLY, BUT THE STRAND FOR EARTH-803--YOUR WORLD--HAS MOVED, AND I CANNOT FIND IT.
THERE WERE HUNDREDS OF WORLD-HOPPING ELECTROS TRYING TO ESCAPE. PLUS THE FINAL SURGE FROM WILLIAM BRADDOCK'S BRACELET. THE FEEDBACK ALONE...
KARN, THE MASTER WEAVER. SUPPOSED TO KNOW EVERYTHING. USUALLY KNOWS NADA.
IS THIS WHY YOU CAN'T FIND BILLY AND MAYDAY?
ANYA--SECOND IN COMMAND, RECENTLY PROMOTED TO LEADER. TOUGH BUT GREEN.
THAT IS POSSIBLE. THERE WAS MUCH CONFUSION, AND I WASN'T HERE IN THE WEB TO MONITOR THE ENERGIES.
EVER SINCE, BILLY AND MAYDAY'S BRACELETS HAVE BEEN NON-FUNCTIONAL, AND I CANNOT TRACK THEM.
WE TRAPPED A COUPLE THOUSAND ELECTROS IN A SPECIAL PRISON, BUT BILLY (OUR LEADER) AND MAYDAY (OUR BOSSY LITTLE SISTER) DIDN'T MAKE IT BACK.
WE DON'T EVEN KNOW IF BILLY AND MAYDAY ARE ALIVE.
BUT MY CITY IS FULL OF INNOCENT PEOPLE, FOR WHOM YOU'VE SO GRACIOUSLY BUILT A MASSIVE METAL MENAGERIE OF ELECTRIC SUPER VILLAINS, AND THERE'S NO ONE THERE TO KEEP AN EYE ON IT.
YOUR PEOPLE ARE SAFE, LADY REILLY. PAVITR'S CALCULATIONS WERE EXACT. THE FARADAY CAGE WILL HOLD.
COLD COMFORT.

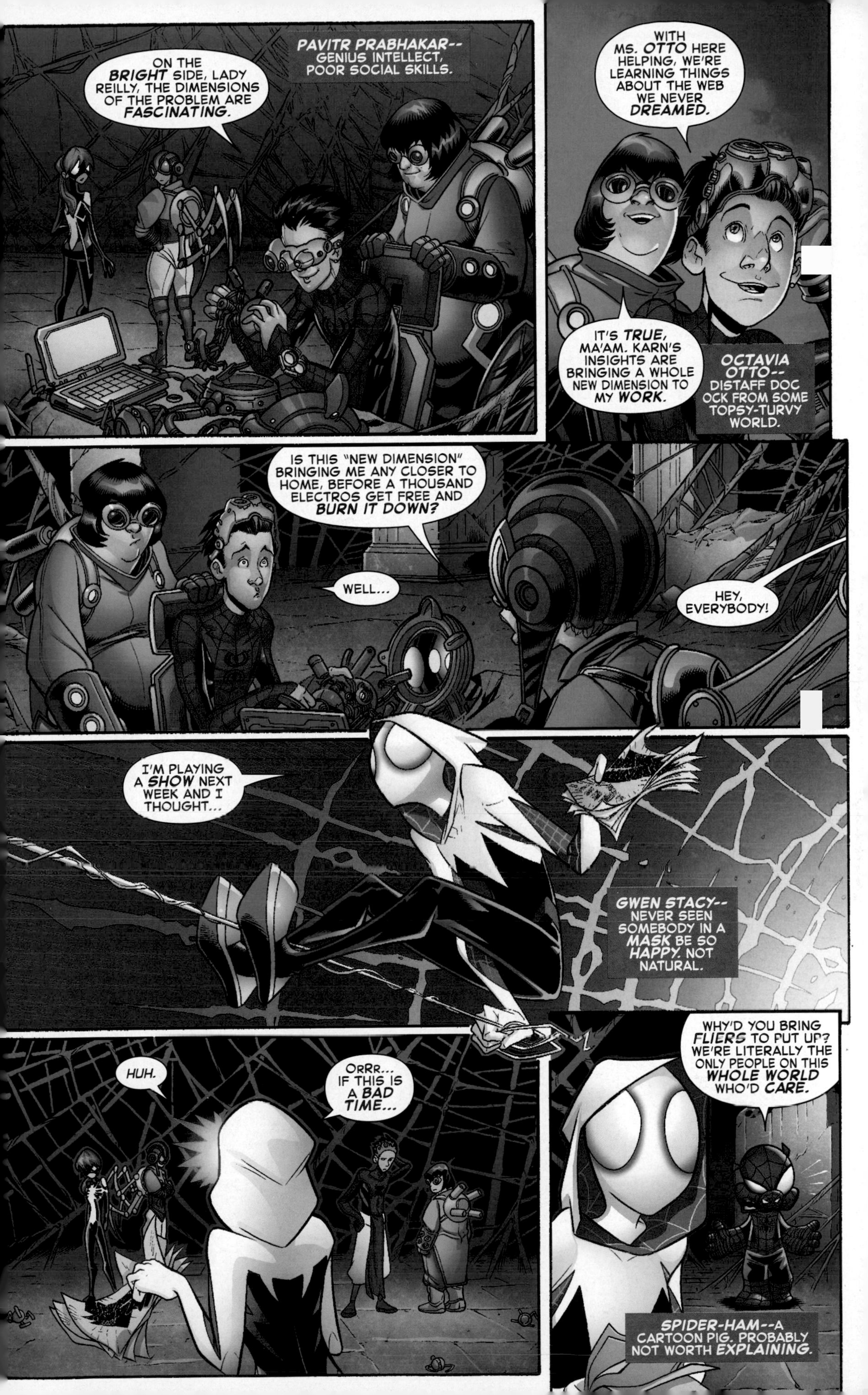
PAVITR PRABHAKAR-- GENIUS INTELLECT, POOR SOCIAL SKILLS.
ON THE BRIGHT SIDE, LADY REILLY, THE DIMENSIONS OF THE PROBLEM ARE FASCINATING.
WITH MS. OTTO HERE HELPING, WE'RE LEARNING THINGS ABOUT THE WEB WE NEVER DREAMED.
IT'S TRUE, MA'AM. KARN'S INSIGHTS ARE BRINGING A WHOLE NEW DIMENSION TO MY WORK.
OCTAVIA OTTO-- DISTAFF DOC OCK FROM SOME TOPSY-TURVY WORLD.
IS THIS "NEW DIMENSION" BRINGING ME ANY CLOSER TO HOME, BEFORE A THOUSAND ELECTROS GET FREE AND BURN IT DOWN?
WELL...
HEY, EVERYBODY!
I'M PLAYING A SHOW NEXT WEEK AND I THOUGHT...
GWEN STACY-- NEVER SEEN SOMEBODY IN A MASK BE SO HAPPY. NOT NATURAL.
HUH.
ORRR... IF THIS IS A BAD TIME...
WHY'D YOU BRING FLIERS TO PUT UP? WE'RE LITERALLY THE ONLY PEOPLE ON THIS WHOLE WORLD WHO'D CARE.
SPIDER-HAM--A CARTOON PIG. PROBABLY NOT WORTH EXPLAINING.

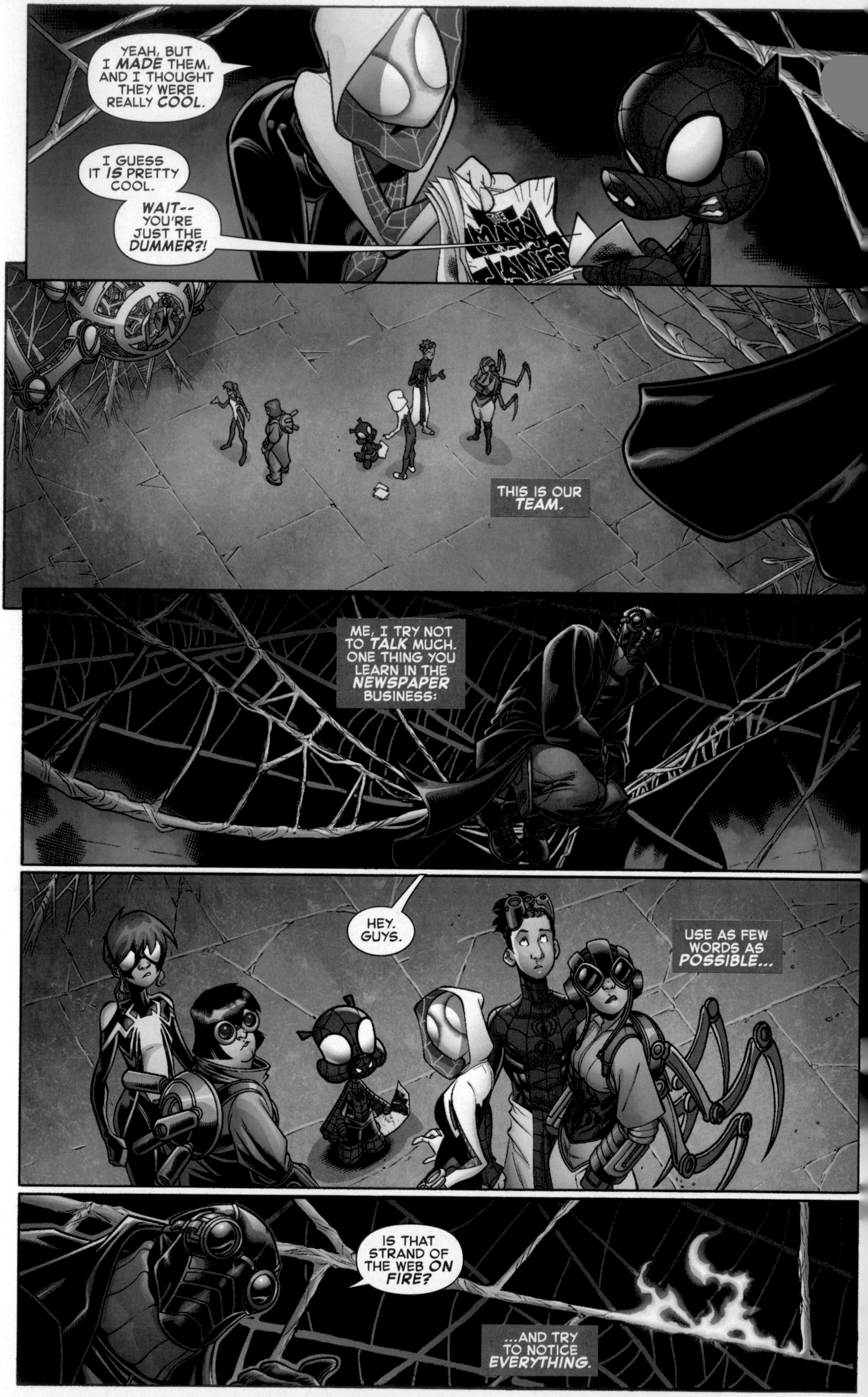
YEAH, BUT I MADE THEM, AND I THOUGHT THEY WERE REALLY COOL.
I GUESS IT IS PRETTY COOL.
WAIT-- YOU'RE JUST THE DUMMER?!
THIS IS OUR TEAM.
ME, I TRY NOT TO TALK MUCH. ONE THING YOU LEARN IN THE NEWSPAPER BUSINESS:
HEY. GUYS.
USE AS FEW WORDS AS POSSIBLE...
IS THAT STRAND OF THE WEB ON FIRE?
...AND TRY TO NOTICE EVERYTHING.

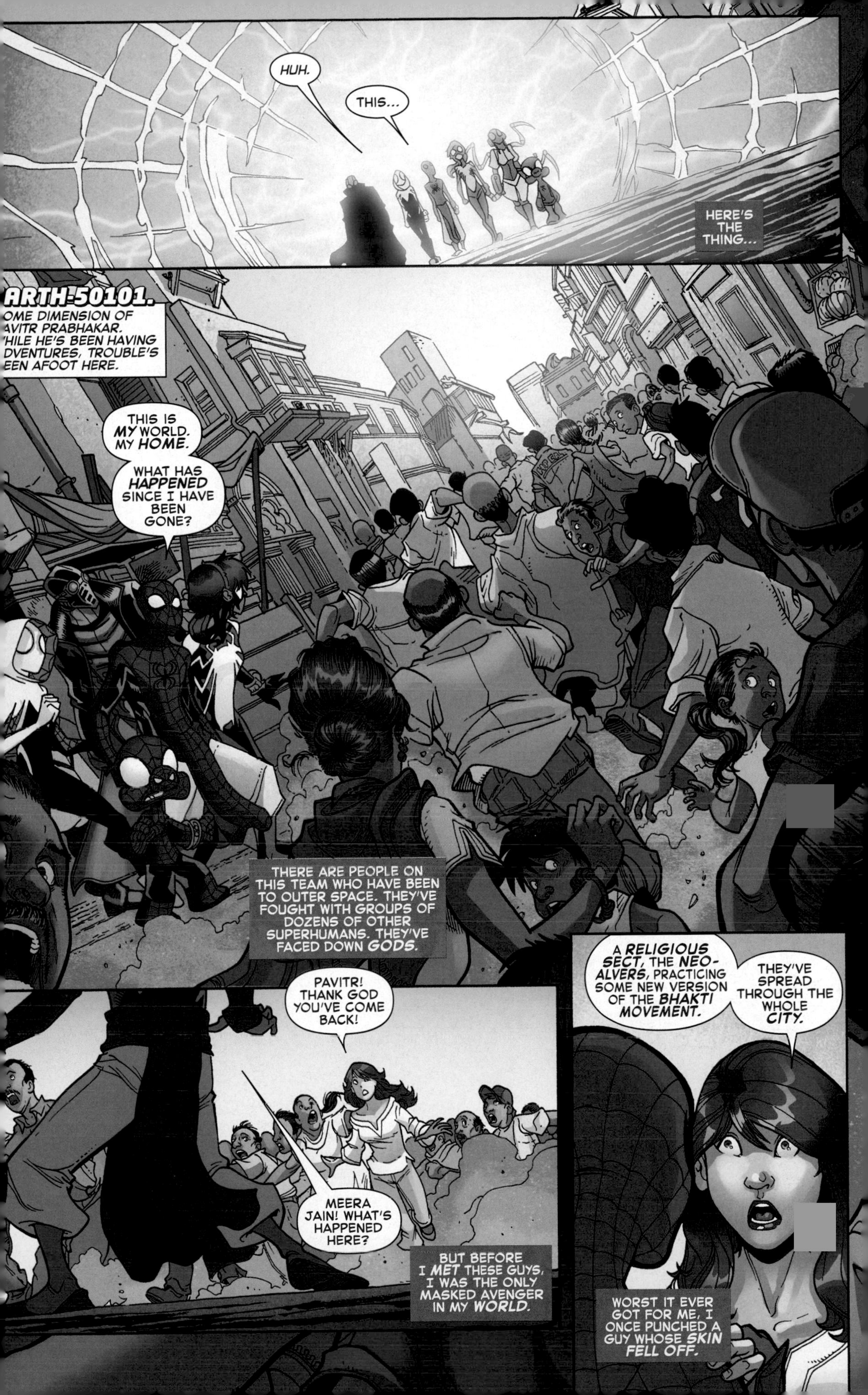

HUH.
THIS...
HERE'S THE THING...
ARTH-50101.
OME DIMENSION OF AVITR PRABHAKAR. HILE HE'S BEEN HAVING DVENTURES, TROUBLE'S EEN AFOOT HERE.
THIS IS MY WORLD. MY HOME.
WHAT HAS HAPPENED SINCE I HAVE BEEN GONE?
THERE ARE PEOPLE ON THIS TEAM WHO HAVE BEEN TO OUTER SPACE. THEY'VE FOUGHT WITH GROUPS OF DOZENS OF OTHER SUPERHUMANS. THEY'VE FACED DOWN GODS.
PAVITR! THANK GOD YOU'VE COME BACK!
MEERA JAIN! WHAT'S HAPPENED HERE?
BUT BEFORE I MET THESE GUYS, I WAS THE ONLY MASKED AVENGER IN MY WORLD.
A RELIGIOUS SECT, THE NEO-ALVERS, PRACTICING SOME NEW VERSION OF THE BHAKTI MOVEMENT.
THEY'VE SPREAD THROUGH THE WHOLE CITY.
WORST IT EVER GOT FOR ME, I ONCE PUNCHED A GUY WHOSE SKIN FELL OFF.

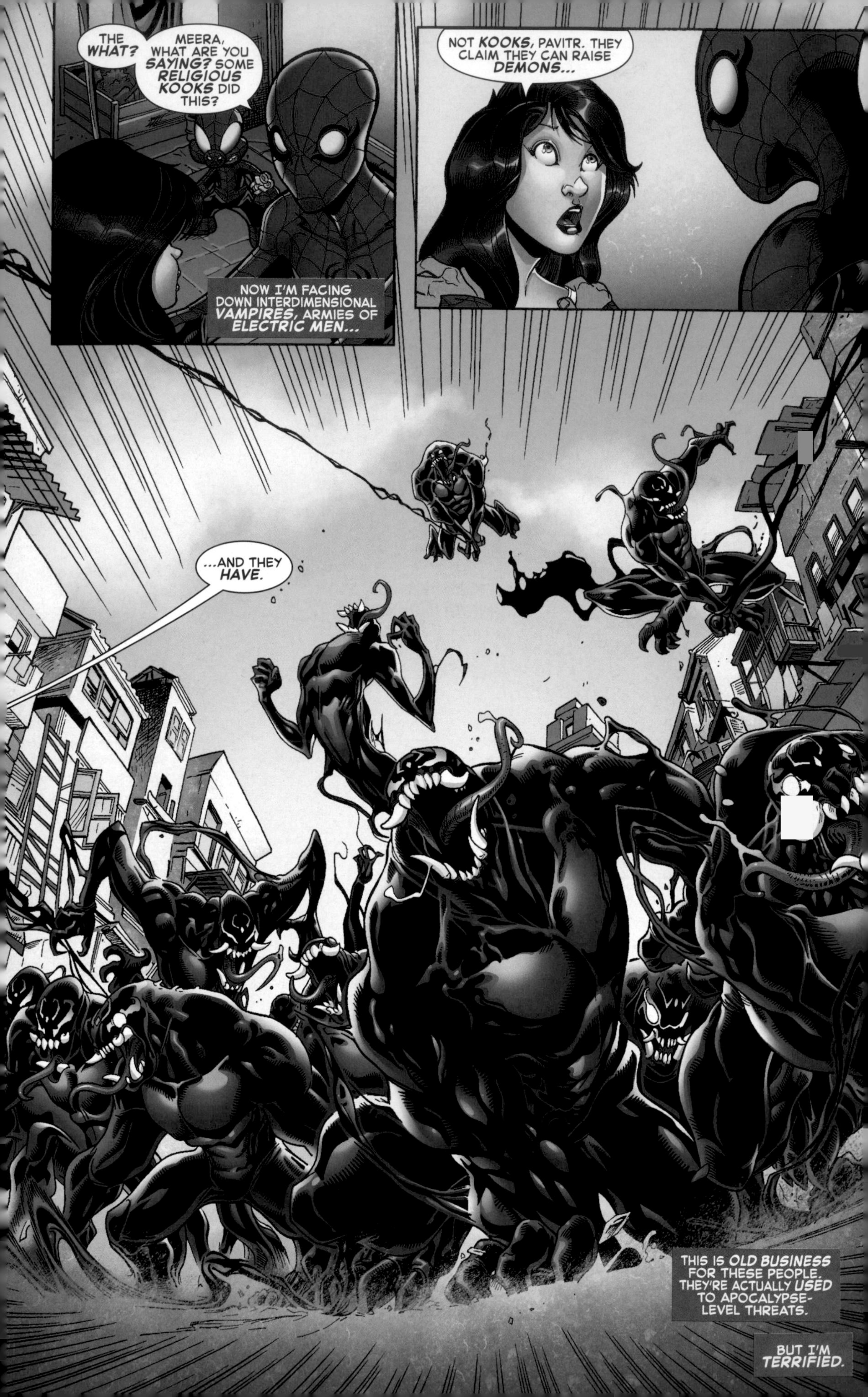
THE WHAT?
MEERA, WHAT ARE YOU SAYING? SOME RELIGIOUS KOOKS DID THIS?
NOW I'M FACING DOWN INTERDIMENSIONAL VAMPIRES, ARMIES OF ELECTRIC MEN...
NOT KOOKS, PAVITR. THEY CLAIM THEY CAN RAISE DEMONS...
...AND THEY HAVE.
THIS IS OLD BUSINESS FOR THESE PEOPLE. THEY'RE ACTUALLY USED TO APOCALYPSE-LEVEL THREATS.
BUT I'M TERRIFIED.

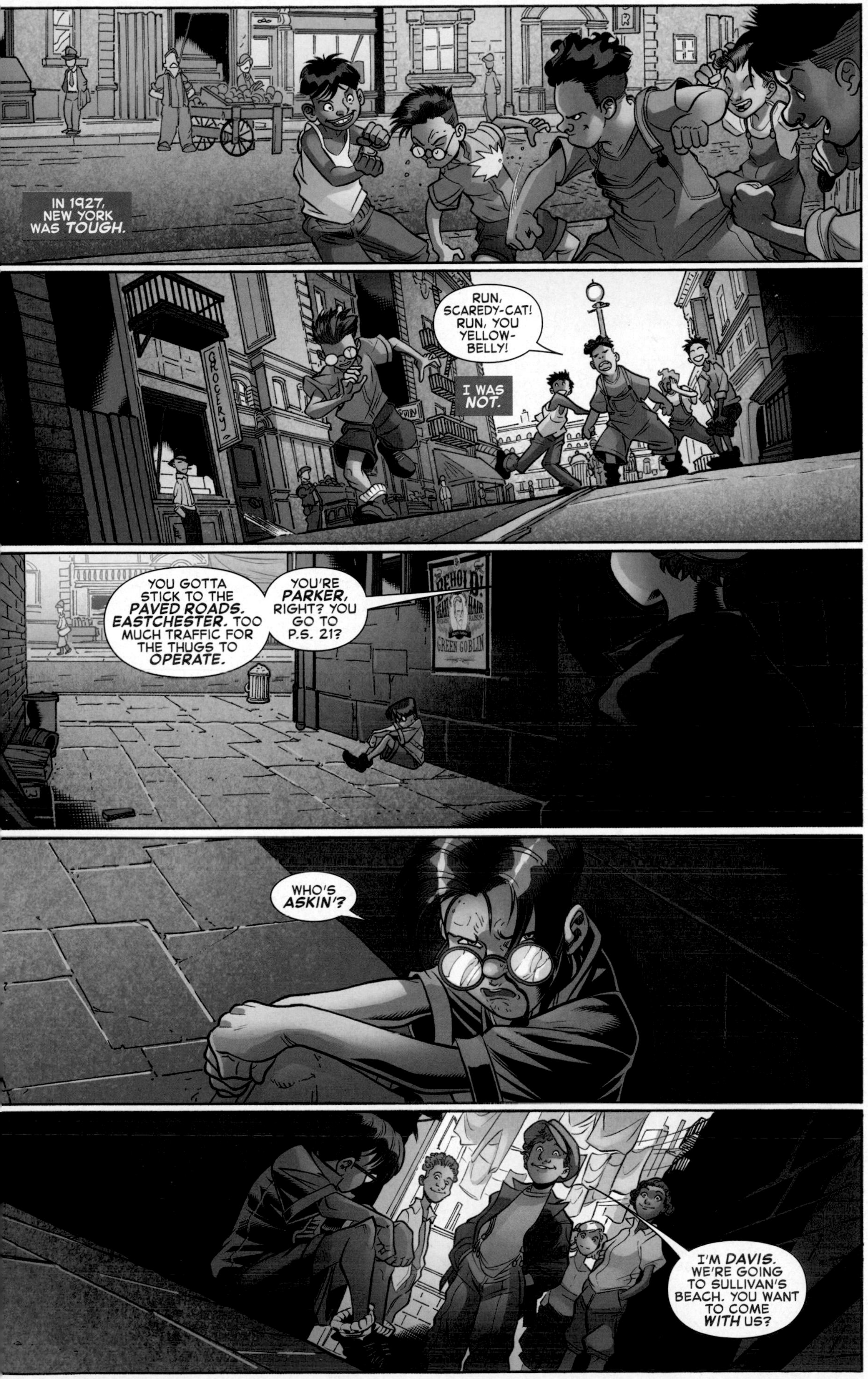
IN 1927, NEW YORK WAS TOUGH.
RUN, SCAREDY-CAT! RUN, YOU YELLOW-BELLY!
I WAS NOT.
GROCERY
YOU GOTTA STICK TO THE PAVED ROADS. EASTCHESTER. TOO MUCH TRAFFIC FOR THE THUGS TO OPERATE.
YOU'RE PARKER, RIGHT? YOU GO TO P.S. 21?
GREEN GOBLIN
WHO'S ASKIN'?
I'M DAVIS. WE'RE GOING TO SULLIVAN'S BEACH. YOU WANT TO COME WITH US?

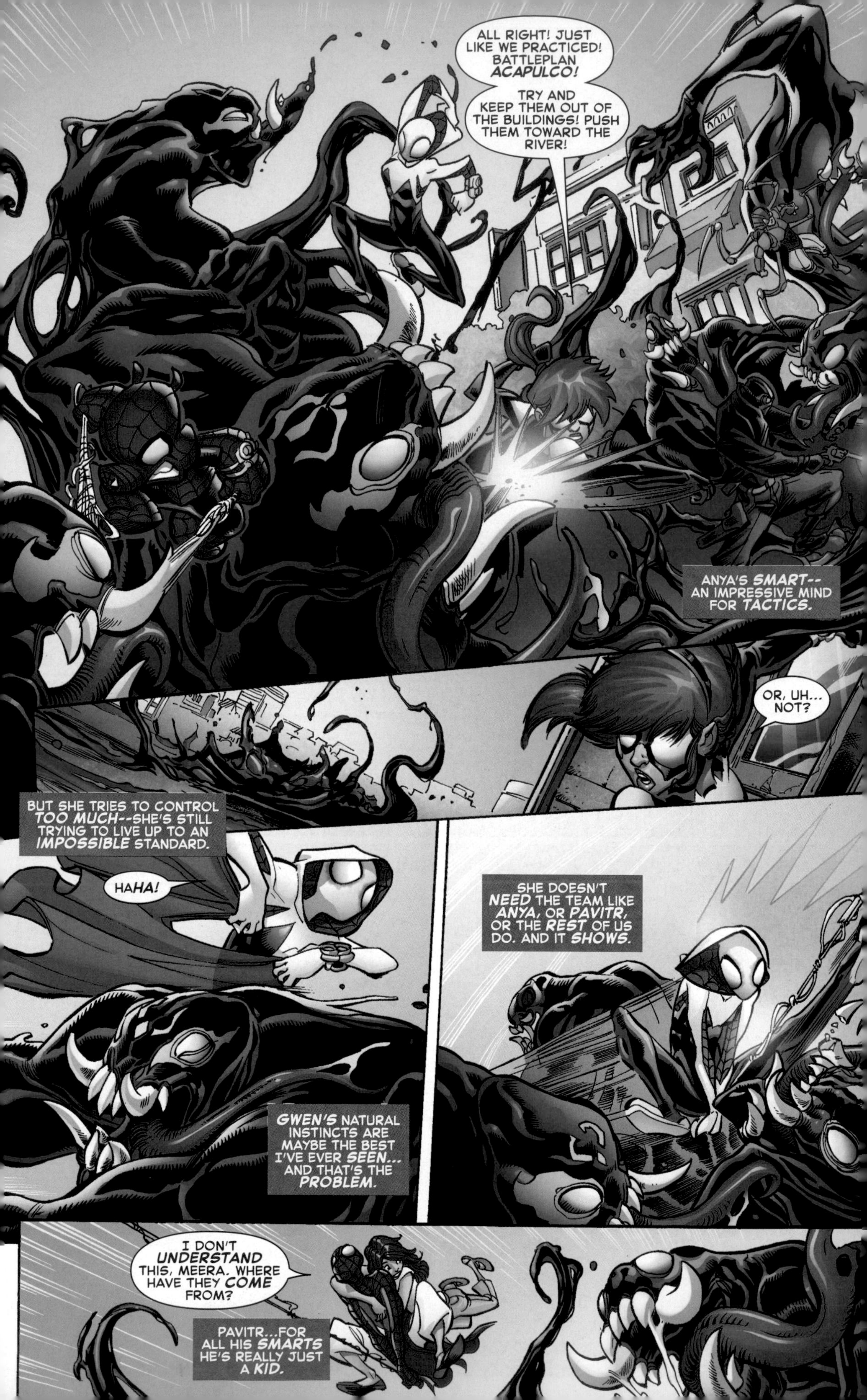
ALL RIGHT! JUST LIKE WE PRACTICED! BATTLEPLAN ACAPULCO!
TRY AND KEEP THEM OUT OF THE BUILDINGS! PUSH THEM TOWARD THE RIVER!
ANYA'S SMART-- AN IMPRESSIVE MIND FOR TACTICS.
OR, UH... NOT?
BUT SHE TRIES TO CONTROL TOO MUCH--SHE'S STILL TRYING TO LIVE UP TO AN IMPOSSIBLE STANDARD.
HAHA!
GWEN'S NATURAL INSTINCTS ARE MAYBE THE BEST I'VE EVER SEEN... AND THAT'S THE PROBLEM.
SHE DOESN'T NEED THE TEAM LIKE ANYA, OR PAVITR, OR THE REST OF US DO. AND IT SHOWS.
I DON'T UNDERSTAND THIS, MEERA. WHERE HAVE THEY COME FROM?
PAVITR...FOR ALL HIS SMARTS HE'S REALLY JUST A KID.

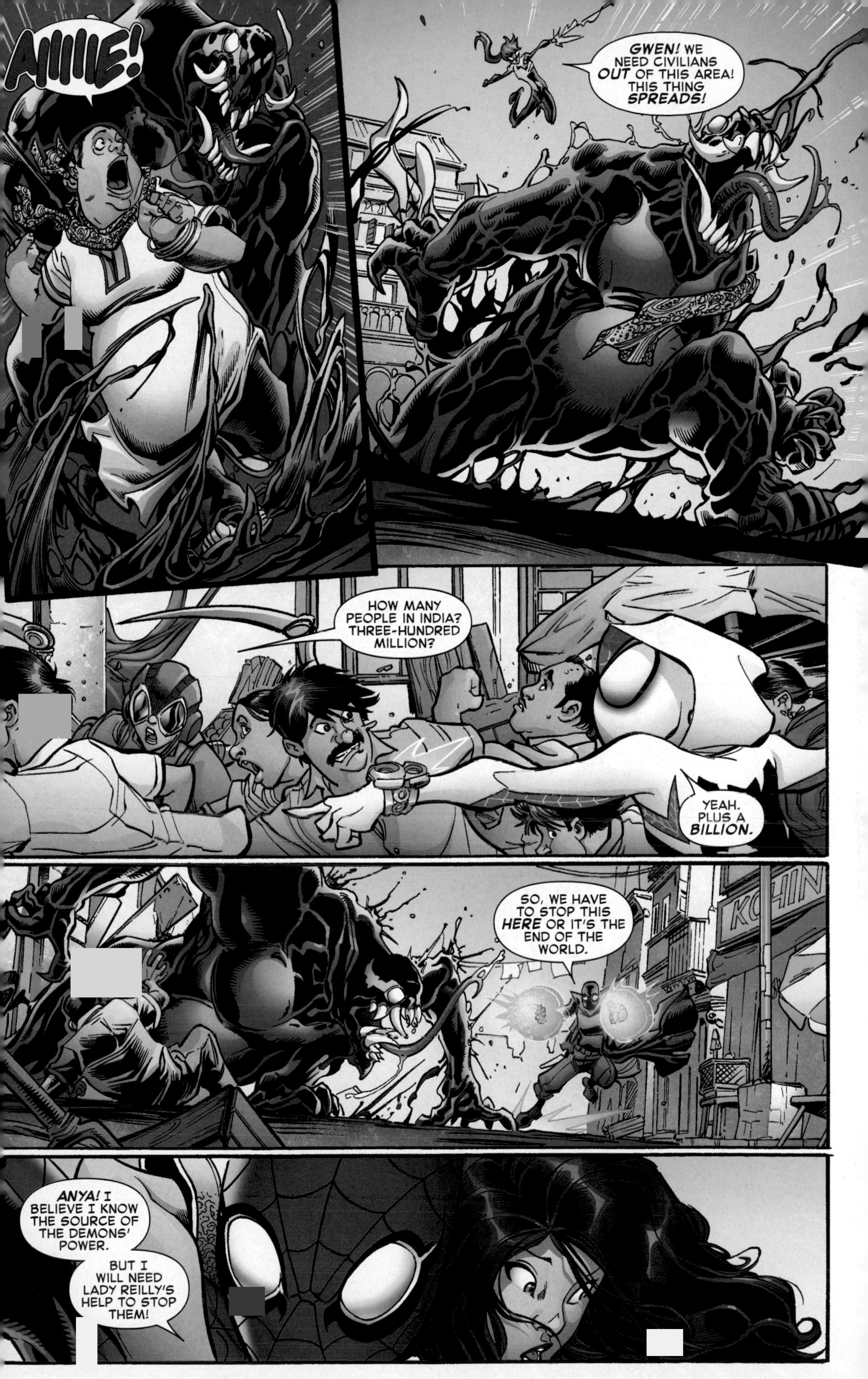
AIIIIE!
GWEN! WE NEED CIVILIANS OUT OF THIS AREA! THIS THING SPREADS!
HOW MANY PEOPLE IN INDIA? THREE-HUNDRED MILLION?
YEAH. PLUS A BILLION.
SO, WE HAVE TO STOP THIS HERE OR IT'S THE END OF THE WORLD.
ANYA! I BELIEVE I KNOW THE SOURCE OF THE DEMONS' POWER.
BUT I WILL NEED LADY REILLY'S HELP TO STOP THEM!

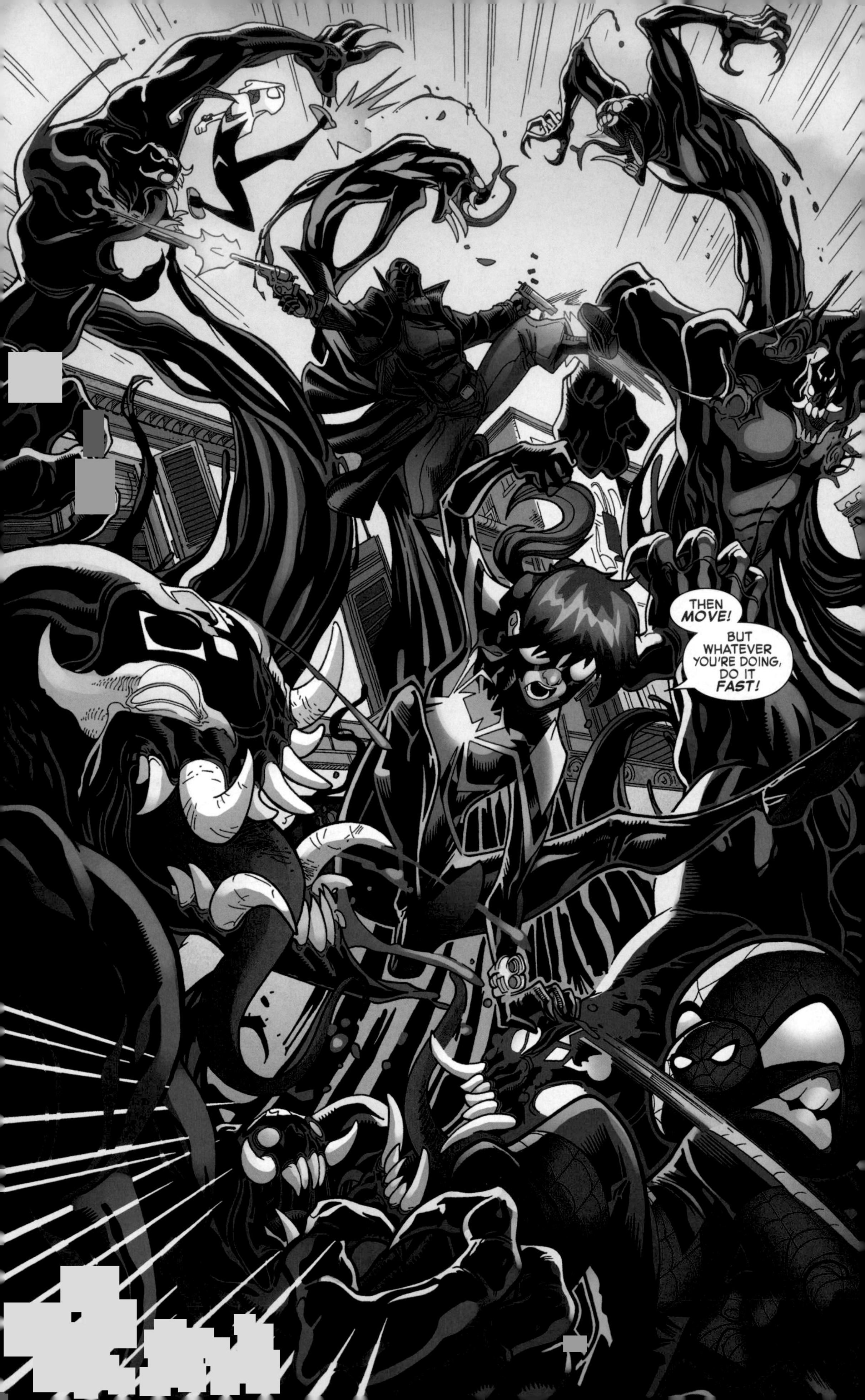
THEN MOVE!
BUT WHATEVER YOU'RE DOING, DO IT FAST!

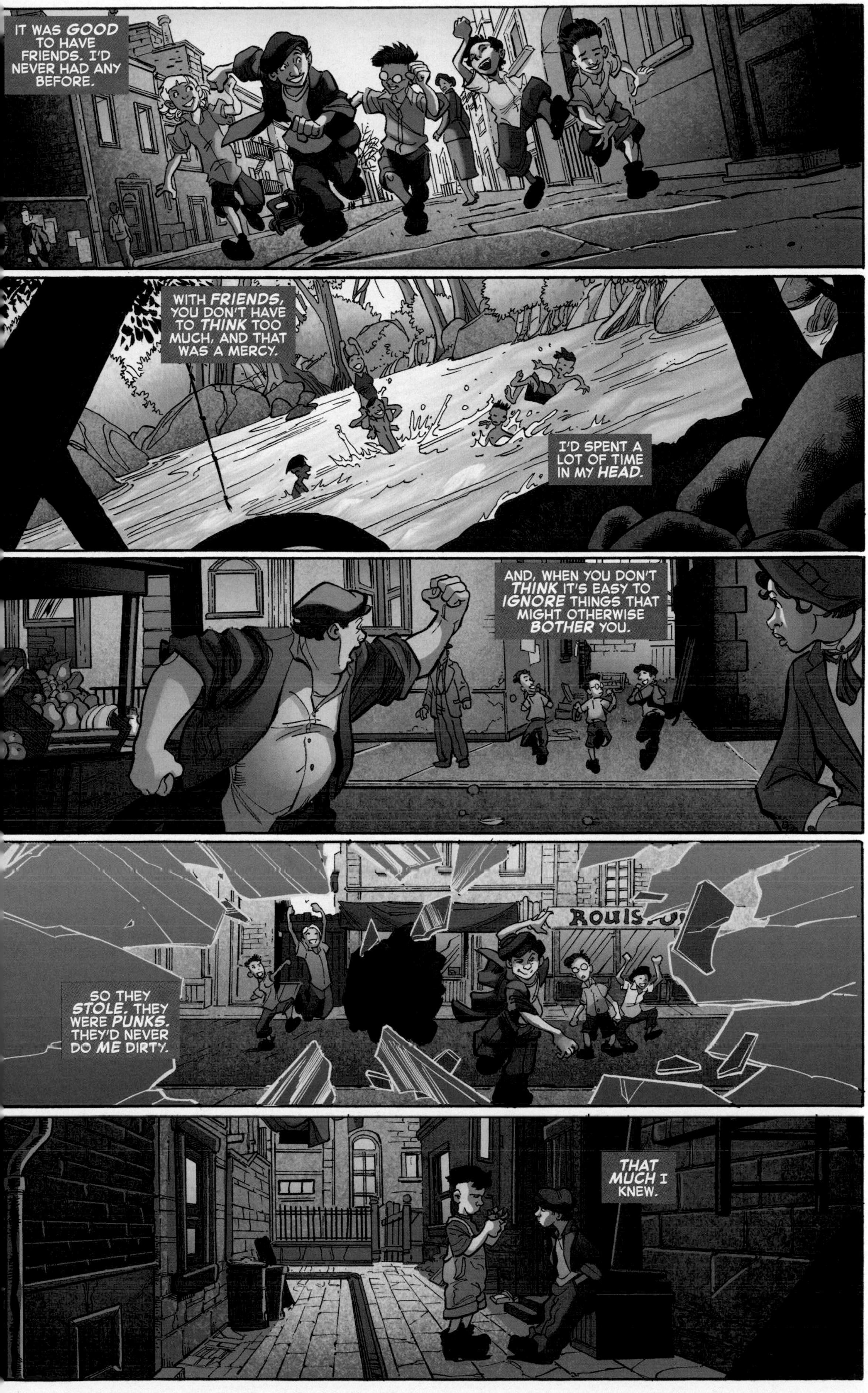
IT WAS GOOD TO HAVE FRIENDS. I'D NEVER HAD ANY BEFORE.
WITH FRIENDS, YOU DON'T HAVE TO THINK TOO MUCH, AND THAT WAS A MERCY.
I'D SPENT A LOT OF TIME IN MY HEAD.
AND, WHEN YOU DON'T THINK IT'S EASY TO IGNORE THINGS THAT MIGHT OTHERWISE BOTHER YOU.
ROUIS
SO THEY STOLE. THEY WERE PUNKS. THEY'D NEVER DO ME DIRTY.
THAT MUCH I KNEW.

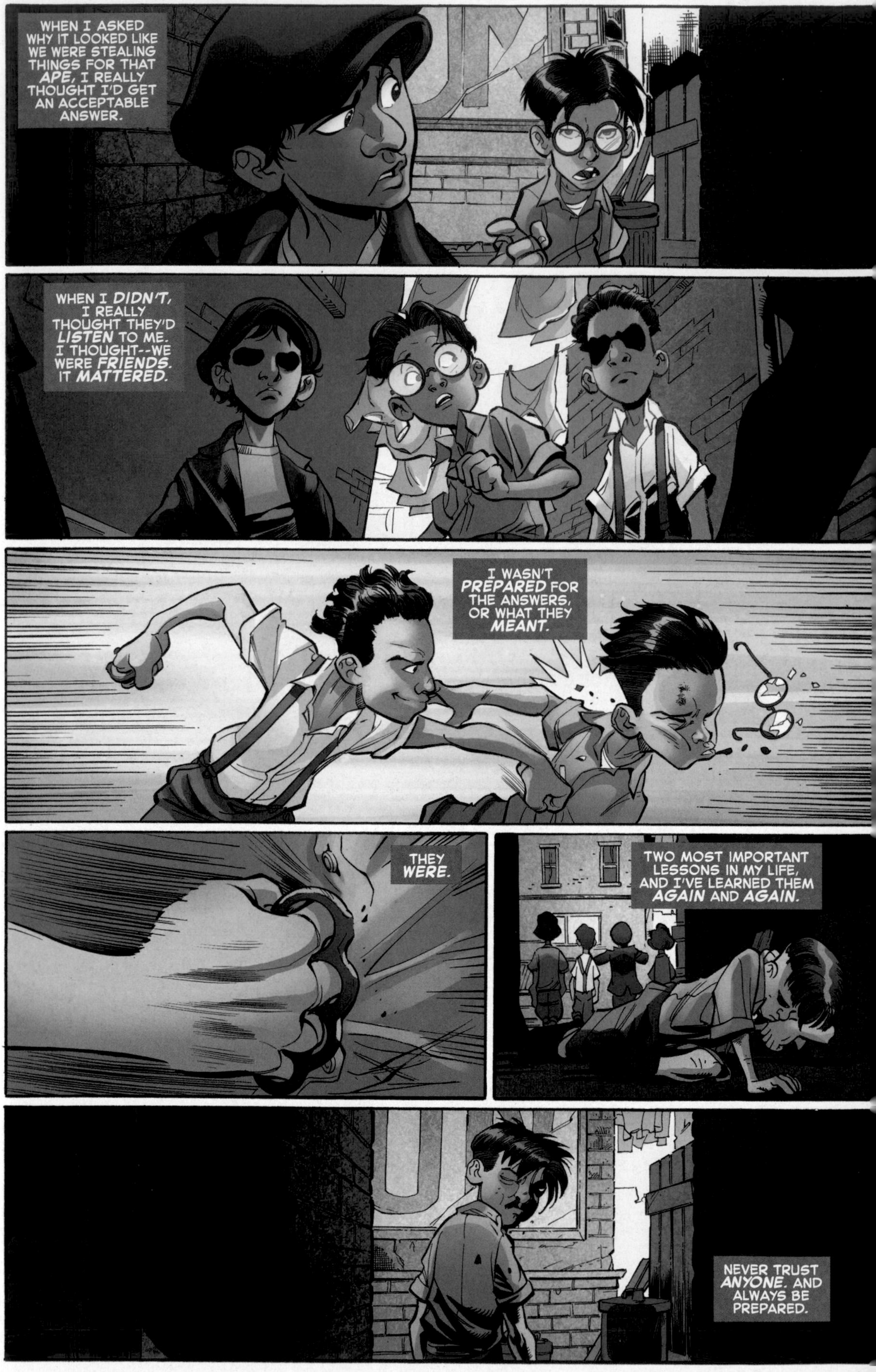
WHEN I ASKED WHY IT LOOKED LIKE WE WERE STEALING THINGS FOR THAT APE, I REALLY THOUGHT I'D GET AN ACCEPTABLE ANSWER.
WHEN I DIDN'T, I REALLY THOUGHT THEY'D LISTEN TO ME. I THOUGHT--WE WERE FRIENDS. IT MATTERED.
I WASN'T PREPARED FOR THE ANSWERS, OR WHAT THEY MEANT.
THEY WERE.
TWO MOST IMPORTANT LESSONS IN MY LIFE, AND I'VE LEARNED THEM AGAIN AND AGAIN.
NEVER TRUST ANYONE. AND ALWAYS BE PREPARED.

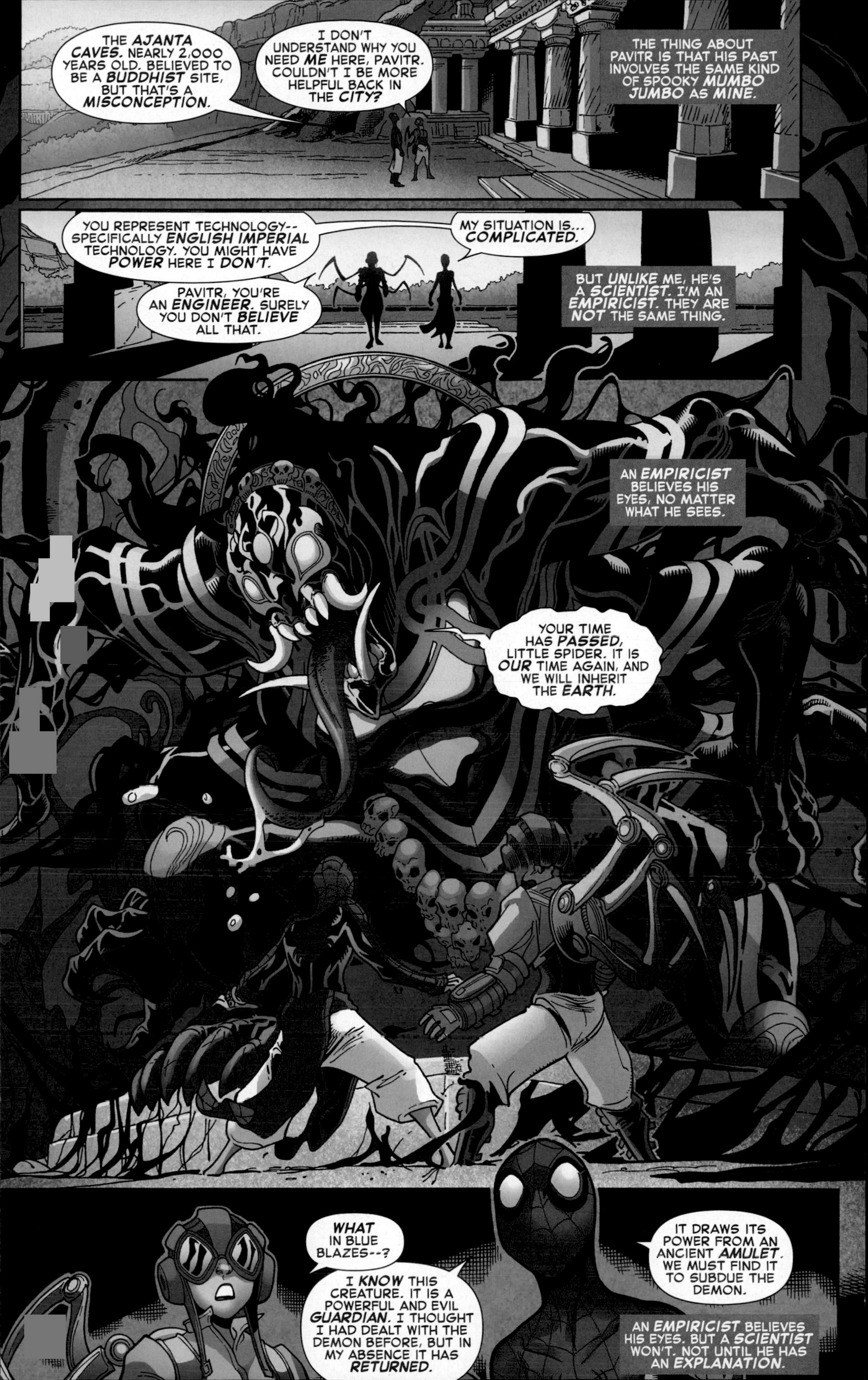
THE AJANTA CAVES. NEARLY 2,000 YEARS OLD. BELIEVED TO BE A BUDDHIST SITE, BUT THAT'S A MISCONCEPTION.
I DON'T UNDERSTAND WHY YOU NEED ME HERE, PAVITR. COULDN'T I BE MORE HELPFUL BACK IN THE CITY?
THE THING ABOUT PAVITR IS THAT HIS PAST INVOLVES THE SAME KIND OF SPOOKY MUMBO JUMBO AS MINE.
YOU REPRESENT TECHNOLOGY-- SPECIFICALLY ENGLISH IMPERIAL TECHNOLOGY. YOU MIGHT HAVE POWER HERE I DON'T.
MY SITUATION IS... COMPLICATED.
PAVITR, YOU'RE AN ENGINEER. SURELY YOU DON'T BELIEVE ALL THAT.
BUT UNLIKE ME, HE'S A SCIENTIST. I'M AN EMPIRICIST. THEY ARE NOT THE SAME THING.
AN EMPIRICIST BELIEVES HIS EYES, NO MATTER WHAT HE SEES.
YOUR TIME HAS PASSED, LITTLE SPIDER. IT IS OUR TIME AGAIN, AND WE WILL INHERIT THE EARTH.
WHAT IN BLUE BLAZES--?
I KNOW THIS CREATURE. IT IS A POWERFUL AND EVIL GUARDIAN. I THOUGHT I HAD DEALT WITH THE DEMON BEFORE, BUT IN MY ABSENCE IT HAS RETURNED.
IT DRAWS ITS POWER FROM AN ANCIENT AMULET. WE MUST FIND IT TO SUBDUE THE DEMON.
AN EMPIRICIST BELIEVES HIS EYES. BUT A SCIENTIST WON'T. NOT UNTIL HE HAS AN EXPLANATION.

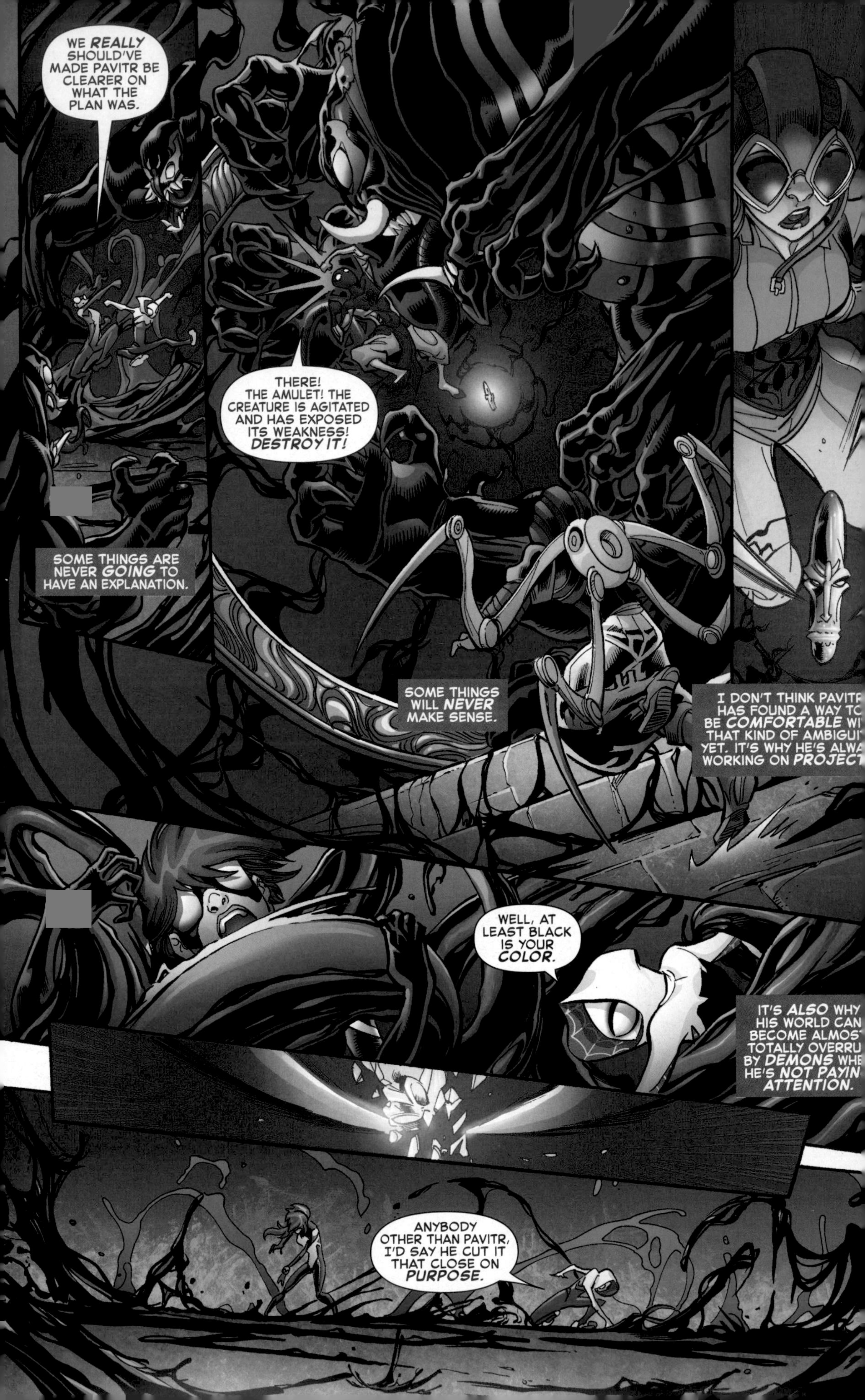
WE REALLY SHOULD'VE MADE PAVITR BE CLEARER ON WHAT THE PLAN WAS.
SOME THINGS ARE NEVER GOING TO HAVE AN EXPLANATION.
THERE! THE AMULET! THE CREATURE IS AGITATED AND HAS EXPOSED ITS WEAKNESS! DESTROY IT!
SOME THINGS WILL NEVER MAKE SENSE.
I DON'T THINK PAVITR HAS FOUND A WAY TO BE COMFORTABLE WI THAT KIND OF AMBIGUIT YET. IT'S WHY HE'S ALWA WORKING ON PROJECT
WELL, AT LEAST BLACK IS YOUR COLOR.
IT'S ALSO WHY HIS WORLD CAN BECOME ALMOS TOTALLY OVERRU BY DEMONS WHE HE'S NOT PAYIN ATTENTION.
ANYBODY OTHER THAN PAVITR, I'D SAY HE CUT IT THAT CLOSE ON PURPOSE.

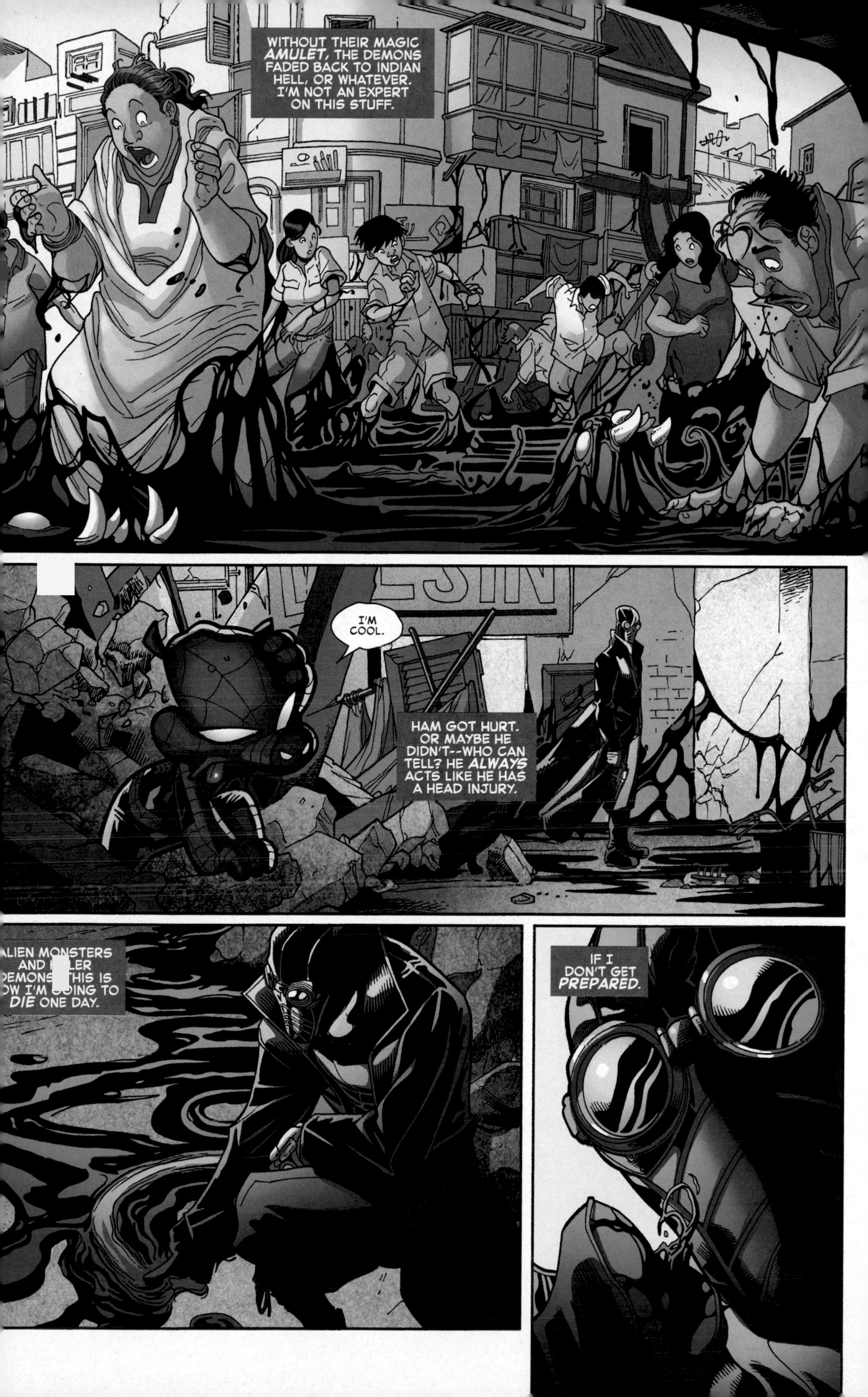
WITHOUT THEIR MAGIC AMULET, THE DEMONS FADED BACK TO INDIAN HELL, OR WHATEVER. I'M NOT AN EXPERT ON THIS STUFF.
I'M COOL.
HAM GOT HURT. OR MAYBE HE DIDN'T--WHO CAN TELL? HE ALWAYS ACTS LIKE HE HAS A HEAD INJURY.
ALIEN MONSTERS AND K LLER DEMONS THIS IS OW I'M OING TO DIE ONE DAY.
IF I DON'T GET PREPARED.

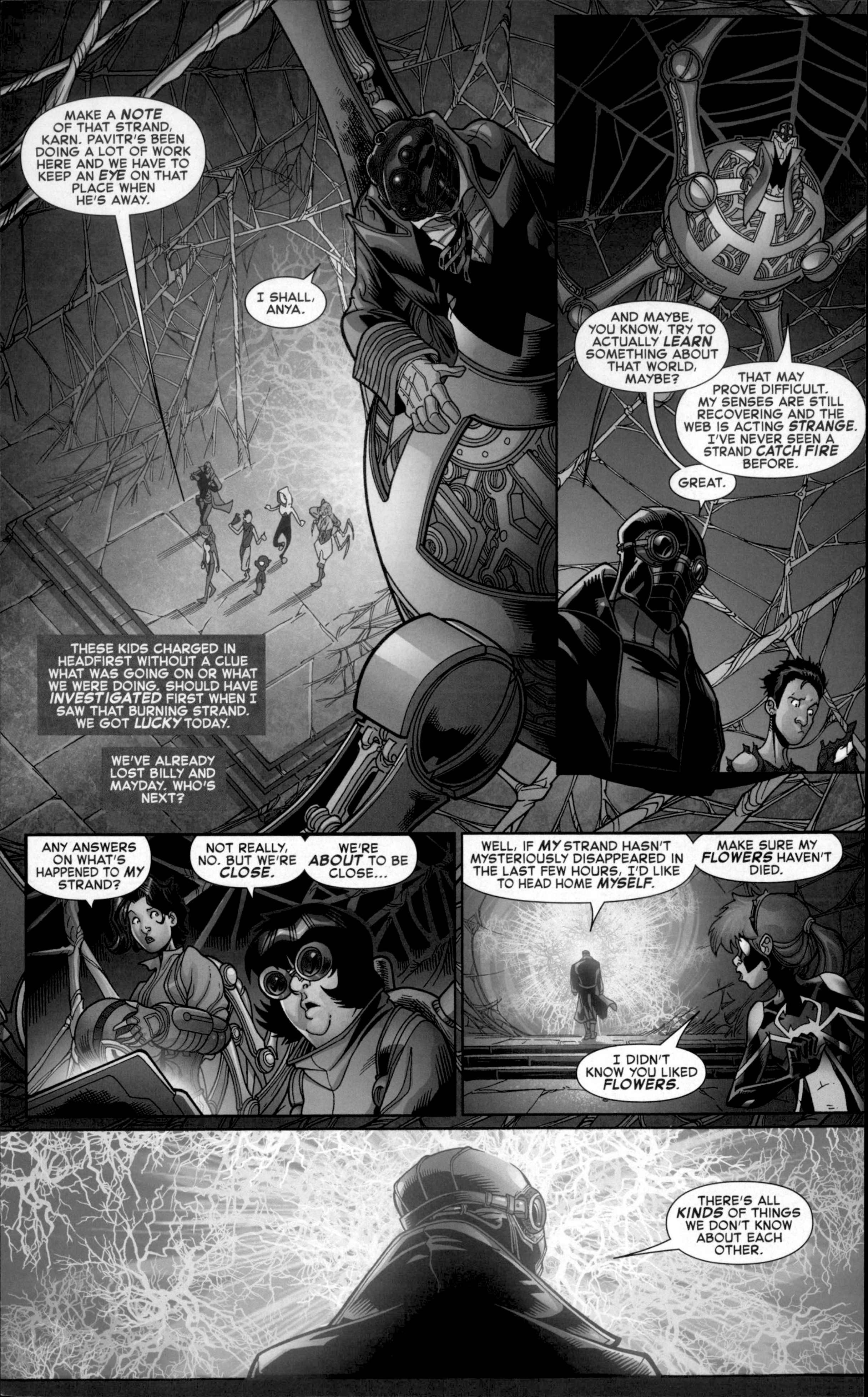
MAKE A NOTE OF THAT STRAND, KARN. PAVITR'S BEEN DOING A LOT OF WORK HERE AND WE HAVE TO KEEP AN EYE ON THAT PLACE WHEN HE'S AWAY.
I SHALL, ANYA.
THESE KIDS CHARGED IN HEADFIRST WITHOUT A CLUE WHAT WAS GOING ON OR WHAT WE WERE DOING. SHOULD HAVE INVESTIGATED FIRST WHEN I SAW THAT BURNING STRAND. WE GOT LUCKY TODAY.
WE'VE ALREADY LOST BILLY AND MAYDAY. WHO'S NEXT?
AND MAYBE, YOU KNOW, TRY TO ACTUALLY LEARN SOMETHING ABOUT THAT WORLD, MAYBE?
THAT MAY PROVE DIFFICULT. MY SENSES ARE STILL RECOVERING AND THE WEB IS ACTING STRANGE. I'VE NEVER SEEN A STRAND CATCH FIRE BEFORE.
GREAT.
ANY ANSWERS ON WHAT'S HAPPENED TO MY STRAND?
NOT REALLY, NO. BUT WE'RE CLOSE.
WE'RE ABOUT TO BE CLOSE...
WELL, IF MY STRAND HASN'T MYSTERIOUSLY DISAPPEARED IN THE LAST FEW HOURS, I'D LIKE TO HEAD HOME MYSELF.
MAKE SURE MY FLOWERS HAVEN'T DIED.
I DIDN'T KNOW YOU LIKED FLOWERS.
THERE'S ALL KINDS OF THINGS WE DON'T KNOW ABOUT EACH OTHER.

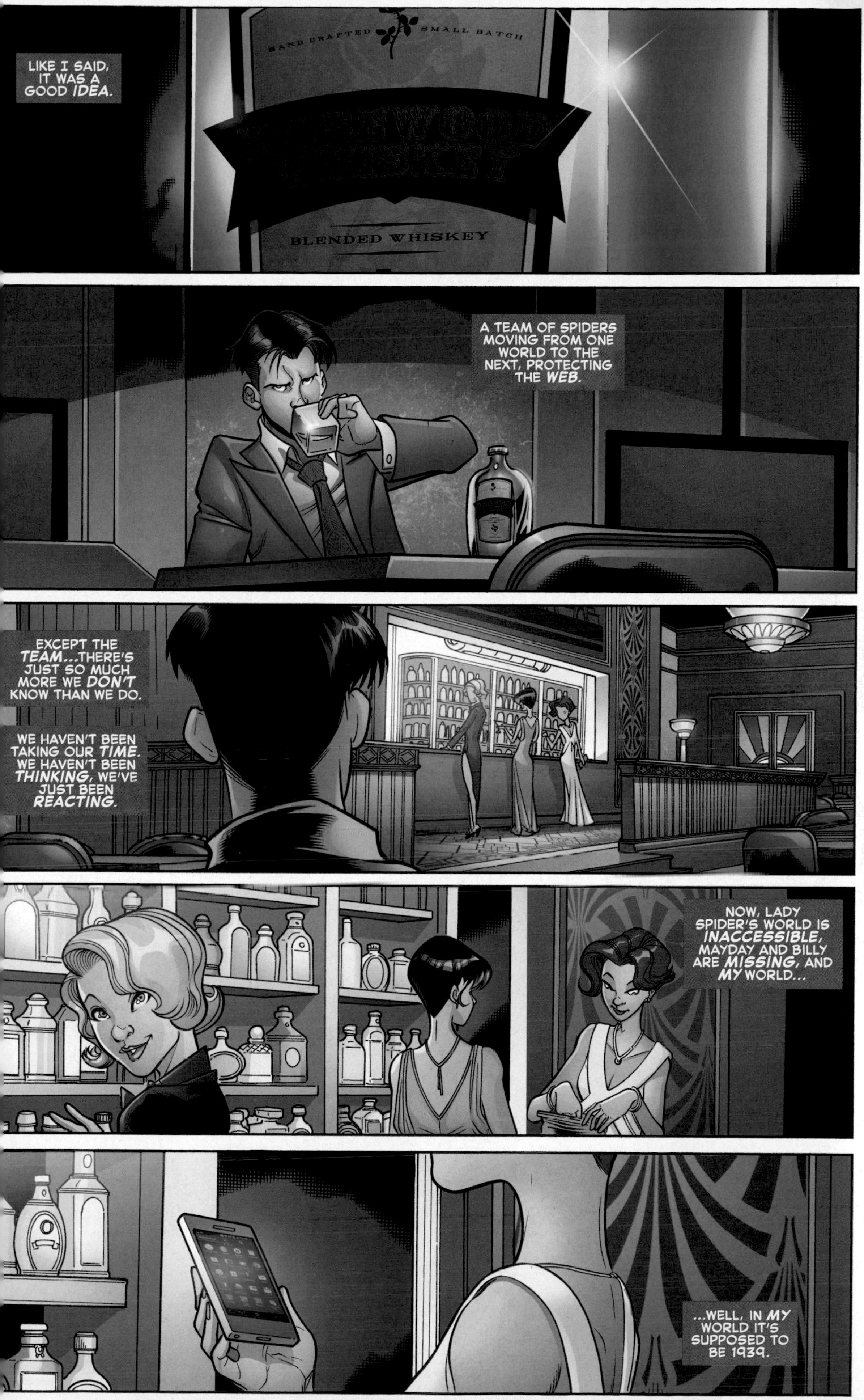
HAND CRAFTED SMALL BATCH
BLENDED WHISKEY
LIKE I SAID, IT WAS A GOOD IDEA.
A TEAM OF SPIDERS MOVING FROM ONE WORLD TO THE NEXT, PROTECTING THE WEB.
EXCEPT THE TEAM...THERE'S JUST SO MUCH MORE WE DON'T KNOW THAN WE DO.
WE HAVEN'T BEEN TAKING OUR TIME. WE HAVEN'T BEEN THINKING, WE'VE JUST BEEN REACTING.
NOW, LADY SPIDER'S WORLD IS INACCESSIBLE, MAYDAY AND BILLY ARE MISSING, AND MY WORLD...
...WELL, IN MY WORLD IT'S SUPPOSED TO BE 1939.

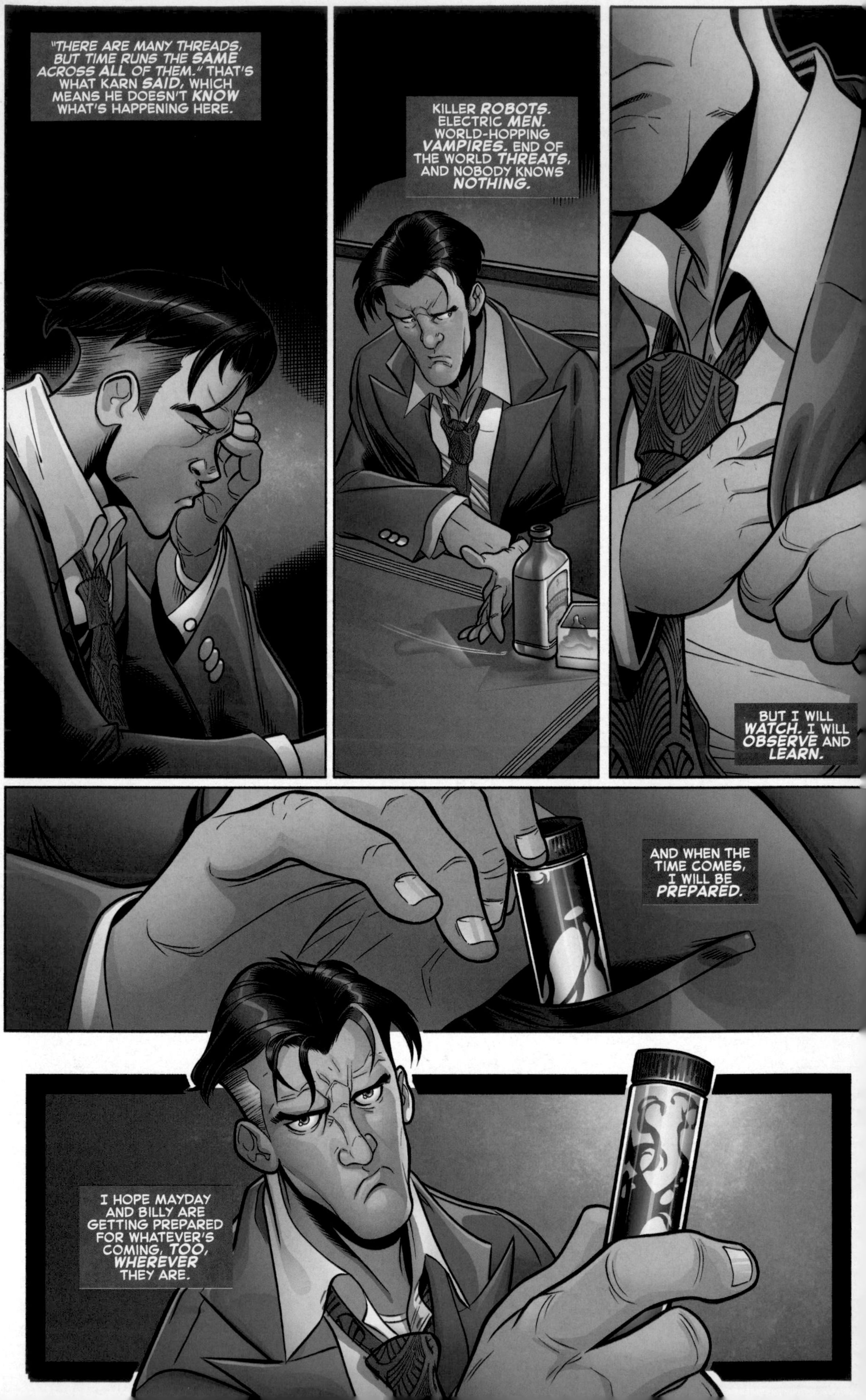
"THERE ARE MANY THREADS, BUT TIME RUNS THE SAME ACROSS ALL OF THEM." THAT'S WHAT KARN SAID, WHICH MEANS HE DOESN'T KNOW WHAT'S HAPPENING HERE.
KILLER ROBOTS. ELECTRIC MEN. WORLD-HOPPING VAMPIRES. END OF THE WORLD THREATS, AND NOBODY KNOWS NOTHING.
BUT I WILL WATCH. I WILL OBSERVE AND LEARN.
AND WHEN THE TIME COMES, I WILL BE PREPARED.
I HOPE MAYDAY AND BILLY ARE GETTING PREPARED FOR WHATEVER'S COMING, TOO, WHEREVER THEY ARE.

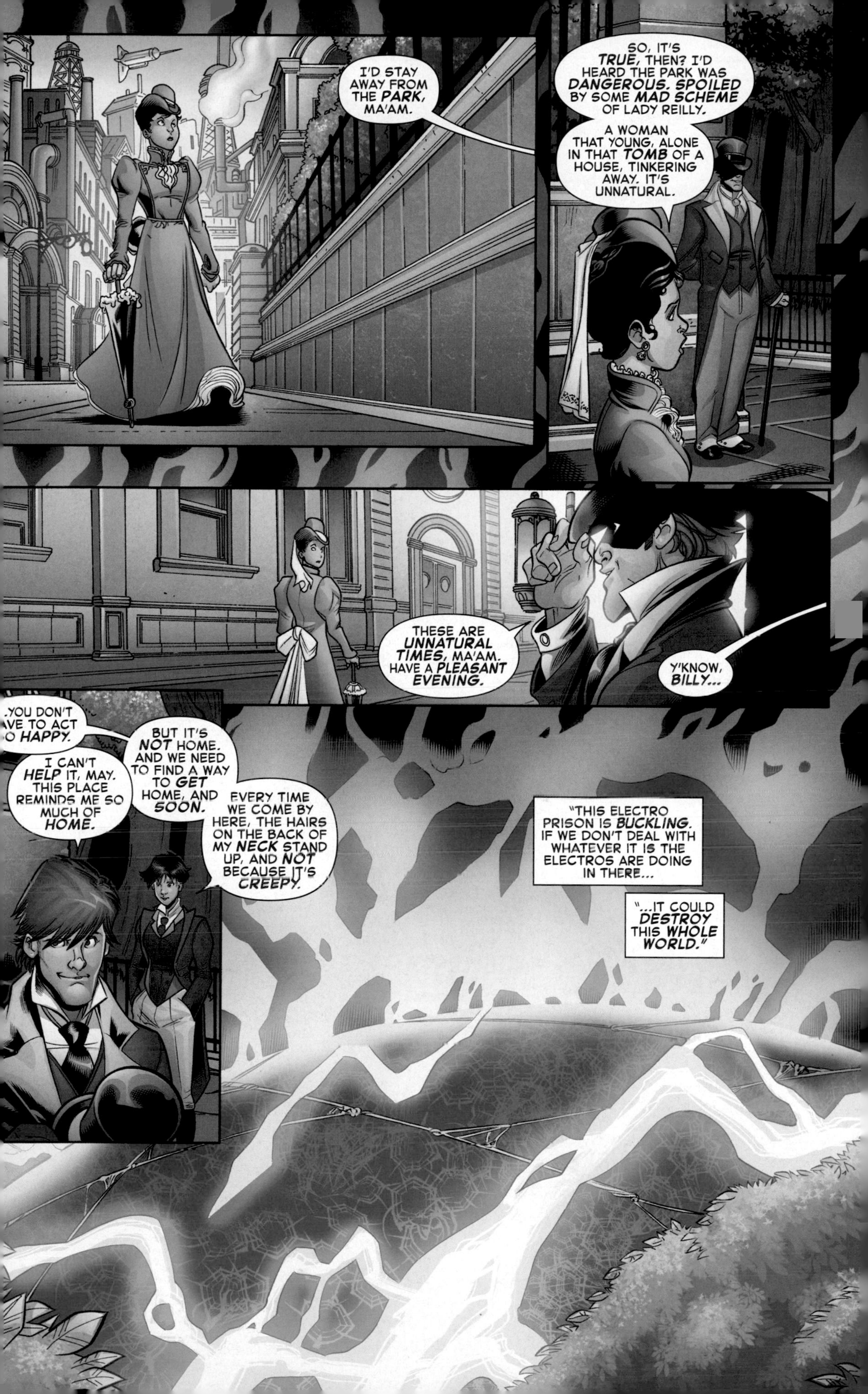
I'D STAY AWAY FROM THE PARK, MA'AM.
SO, IT'S TRUE, THEN? I'D HEARD THE PARK WAS DANGEROUS. SPOILED BY SOME MAD SCHEME OF LADY REILLY.
A WOMAN THAT YOUNG, ALONE IN THAT TOMB OF A HOUSE, TINKERING AWAY. IT'S UNNATURAL.
THESE ARE UNNATURAL TIMES, MA'AM. HAVE A PLEASANT EVENING.
Y'KNOW, BILLY...
...YOU DON'T HAVE TO ACT SO HAPPY.
I CAN'T HELP IT, MAY. THIS PLACE REMINDS ME SO MUCH OF HOME.
BUT IT'S NOT HOME. AND WE NEED TO FIND A WAY TO GET HOME, AND SOON.
EVERY TIME WE COME BY HERE, THE HAIRS ON THE BACK OF MY NECK STAND UP, AND NOT BECAUSE IT'S CREEPY.
"THIS ELECTRO PRISON IS BUCKLING. IF WE DON'T DEAL WITH WHATEVER IT IS THE ELECTROS ARE DOING IN THERE...
"...IT COULD DESTROY THIS WHOLE WORLD."

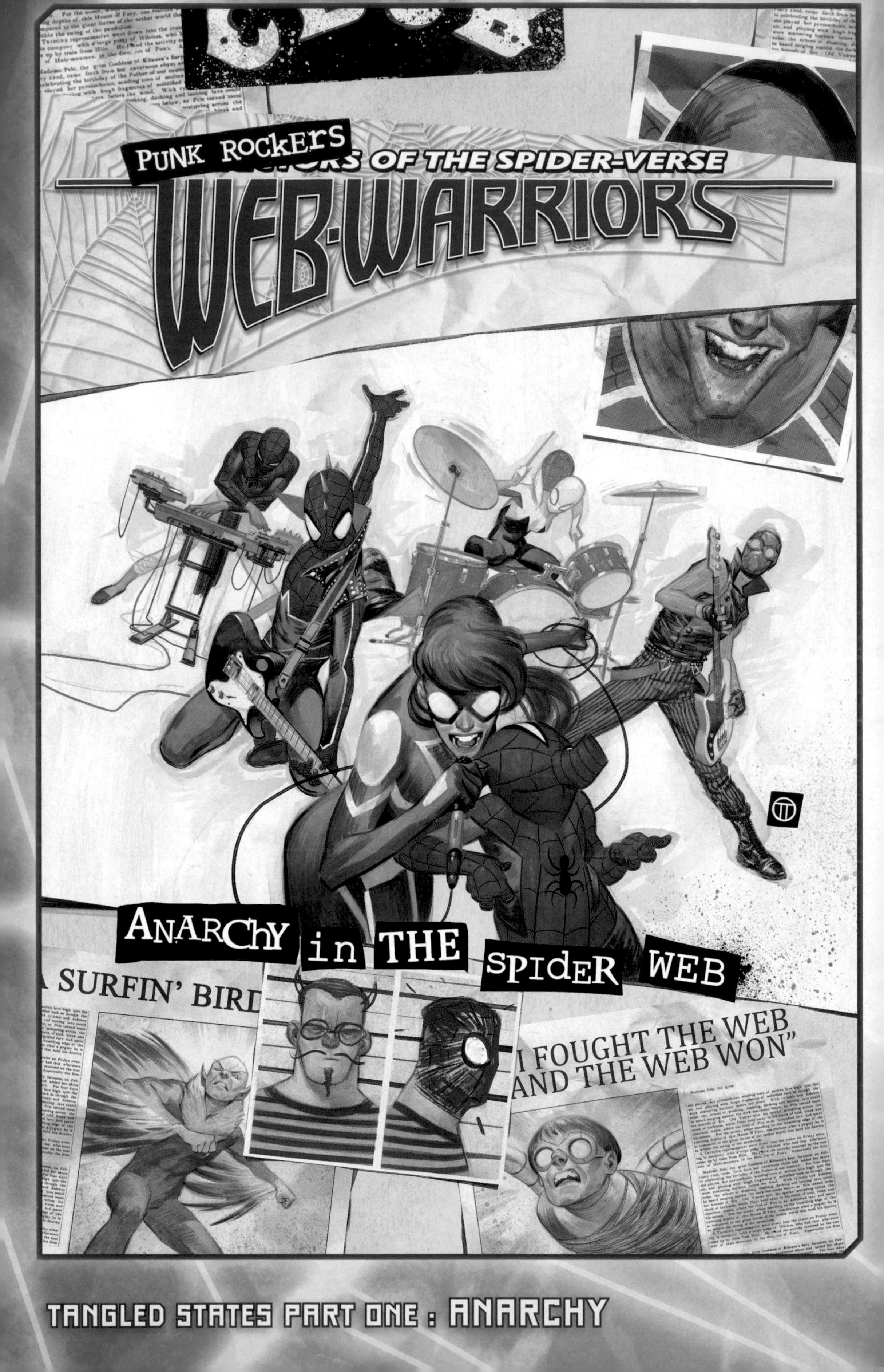
PUNK ROCKERS
OF THE SPIDER-VERSE
WEB-WARRIORS
ANARCHY in THE spider WEB
A SURFIN' BIRD
I FOUGHT THE WEB AND THE WEB WON"

TANGLED STATES PART ONE : ANARCHY

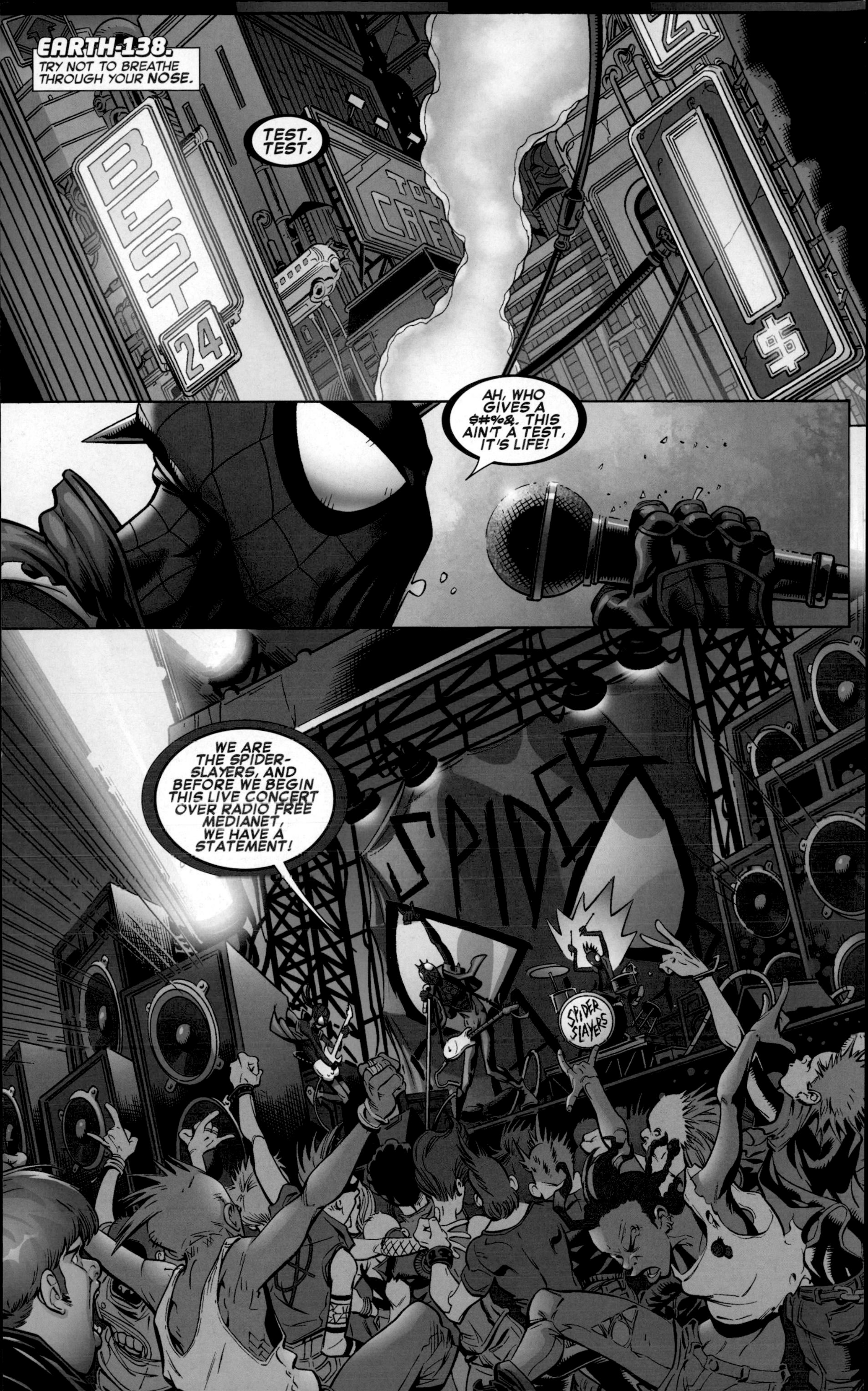
EARTH-138.
TRY NOT TO BREATHE THROUGH YOUR NOSE.
TEST. TEST.
BEST
24
$
AH, WHO GIVES A $#%&. THIS AIN'T A TEST, IT'S LIFE!
WE ARE THE SPIDER-SLAYERS, AND BEFORE WE BEGIN THIS LIVE CONCERT OVER RADIO FREE MEDIANET, WE HAVE A STATEMENT!
SPIDER
SPIDER SLAYERS

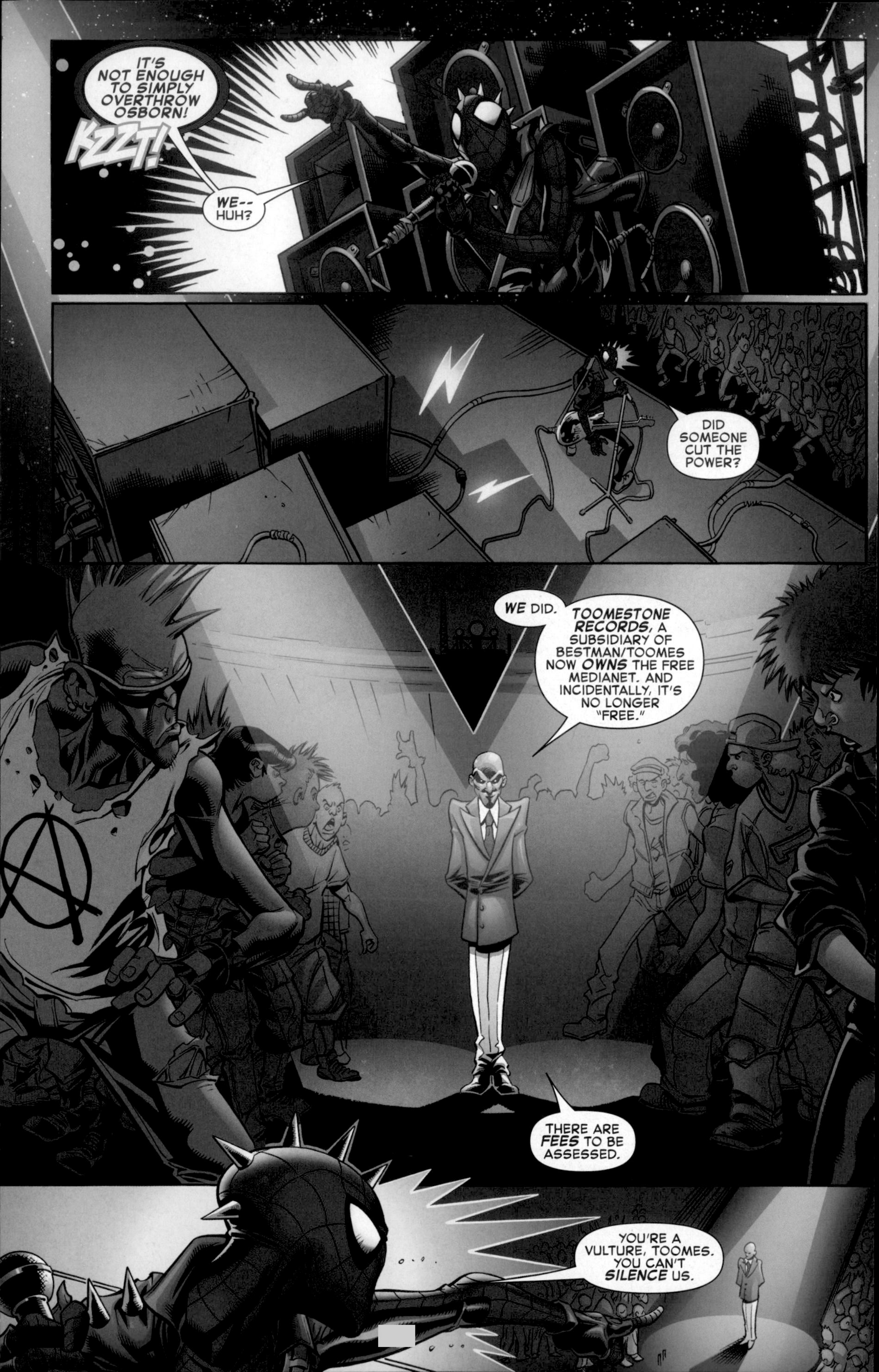
IT'S NOT ENOUGH TO SIMPLY OVERTHROW OSBORN!
KZZT!
WE-- HUH?
DID SOMEONE CUT THE POWER?
WE DID. TOOMESTONE RECORDS, A SUBSIDIARY OF BESTMAN/TOOMES NOW OWNS THE FREE MEDIANET. AND INCIDENTALLY, IT'S NO LONGER "FREE."
THERE ARE FEES TO BE ASSESSED.
YOU'RE A VULTURE, TOOMES. YOU CAN'T SILENCE US.

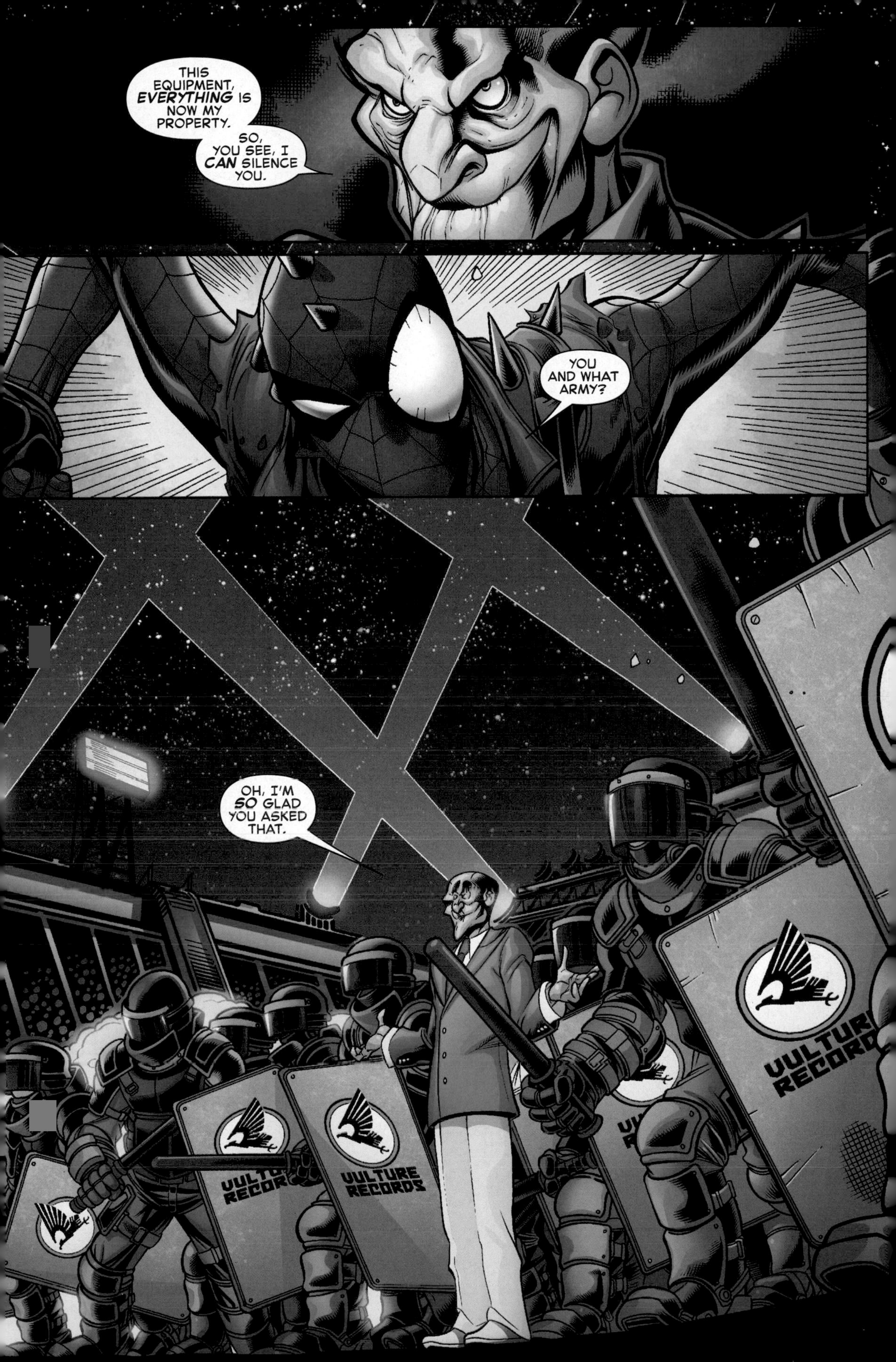
THIS EQUIPMENT, EVERYTHING IS NOW MY PROPERTY.
SO, YOU SEE, I CAN SILENCE YOU.
YOU AND WHAT ARMY?
OH, I'M SO GLAD YOU ASKED THAT.
VULTURE RECORDS

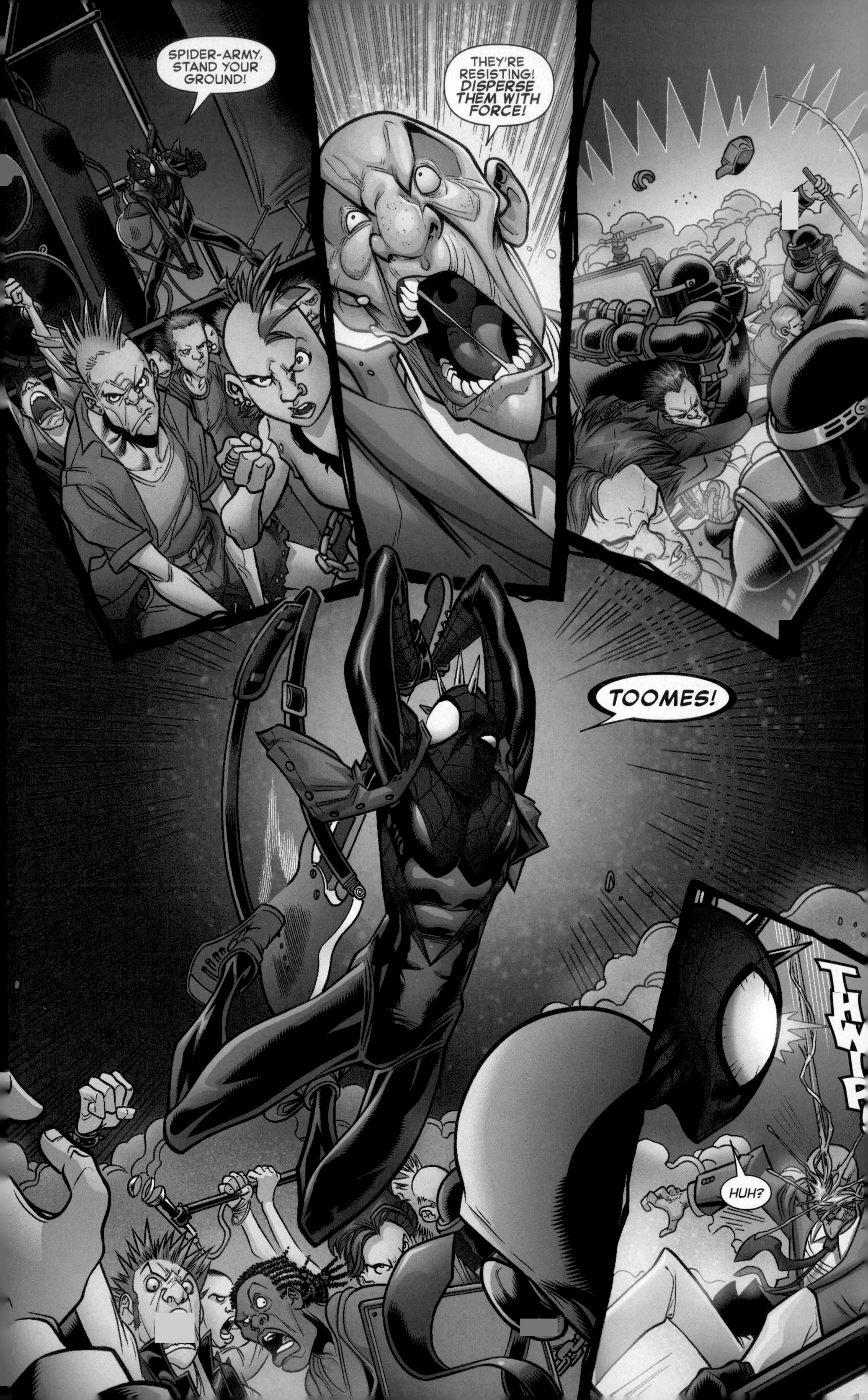
SPIDER-ARMY, STAND YOUR GROUND!
THEY'RE RESISTING! DISPERSE THEM WITH FORCE!
TOOMES!
THWIP!
HUH?

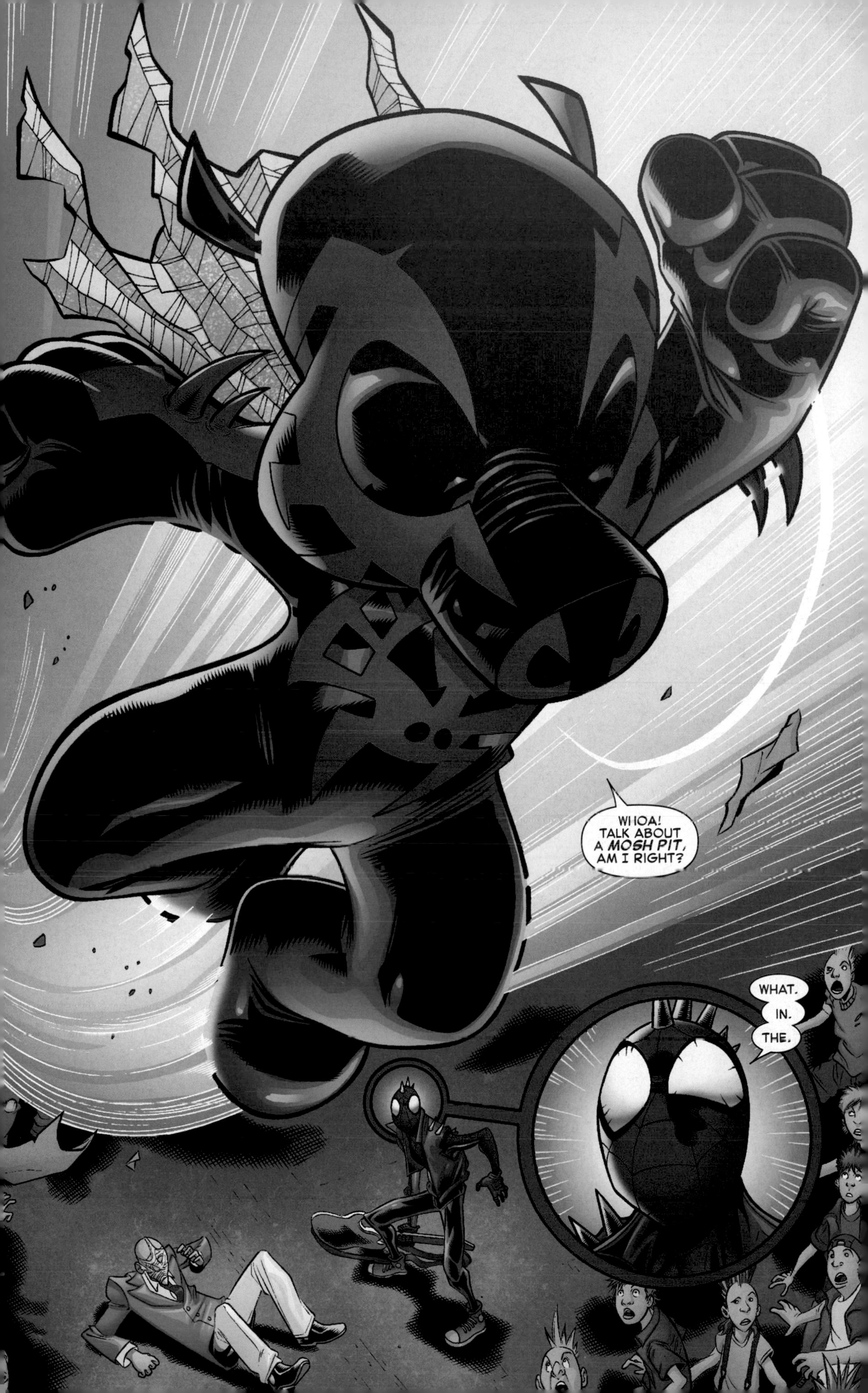
WHOA! TALK ABOUT A *MOSH PIT*, AM I RIGHT?
WHAT. IN. THE.

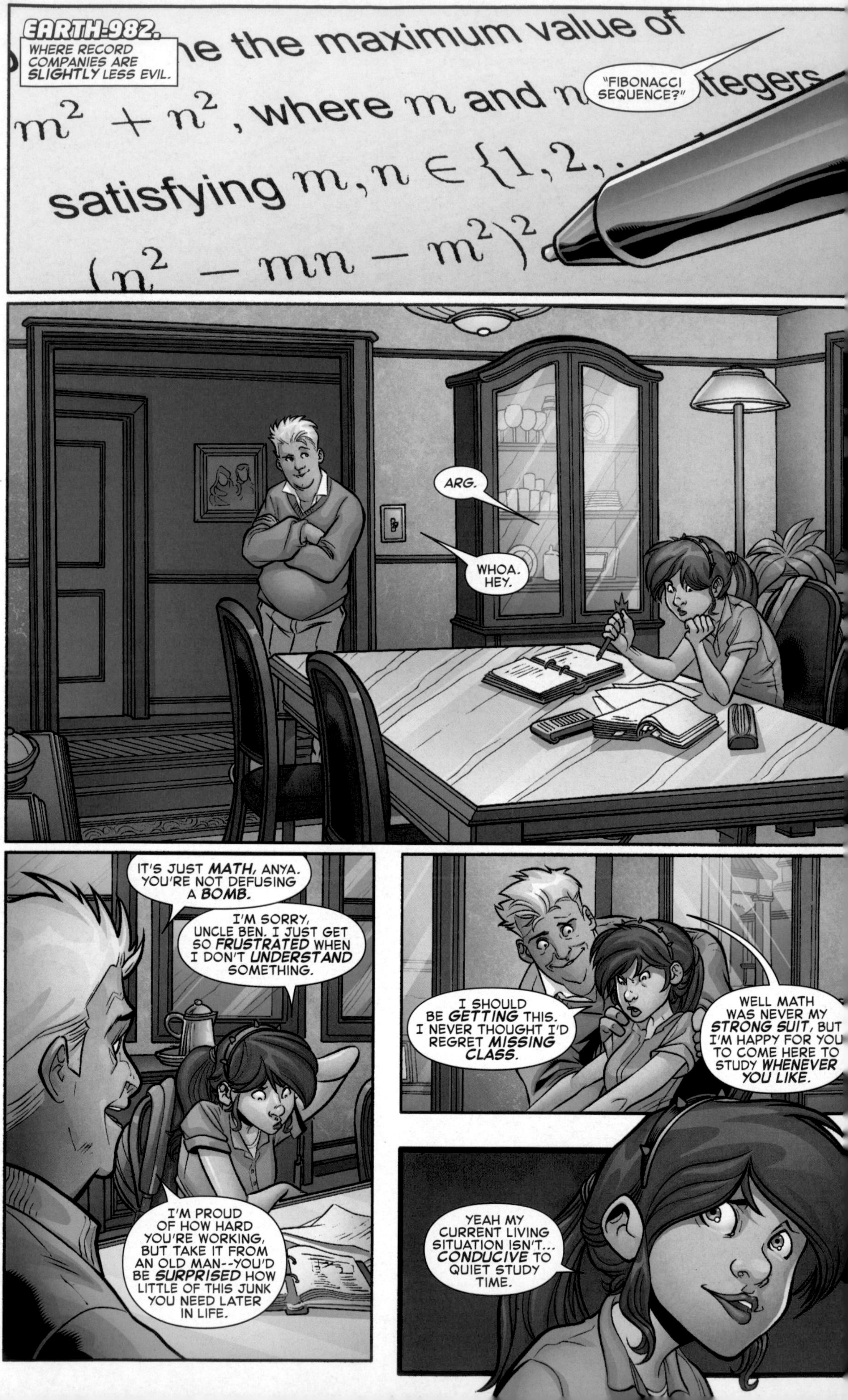
EARTH-982.
WHERE RECORD COMPANIES ARE SLIGHTLY LESS EVIL.
"FIBONACCI SEQUENCE?"
ARG.
WHOA. HEY.
IT'S JUST MATH, ANYA. YOU'RE NOT DEFUSING A BOMB.
I'M SORRY, UNCLE BEN. I JUST GET SO FRUSTRATED WHEN I DON'T UNDERSTAND SOMETHING.
I'M PROUD OF HOW HARD YOU'RE WORKING, BUT TAKE IT FROM AN OLD MAN--YOU'D BE SURPRISED HOW LITTLE OF THIS JUNK YOU NEED LATER IN LIFE.
I SHOULD BE GETTING THIS. I NEVER THOUGHT I'D REGRET MISSING CLASS.
WELL MATH WAS NEVER MY STRONG SUIT, BUT I'M HAPPY FOR YOU TO COME HERE TO STUDY WHENEVER YOU LIKE.
YEAH MY CURRENT LIVING SITUATION ISN'T... CONDUCIVE TO QUIET STUDY TIME.

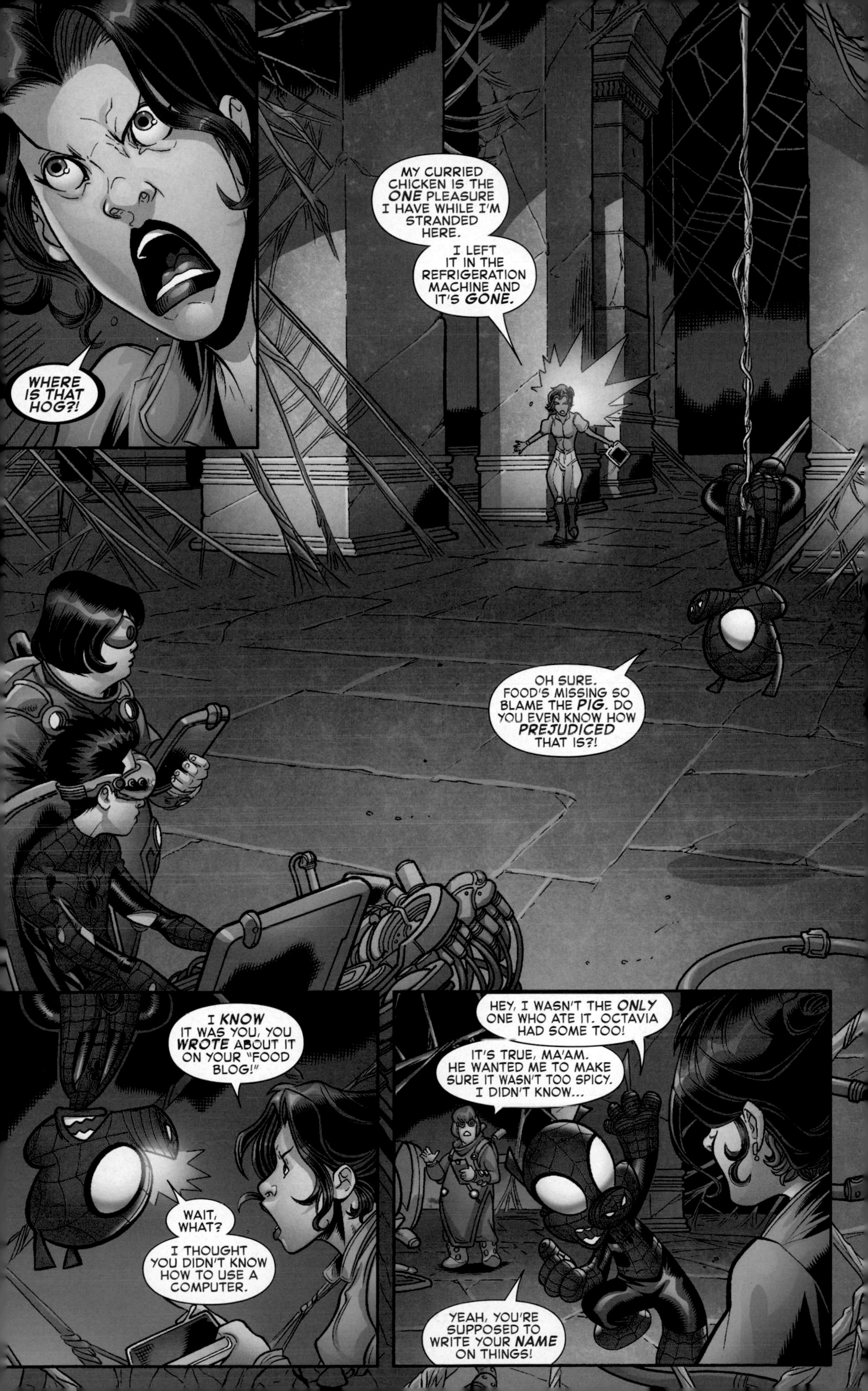
WHERE IS THAT HOG?!
MY CURRIED CHICKEN IS THE ONE PLEASURE I HAVE WHILE I'M STRANDED HERE.
I LEFT IT IN THE REFRIGERATION MACHINE AND IT'S GONE.
OH SURE. FOOD'S MISSING SO BLAME THE PIG. DO YOU EVEN KNOW HOW PREJUDICED THAT IS?!
I KNOW IT WAS YOU, YOU WROTE ABOUT IT ON YOUR "FOOD BLOG!"
WAIT, WHAT?
I THOUGHT YOU DIDN'T KNOW HOW TO USE A COMPUTER.
HEY, I WASN'T THE ONLY ONE WHO ATE IT. OCTAVIA HAD SOME TOO!
IT'S TRUE, MA'AM. HE WANTED ME TO MAKE SURE IT WASN'T TOO SPICY. I DIDN'T KNOW...
YEAH, YOU'RE SUPPOSED TO WRITE YOUR NAME ON THINGS!

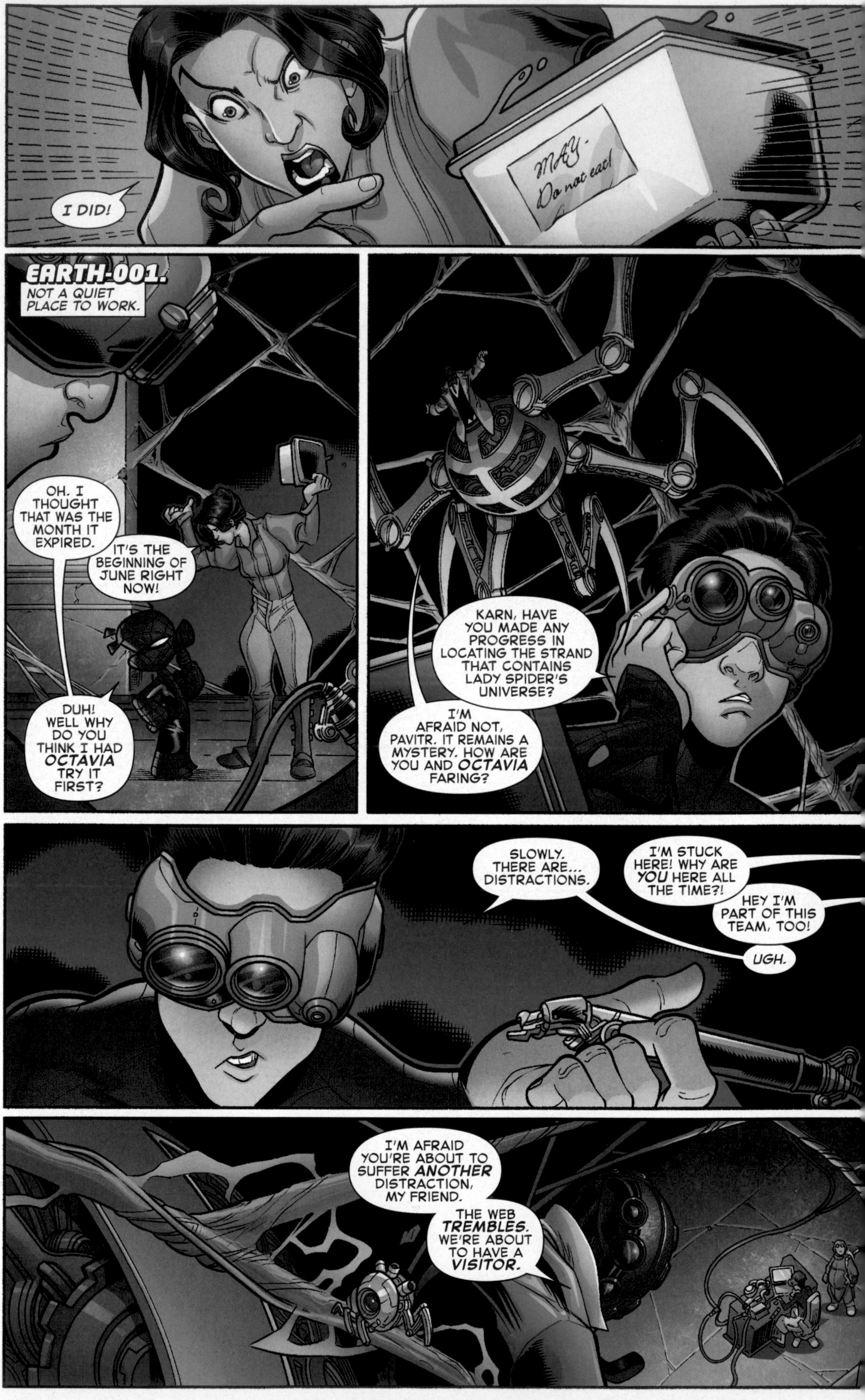
I DID!
MAY - Do not eat!
EARTH-001. NOT A QUIET PLACE TO WORK.
OH. I THOUGHT THAT WAS THE MONTH IT EXPIRED.
IT'S THE BEGINNING OF JUNE RIGHT NOW!
DUH! WELL WHY DO YOU THINK I HAD OCTAVIA TRY IT FIRST?
KARN, HAVE YOU MADE ANY PROGRESS IN LOCATING THE STRAND THAT CONTAINS LADY SPIDER'S UNIVERSE?
I'M AFRAID NOT, PAVITR. IT REMAINS A MYSTERY. HOW ARE YOU AND OCTAVIA FARING?
SLOWLY. THERE ARE... DISTRACTIONS.
I'M STUCK HERE! WHY ARE YOU HERE ALL THE TIME?!
HEY I'M PART OF THIS TEAM, TOO!
UGH.
I'M AFRAID YOU'RE ABOUT TO SUFFER ANOTHER DISTRACTION, MY FRIEND.
THE WEB TREMBLES. WE'RE ABOUT TO HAVE A VISITOR.

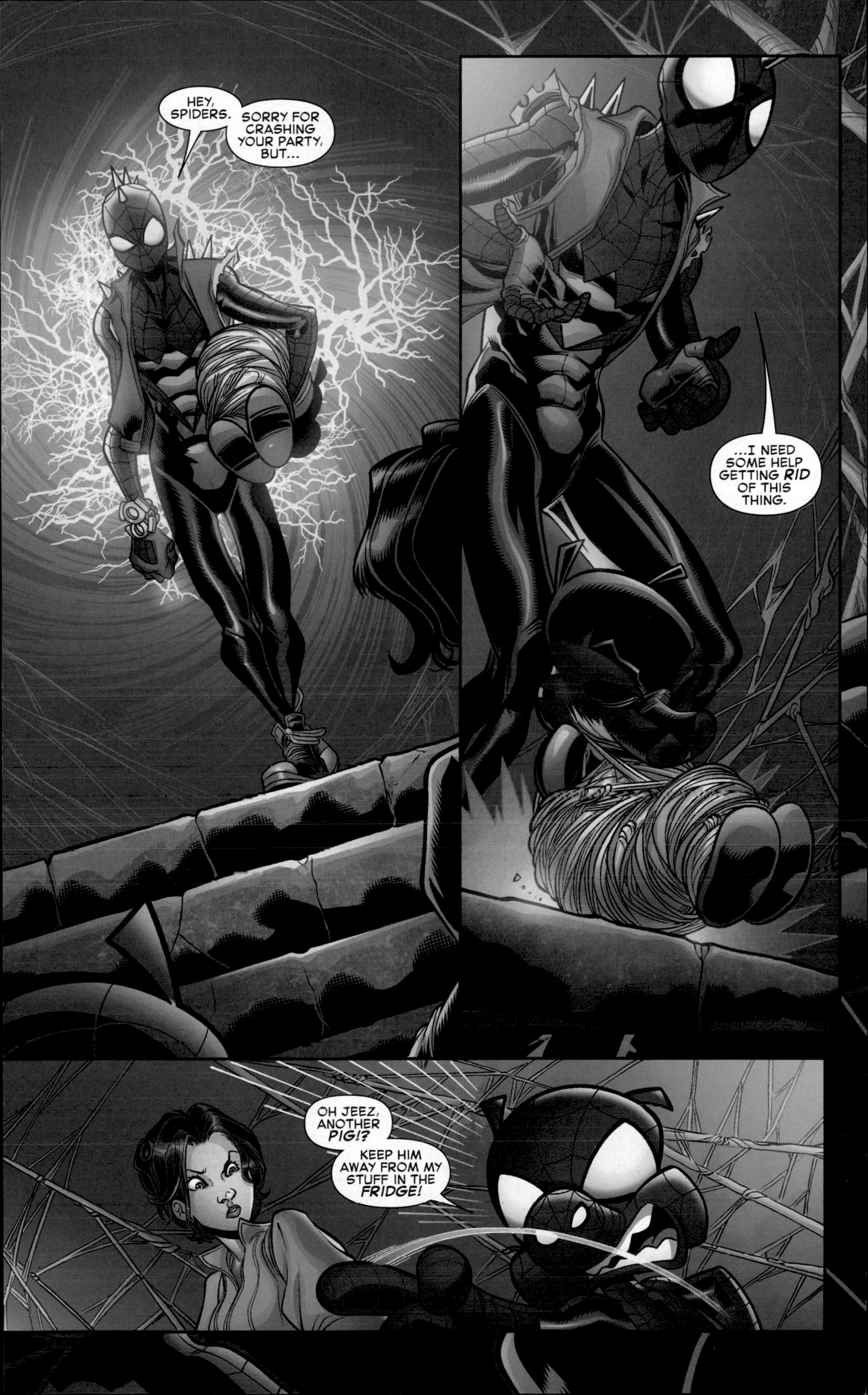
HEY, SPIDERS.
SORRY FOR CRASHING YOUR PARTY, BUT...
...I NEED SOME HELP GETTING RID OF THIS THING.
OH JEEZ, ANOTHER PIG!?
KEEP HIM AWAY FROM MY STUFF IN THE FRIDGE!

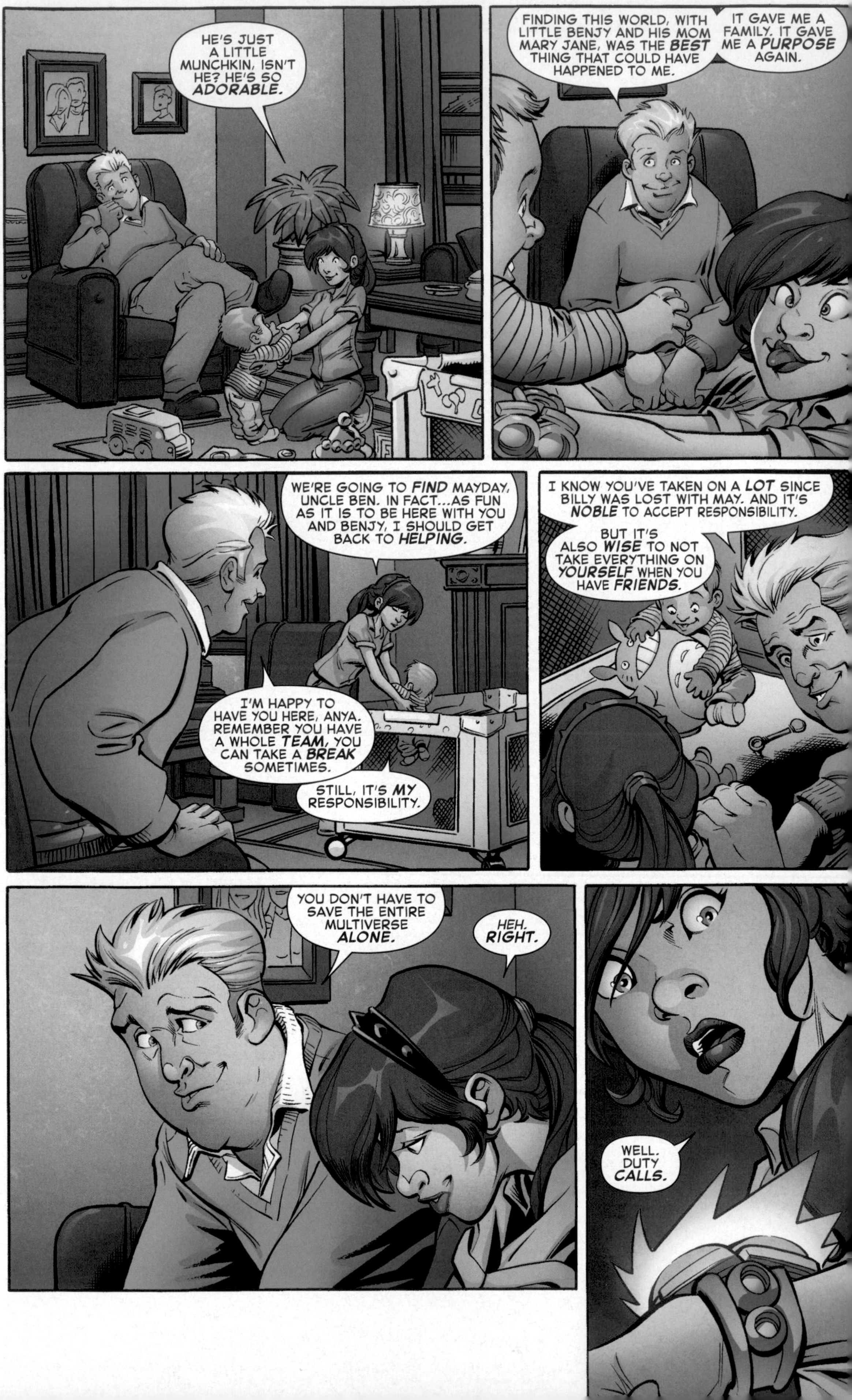
HE'S JUST A LITTLE MUNCHKIN, ISN'T HE? HE'S SO ADORABLE.
FINDING THIS WORLD, WITH LITTLE BENJY AND HIS MOM MARY JANE, WAS THE BEST THING THAT COULD HAVE HAPPENED TO ME.
IT GAVE ME A FAMILY. IT GAVE ME A PURPOSE AGAIN.
WE'RE GOING TO FIND MAYDAY, UNCLE BEN. IN FACT...AS FUN AS IT IS TO BE HERE WITH YOU AND BENJY, I SHOULD GET BACK TO HELPING.
I'M HAPPY TO HAVE YOU HERE, ANYA. REMEMBER YOU HAVE A WHOLE TEAM, YOU CAN TAKE A BREAK SOMETIMES.
STILL, IT'S MY RESPONSIBILITY.
I KNOW YOU'VE TAKEN ON A LOT SINCE BILLY WAS LOST WITH MAY. AND IT'S NOBLE TO ACCEPT RESPONSIBILITY.
BUT IT'S ALSO WISE TO NOT TAKE EVERYTHING ON YOURSELF WHEN YOU HAVE FRIENDS.
YOU DON'T HAVE TO SAVE THE ENTIRE MULTIVERSE ALONE.
HEH. RIGHT.
WELL. DUTY CALLS.

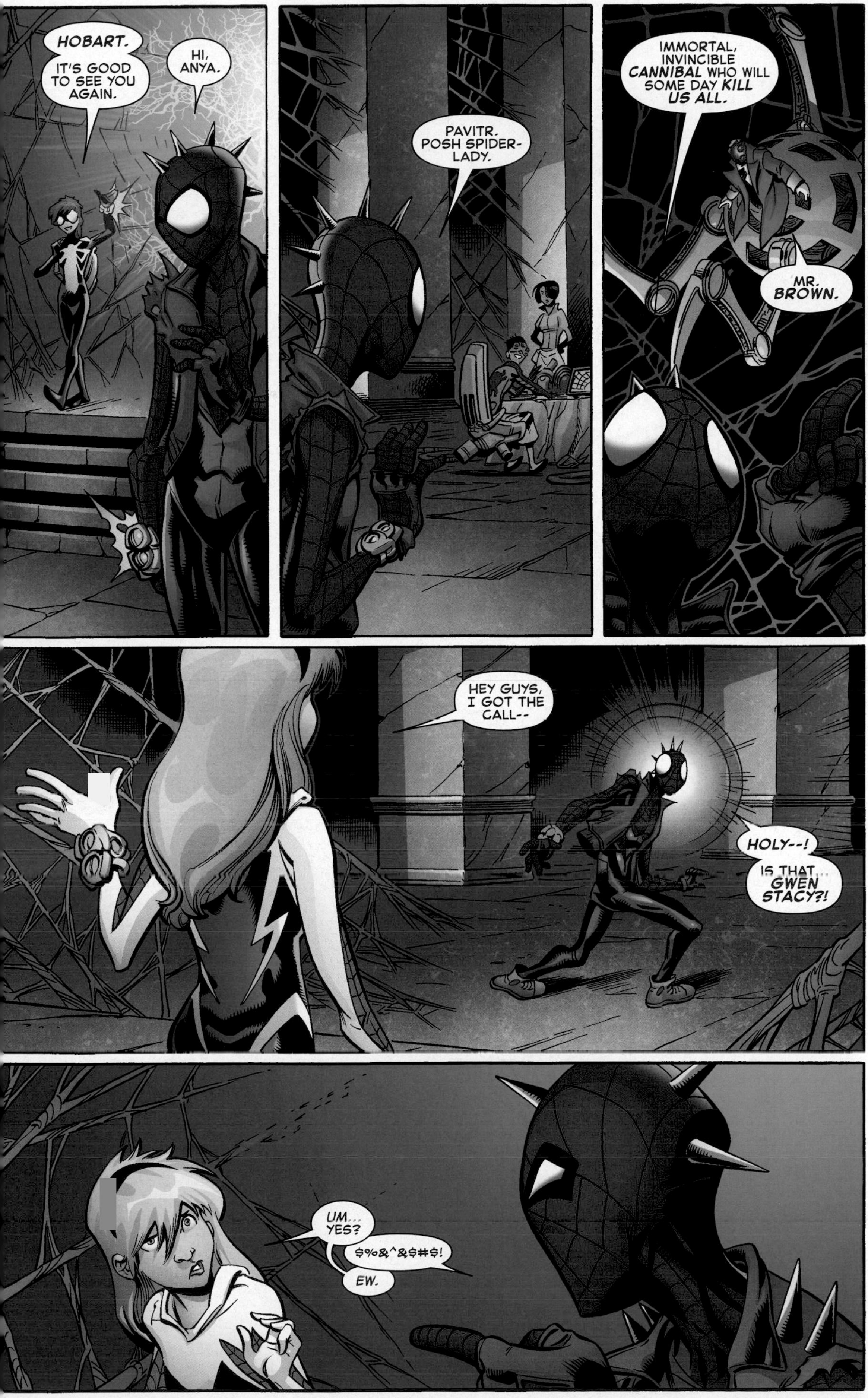
HOBART.
IT'S GOOD TO SEE YOU AGAIN.
HI, ANYA.
PAVITR. POSH SPIDER-LADY.
IMMORTAL, INVINCIBLE CANNIBAL WHO WILL SOME DAY KILL US ALL.
MR. BROWN.
HEY GUYS, I GOT THE CALL--
HOLY--!
IS THAT... GWEN STACY?!
UM... YES?
$%&^&$#$!
EW.

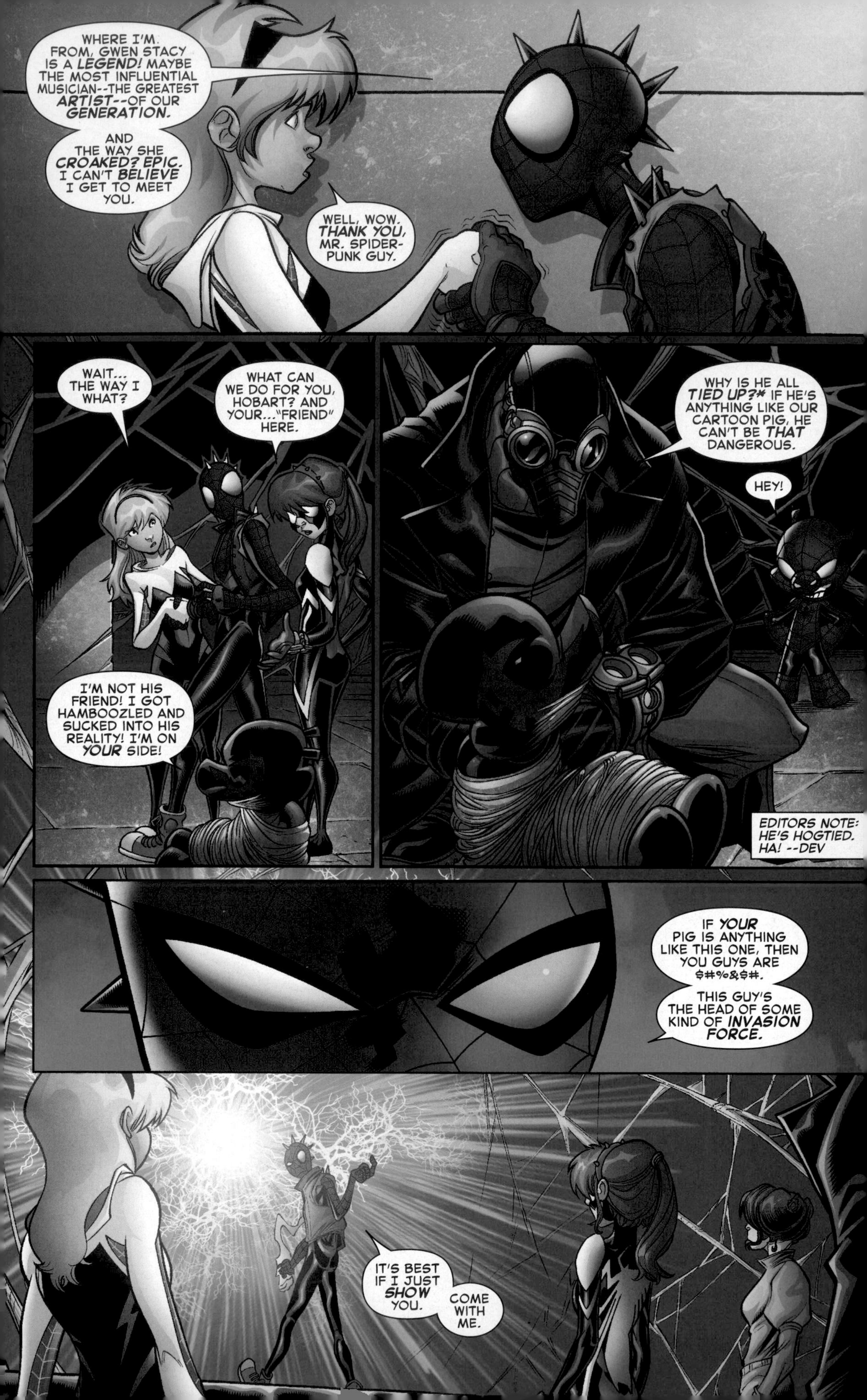
WHERE I'M FROM, GWEN STACY IS A LEGEND! MAYBE THE MOST INFLUENTIAL MUSICIAN--THE GREATEST ARTIST--OF OUR GENERATION.
AND THE WAY SHE CROAKED? EPIC. I CAN'T BELIEVE I GET TO MEET YOU.
WELL, WOW. THANK YOU, MR. SPIDER-PUNK GUY.
WAIT... THE WAY I WHAT?
WHAT CAN WE DO FOR YOU, HOBART? AND YOUR..."FRIEND" HERE.
I'M NOT HIS FRIEND! I GOT HAMBOOZLED AND SUCKED INTO HIS REALITY! I'M ON YOUR SIDE!
WHY IS HE ALL TIED UP?* IF HE'S ANYTHING LIKE OUR CARTOON PIG, HE CAN'T BE THAT DANGEROUS.
HEY!
EDITORS NOTE: HE'S HOGTIED. HA! --DEV
IF YOUR PIG IS ANYTHING LIKE THIS ONE, THEN YOU GUYS ARE $#%&$#.
THIS GUY'S THE HEAD OF SOME KIND OF INVASION FORCE.
IT'S BEST IF I JUST SHOW YOU.
COME WITH ME.

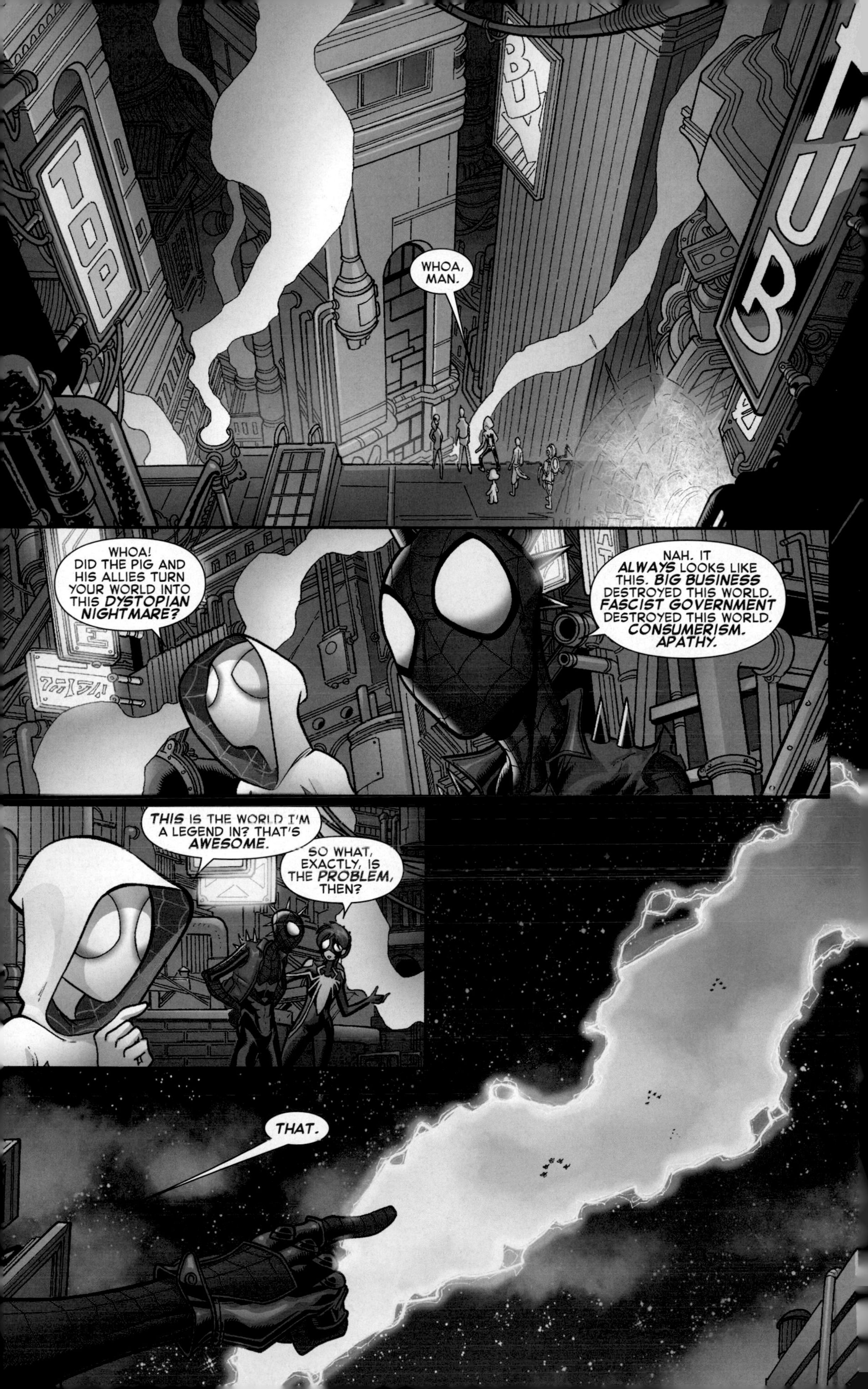
TOP
HUB
WHOA, MAN.
WHOA! DID THE PIG AND HIS ALLIES TURN YOUR WORLD INTO THIS DYSTOPIAN NIGHTMARE?
NAH. IT ALWAYS LOOKS LIKE THIS. BIG BUSINESS DESTROYED THIS WORLD. FASCIST GOVERNMENT DESTROYED THIS WORLD. CONSUMERISM. APATHY.
THIS IS THE WORLD I'M A LEGEND IN? THAT'S AWESOME.
SO WHAT, EXACTLY, IS THE PROBLEM, THEN?
THAT.

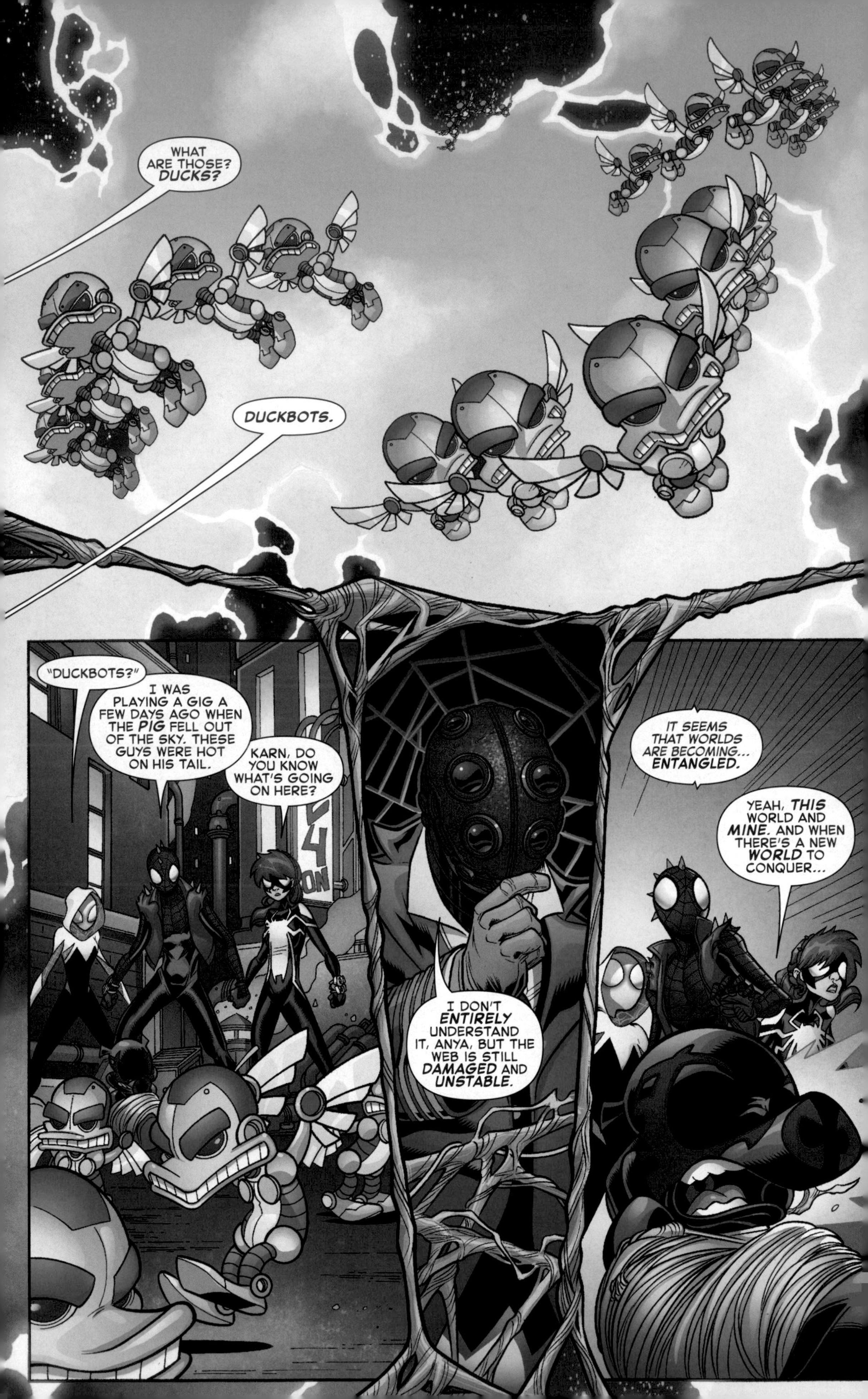

WHAT ARE THOSE? *DUCKS?*
DUCKBOTS.
"DUCKBOTS?"
I WAS PLAYING A GIG A FEW DAYS AGO WHEN THE *PIG* FELL OUT OF THE SKY. THESE GUYS WERE HOT ON HIS TAIL.
KARN, DO YOU KNOW WHAT'S GOING ON HERE?
I DON'T *ENTIRELY* UNDERSTAND IT, ANYA, BUT THE WEB IS STILL *DAMAGED* AND *UNSTABLE.*
IT SEEMS THAT WORLDS ARE BECOMING... **ENTANGLED.**
YEAH, **THIS** WORLD AND **MINE.** AND WHEN THERE'S A NEW **WORLD** TO CONQUER...

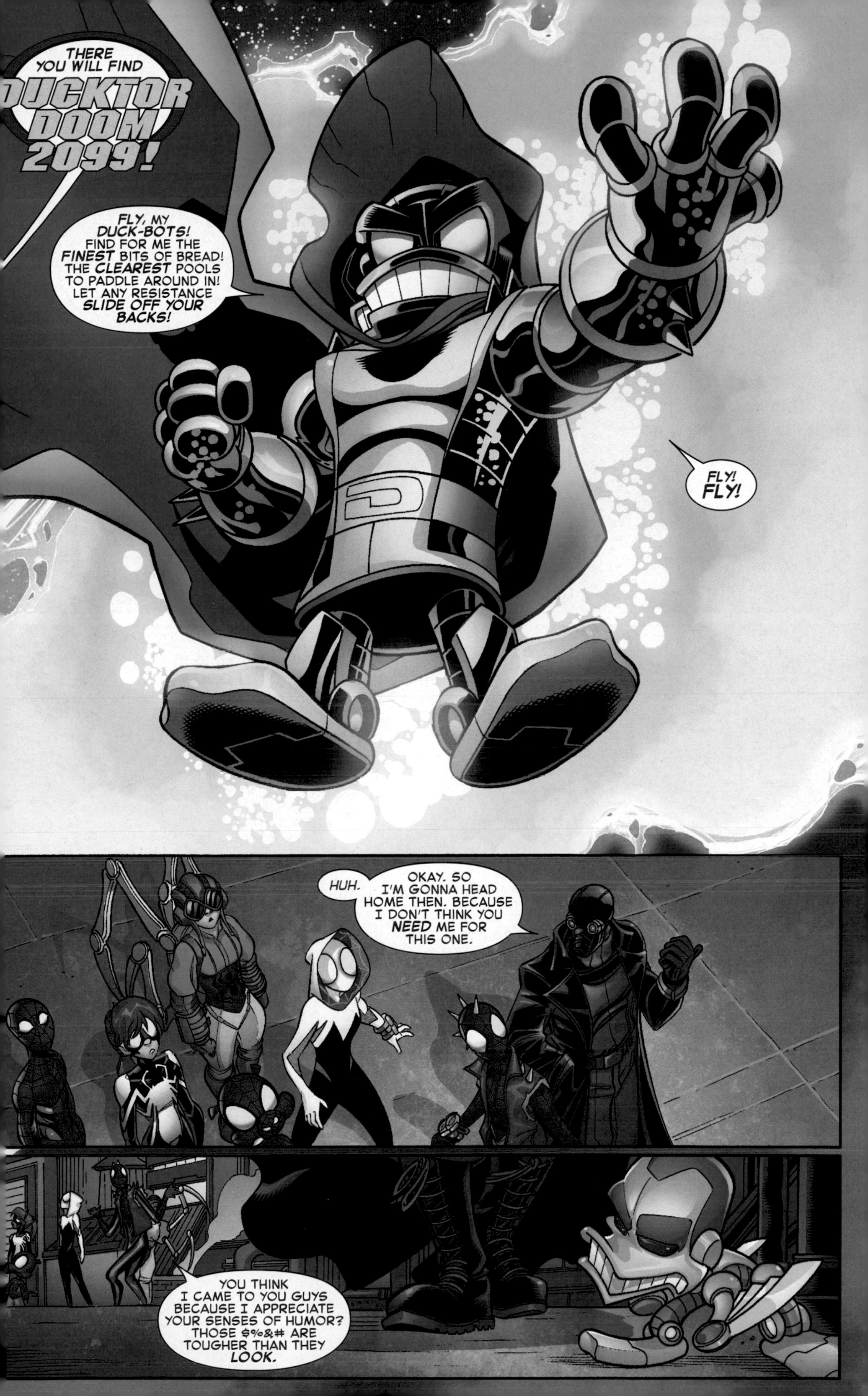
THERE YOU WILL FIND DUCKTOR DOOM 2099!
FLY, MY DUCK-BOTS! FIND FOR ME THE FINEST BITS OF BREAD! THE CLEAREST POOLS TO PADDLE AROUND IN! LET ANY RESISTANCE SLIDE OFF YOUR BACKS!
FLY! FLY!
HUH.
OKAY. SO I'M GONNA HEAD HOME THEN. BECAUSE I DON'T THINK YOU NEED ME FOR THIS ONE.
YOU THINK I CAME TO YOU GUYS BECAUSE I APPRECIATE YOUR SENSES OF HUMOR? THOSE $%&# ARE TOUGHER THAN THEY LOOK.

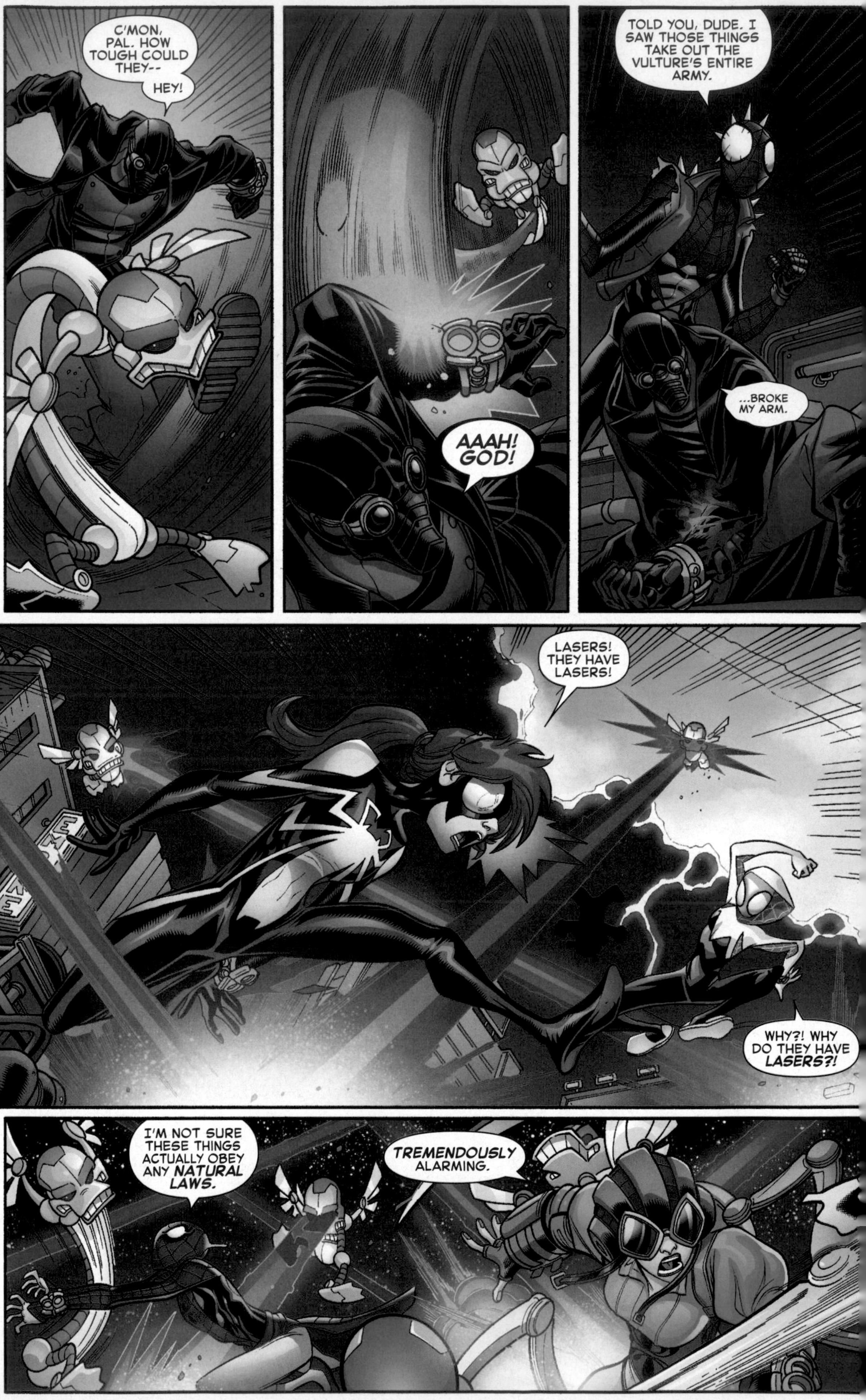
C'MON, PAL. HOW TOUGH COULD THEY--
HEY!
AAAH! GOD!
TOLD YOU, DUDE. I SAW THOSE THINGS TAKE OUT THE VULTURE'S ENTIRE ARMY.
...BROKE MY ARM.
LASERS! THEY HAVE LASERS!
WHY?! WHY DO THEY HAVE *LASERS?!*
I'M NOT SURE THESE THINGS ACTUALLY OBEY ANY *NATURAL LAWS.*
TREMENDOUSLY ALARMING.

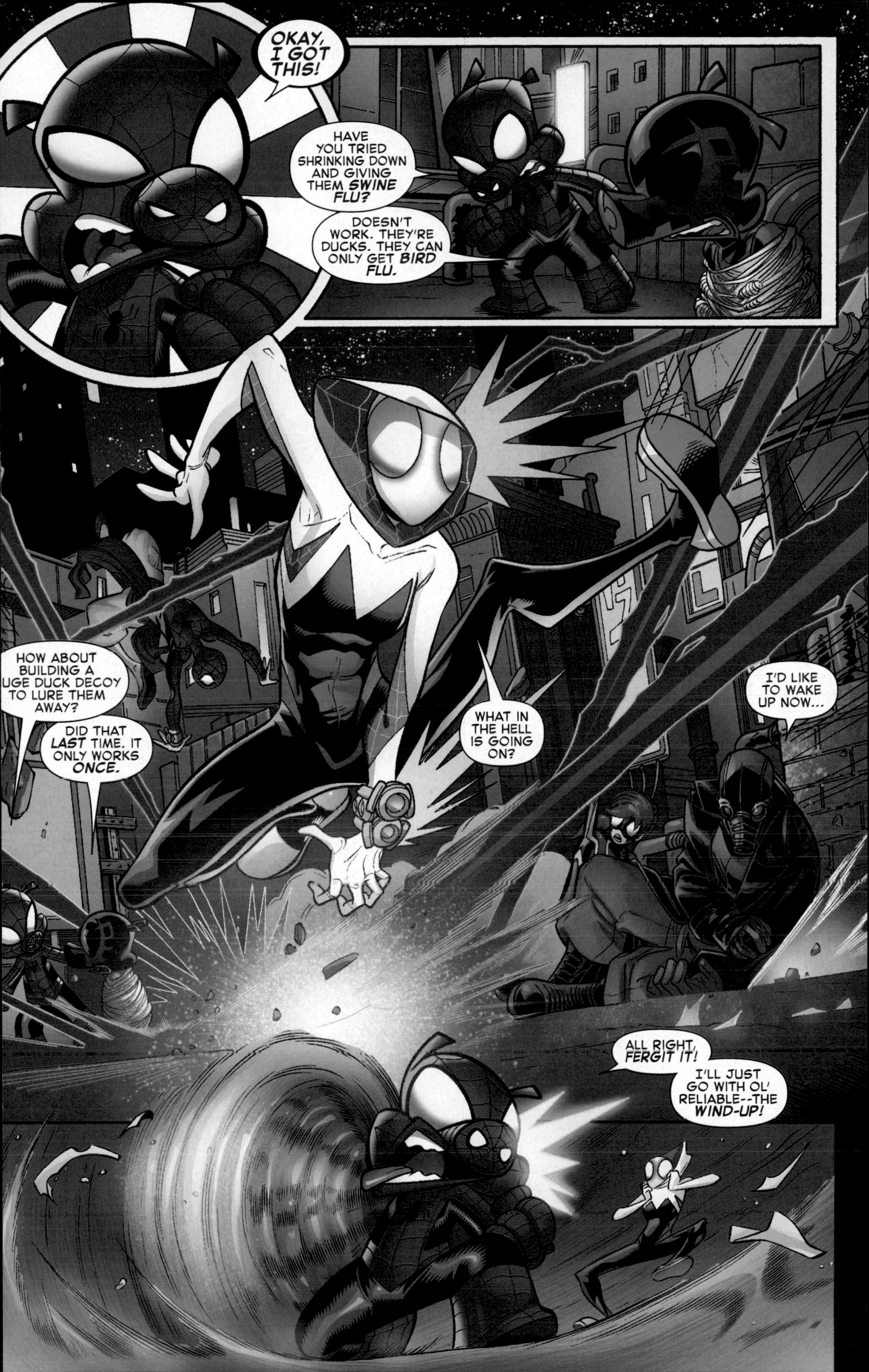
OKAY, I GOT THIS!
HAVE YOU TRIED SHRINKING DOWN AND GIVING THEM SWINE FLU?
DOESN'T WORK. THEY'RE DUCKS. THEY CAN ONLY GET BIRD FLU.
HOW ABOUT BUILDING A UGE DUCK DECOY TO LURE THEM AWAY?
DID THAT LAST TIME. IT ONLY WORKS ONCE.
WHAT IN THE HELL IS GOING ON?
I'D LIKE TO WAKE UP NOW...
ALL RIGHT, FERGIT IT!
I'LL JUST GO WITH OL' RELIABLE--THE WIND-UP!

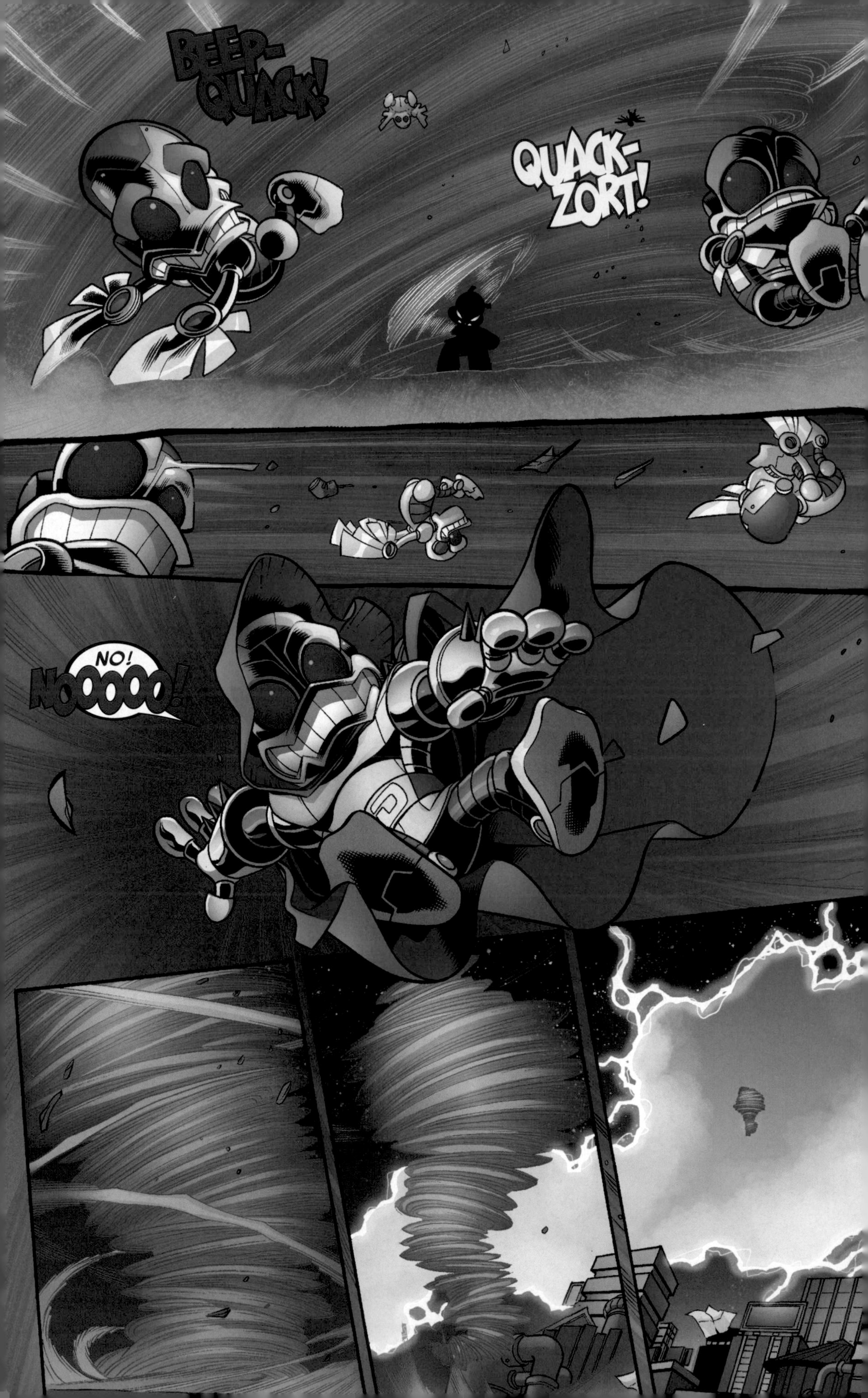
BEEP-QUACK!
QUACK-ZORT!
NO!
NOOOOO!

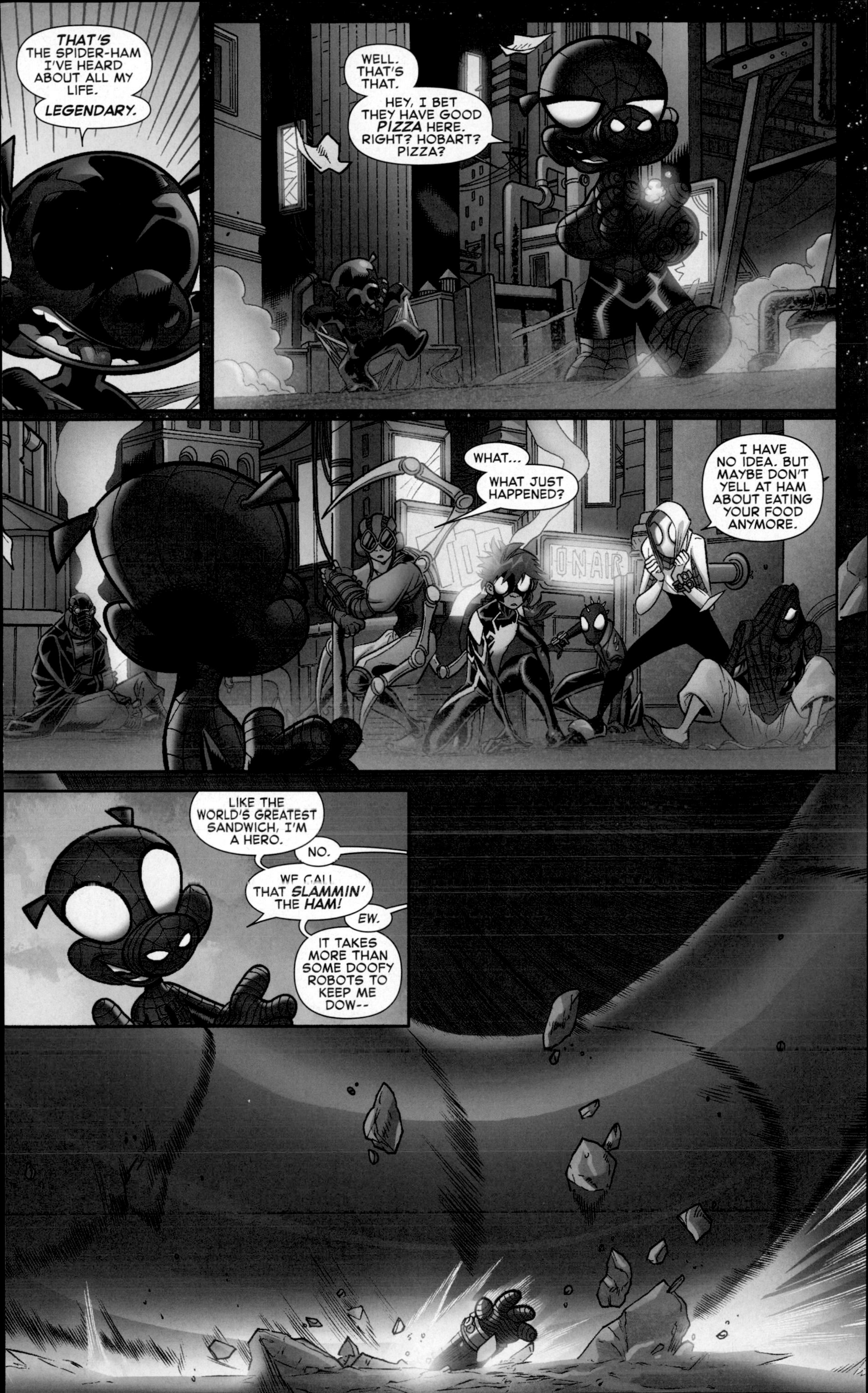
THAT'S THE SPIDER-HAM I'VE HEARD ABOUT ALL MY LIFE.
LEGENDARY.
WELL. THAT'S THAT.
HEY, I BET THEY HAVE GOOD PIZZA HERE. RIGHT? HOBART? PIZZA?
WHAT...
WHAT JUST HAPPENED?
I HAVE NO IDEA. BUT MAYBE DON'T YELL AT HAM ABOUT EATING YOUR FOOD ANYMORE.
ON AIR
LIKE THE WORLD'S GREATEST SANDWICH, I'M A HERO.
NO.
WE CALL THAT SLAMMIN' THE HAM!
EW.
IT TAKES MORE THAN SOME DOOFY ROBOTS TO KEEP ME DOW--

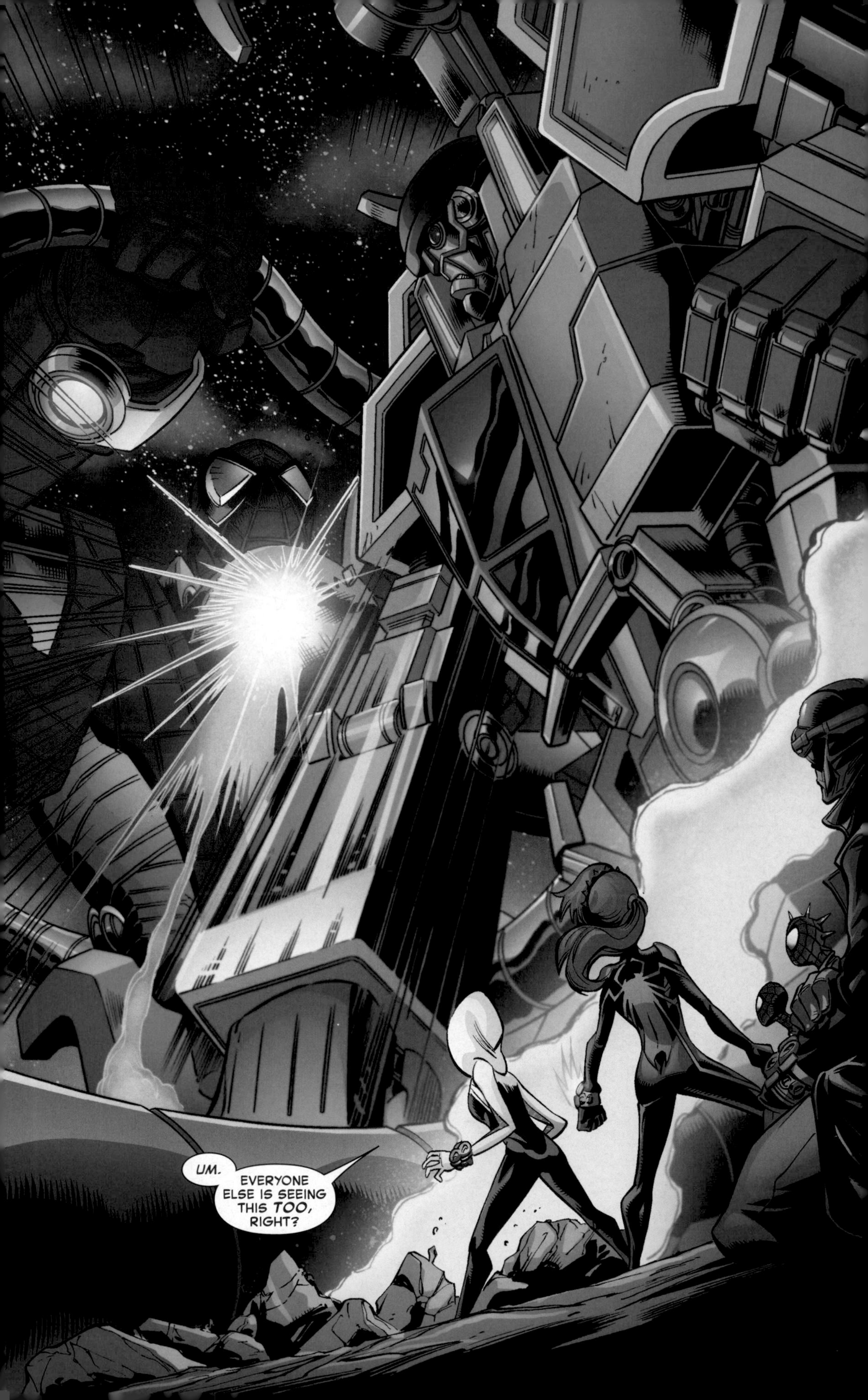
UM.
EVERYONE ELSE IS SEEING THIS TOO, RIGHT?

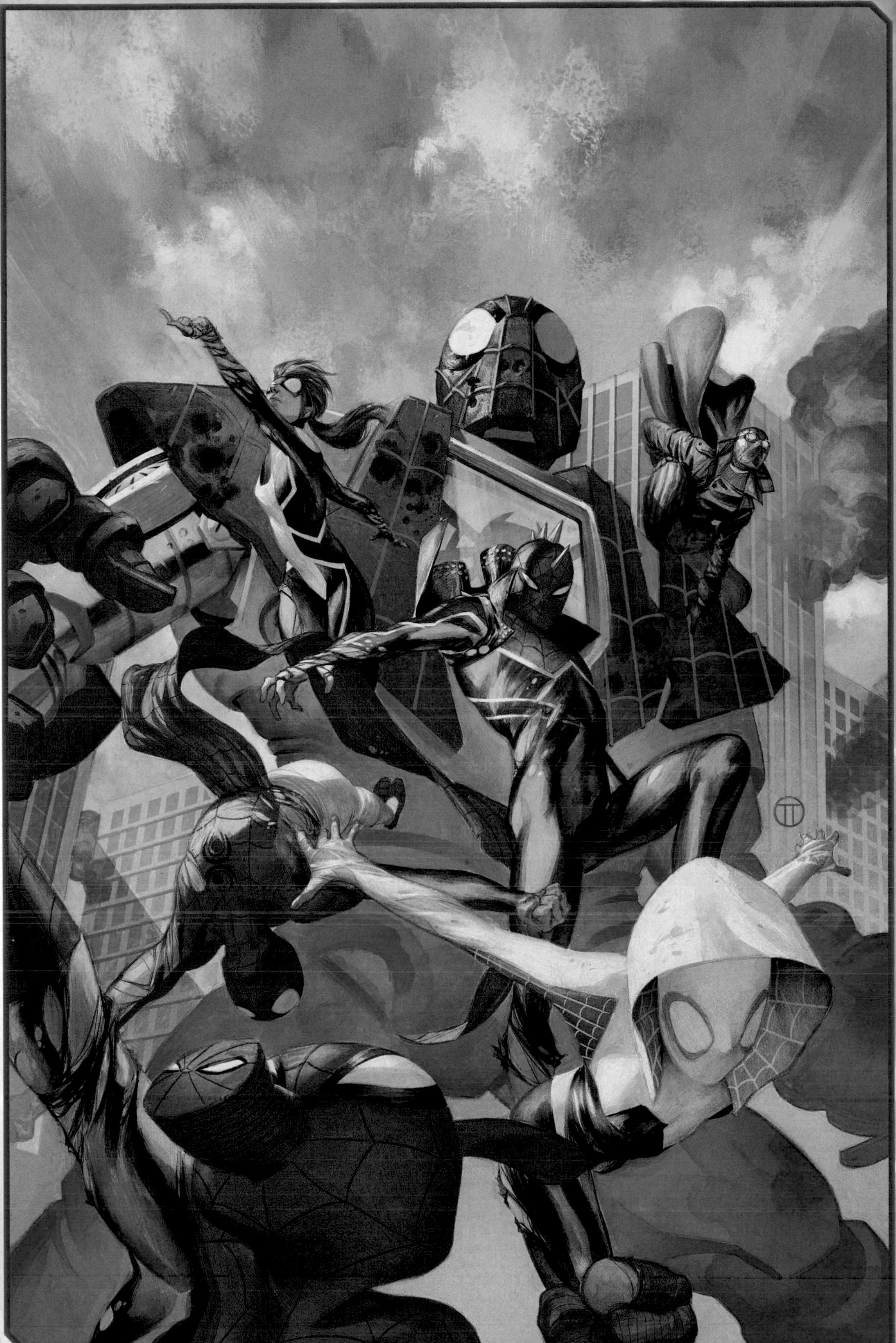

TANGLED STATES PART TWO : TECHNOCRACY

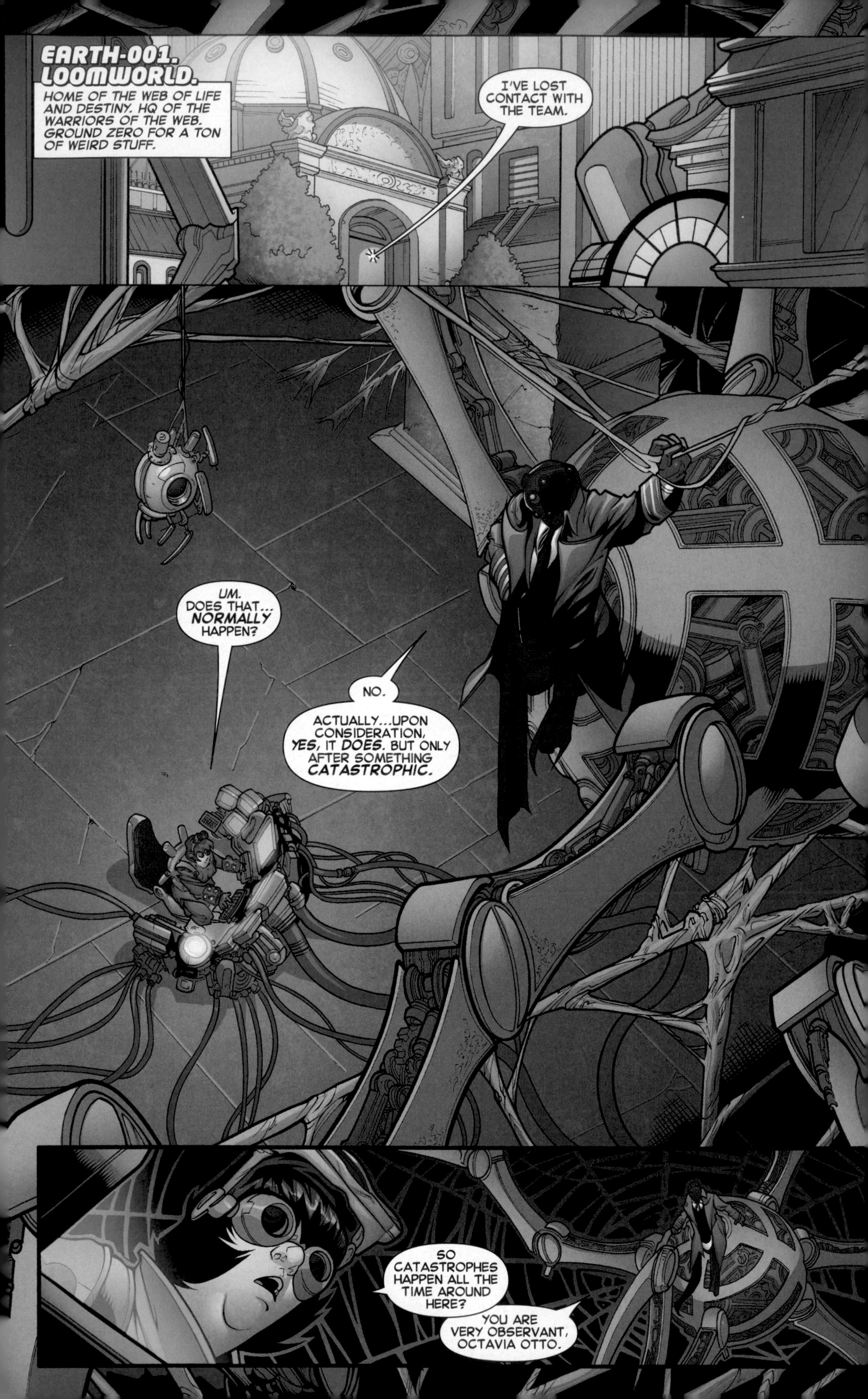
EARTH-001. LOOMWORLD.
HOME OF THE WEB OF LIFE AND DESTINY. HQ OF THE WARRIORS OF THE WEB. GROUND ZERO FOR A TON OF WEIRD STUFF.
I'VE LOST CONTACT WITH THE TEAM.
UM. DOES THAT... NORMALLY HAPPEN?
NO.
ACTUALLY...UPON CONSIDERATION, YES, IT DOES. BUT ONLY AFTER SOMETHING CATASTROPHIC.
SO CATASTROPHES HAPPEN ALL THE TIME AROUND HERE?
YOU ARE VERY OBSERVANT, OCTAVIA OTTO.

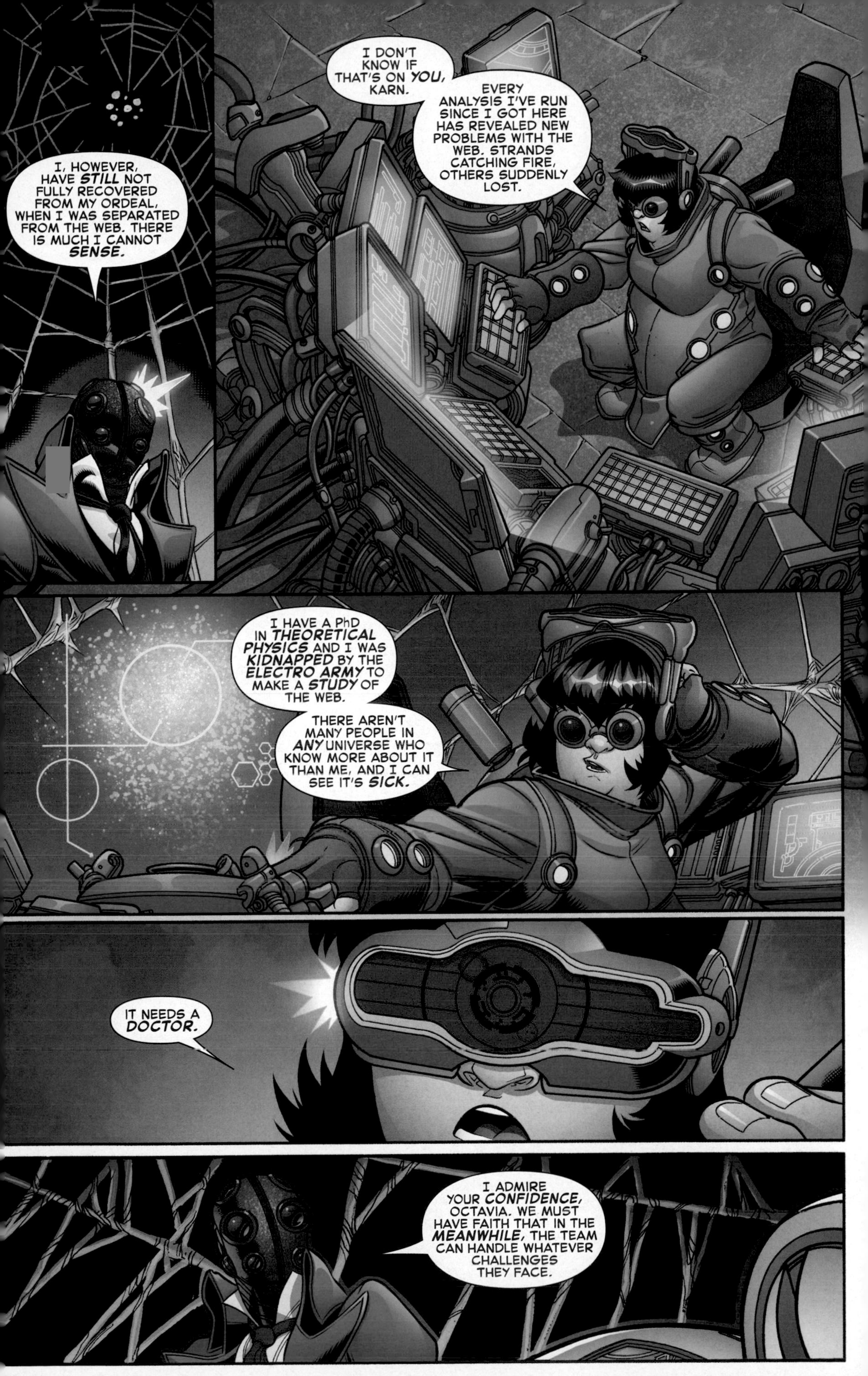
I, HOWEVER, HAVE STILL NOT FULLY RECOVERED FROM MY ORDEAL, WHEN I WAS SEPARATED FROM THE WEB. THERE IS MUCH I CANNOT SENSE.
I DON'T KNOW IF THAT'S ON YOU, KARN.
EVERY ANALYSIS I'VE RUN SINCE I GOT HERE HAS REVEALED NEW PROBLEMS WITH THE WEB. STRANDS CATCHING FIRE, OTHERS SUDDENLY LOST.
I HAVE A PhD IN THEORETICAL PHYSICS AND I WAS KIDNAPPED BY THE ELECTRO ARMY TO MAKE A STUDY OF THE WEB.
THERE AREN'T MANY PEOPLE IN ANY UNIVERSE WHO KNOW MORE ABOUT IT THAN ME, AND I CAN SEE IT'S SICK.
IT NEEDS A DOCTOR.
I ADMIRE YOUR CONFIDENCE, OCTAVIA. WE MUST HAVE FAITH THAT IN THE MEANWHILE, THE TEAM CAN HANDLE WHATEVER CHALLENGES THEY FACE.

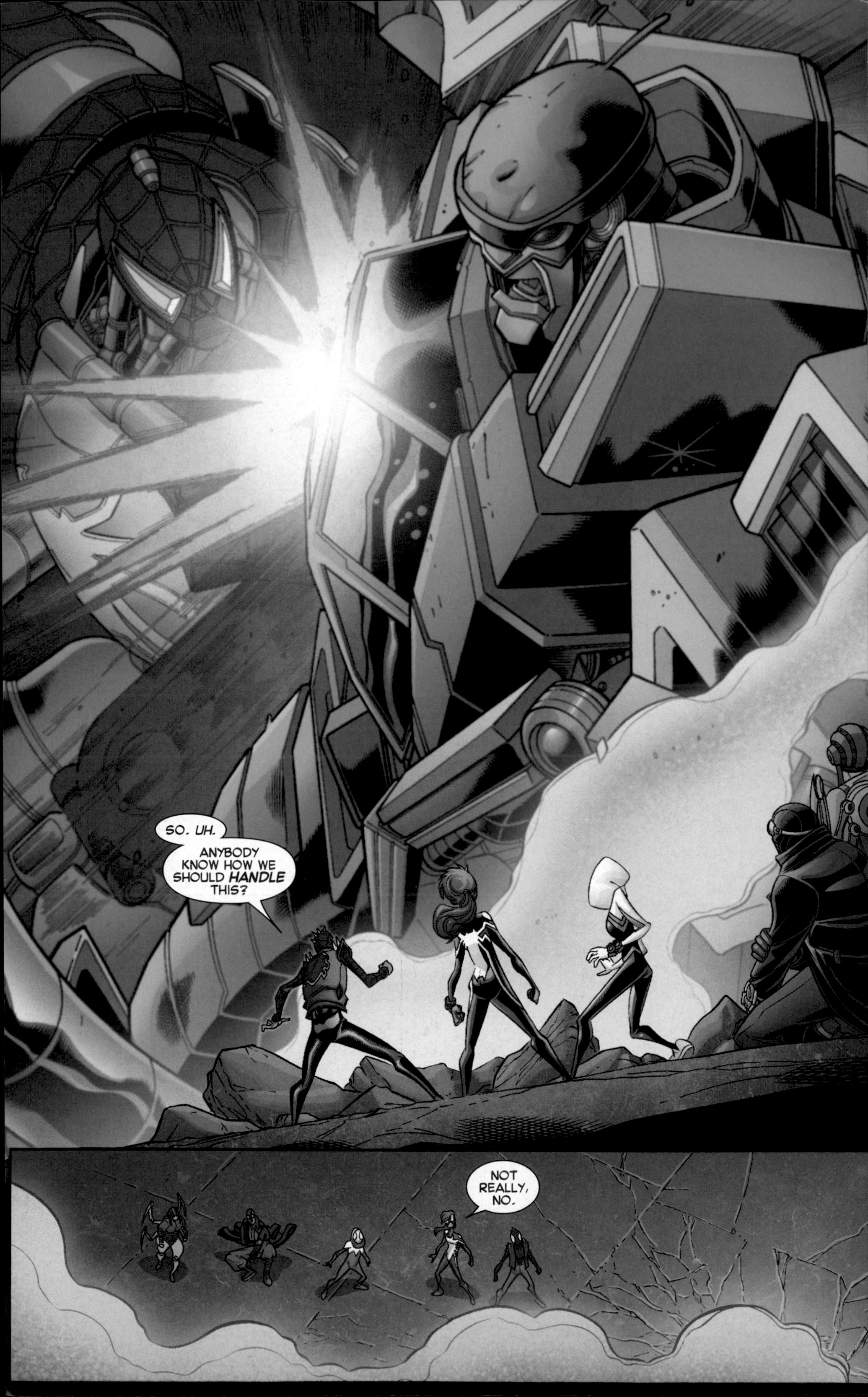
SO. UH.
ANYBODY KNOW HOW WE SHOULD HANDLE THIS?
NOT REALLY, NO.

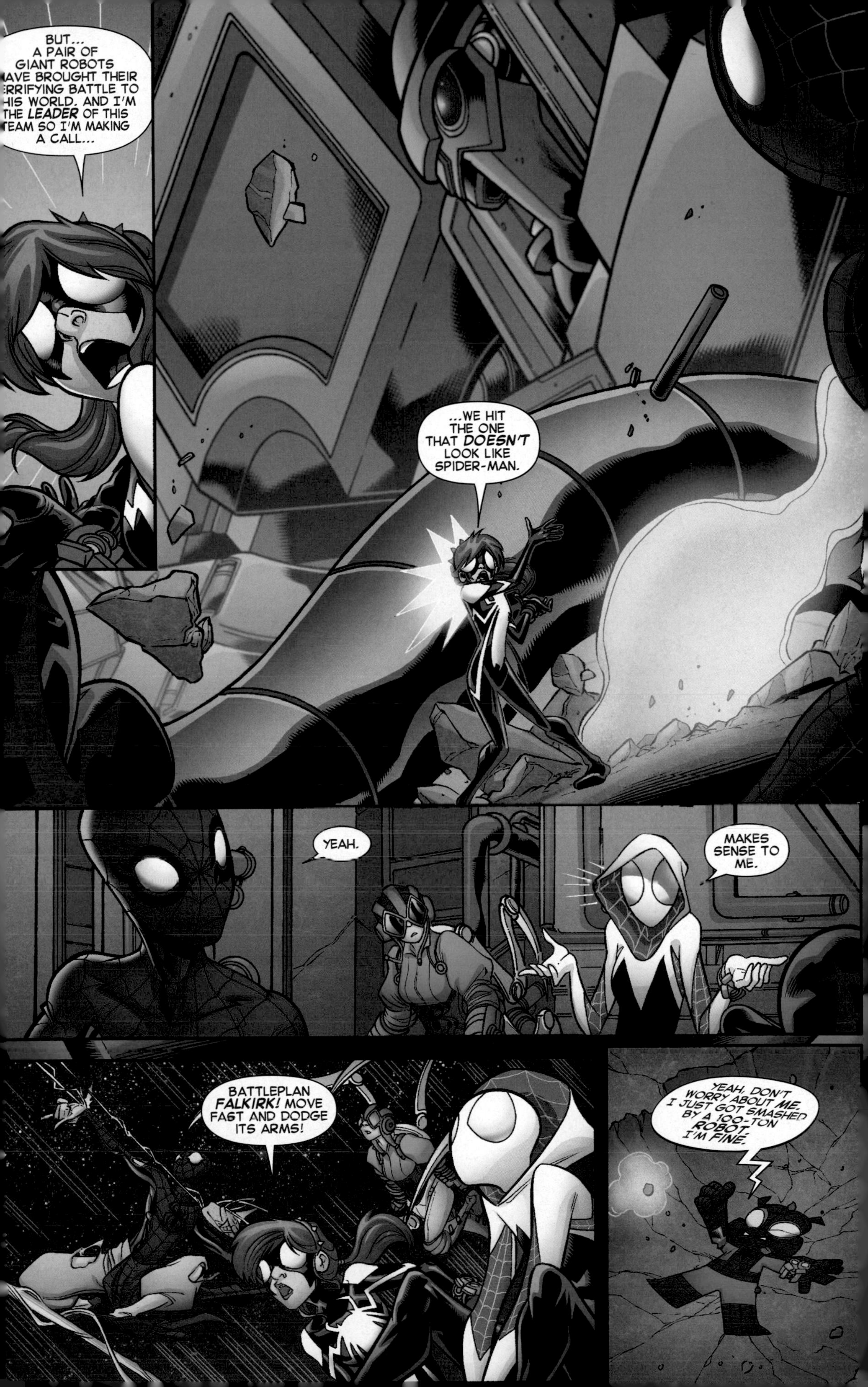
BUT... A PAIR OF GIANT ROBOTS HAVE BROUGHT THEIR TERRIFYING BATTLE TO THIS WORLD. AND I'M THE LEADER OF THIS TEAM SO I'M MAKING A CALL...
...WE HIT THE ONE THAT DOESN'T LOOK LIKE SPIDER-MAN.
YEAH.
MAKES SENSE TO ME.
BATTLEPLAN FALKIRK! MOVE FAST AND DODGE ITS ARMS!
YEAH, DON'T WORRY ABOUT ME. I JUST GOT SMASHED BY A 100-TON ROBOT. I'M FINE.

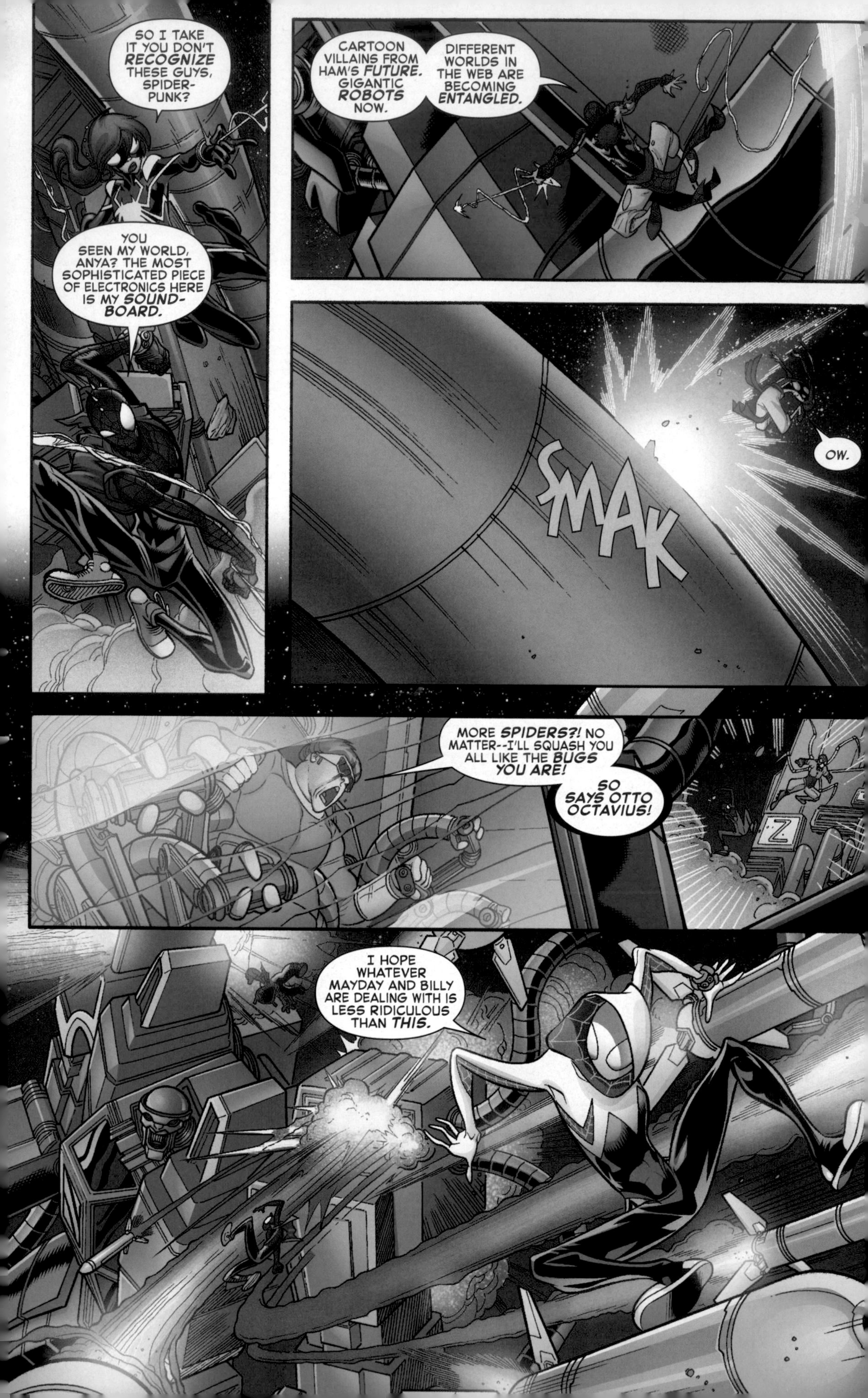
SO I TAKE IT YOU DON'T RECOGNIZE THESE GUYS, SPIDER-PUNK?
YOU SEEN MY WORLD, ANYA? THE MOST SOPHISTICATED PIECE OF ELECTRONICS HERE IS MY SOUND-BOARD.
CARTOON VILLAINS FROM HAM'S FUTURE. GIGANTIC ROBOTS NOW.
DIFFERENT WORLDS IN THE WEB ARE BECOMING ENTANGLED.
SMAK
OW.
MORE SPIDERS?! NO MATTER--I'LL SQUASH YOU ALL LIKE THE BUGS YOU ARE!
SO SAYS OTTO OCTAVIUS!
I HOPE WHATEVER MAYDAY AND BILLY ARE DEALING WITH IS LESS RIDICULOUS THAN THIS.

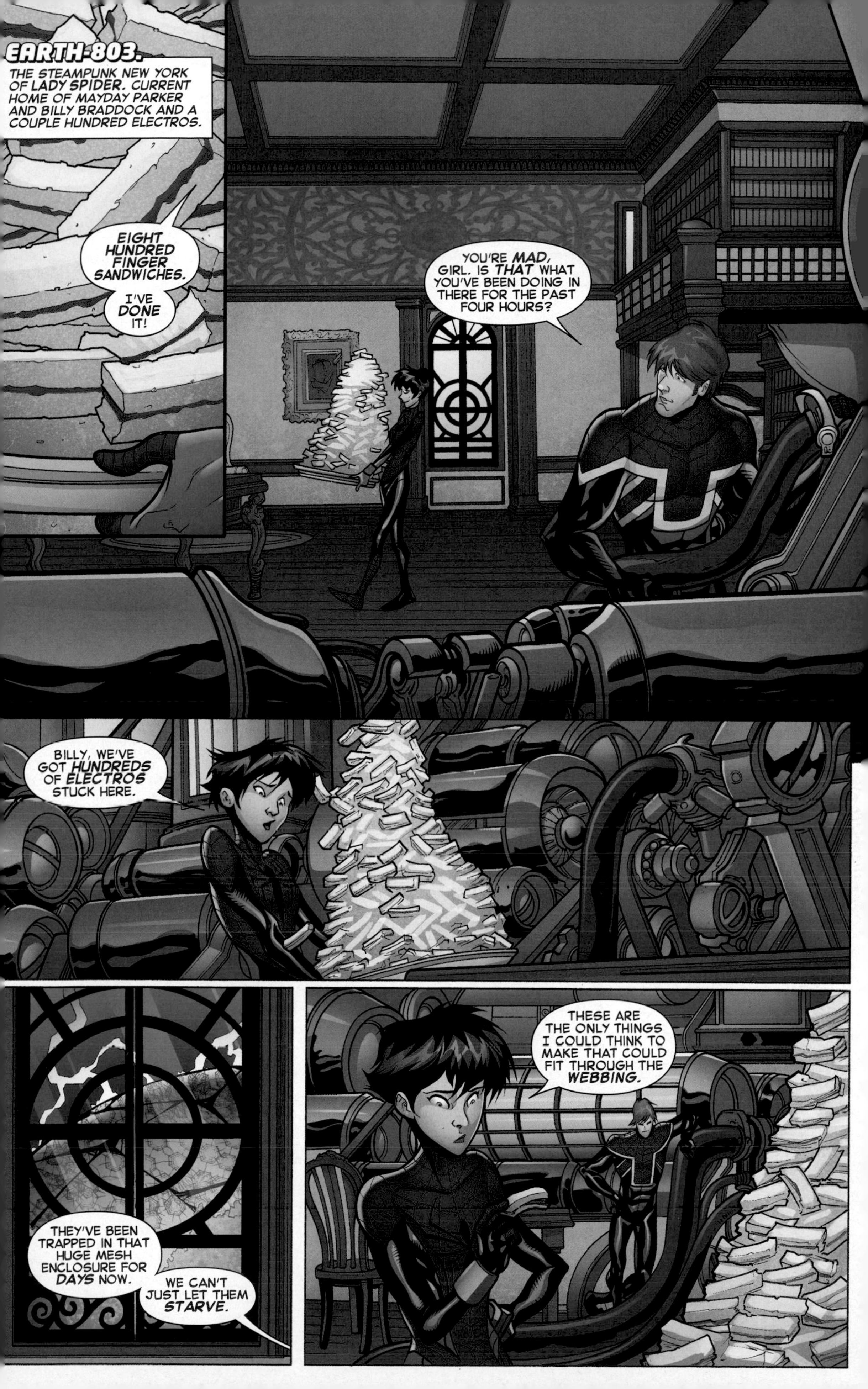
EARTH-803.
THE STEAMPUNK NEW YORK OF LADY SPIDER. CURRENT HOME OF MAYDAY PARKER AND BILLY BRADDOCK AND A COUPLE HUNDRED ELECTROS.
EIGHT HUNDRED FINGER SANDWICHES.
I'VE DONE IT!
YOU'RE MAD, GIRL. IS THAT WHAT YOU'VE BEEN DOING IN THERE FOR THE PAST FOUR HOURS?
BILLY, WE'VE GOT HUNDREDS OF ELECTROS STUCK HERE.
THEY'VE BEEN TRAPPED IN THAT HUGE MESH ENCLOSURE FOR DAYS NOW.
WE CAN'T JUST LET THEM STARVE.
THESE ARE THE ONLY THINGS I COULD THINK TO MAKE THAT COULD FIT THROUGH THE WEBBING.

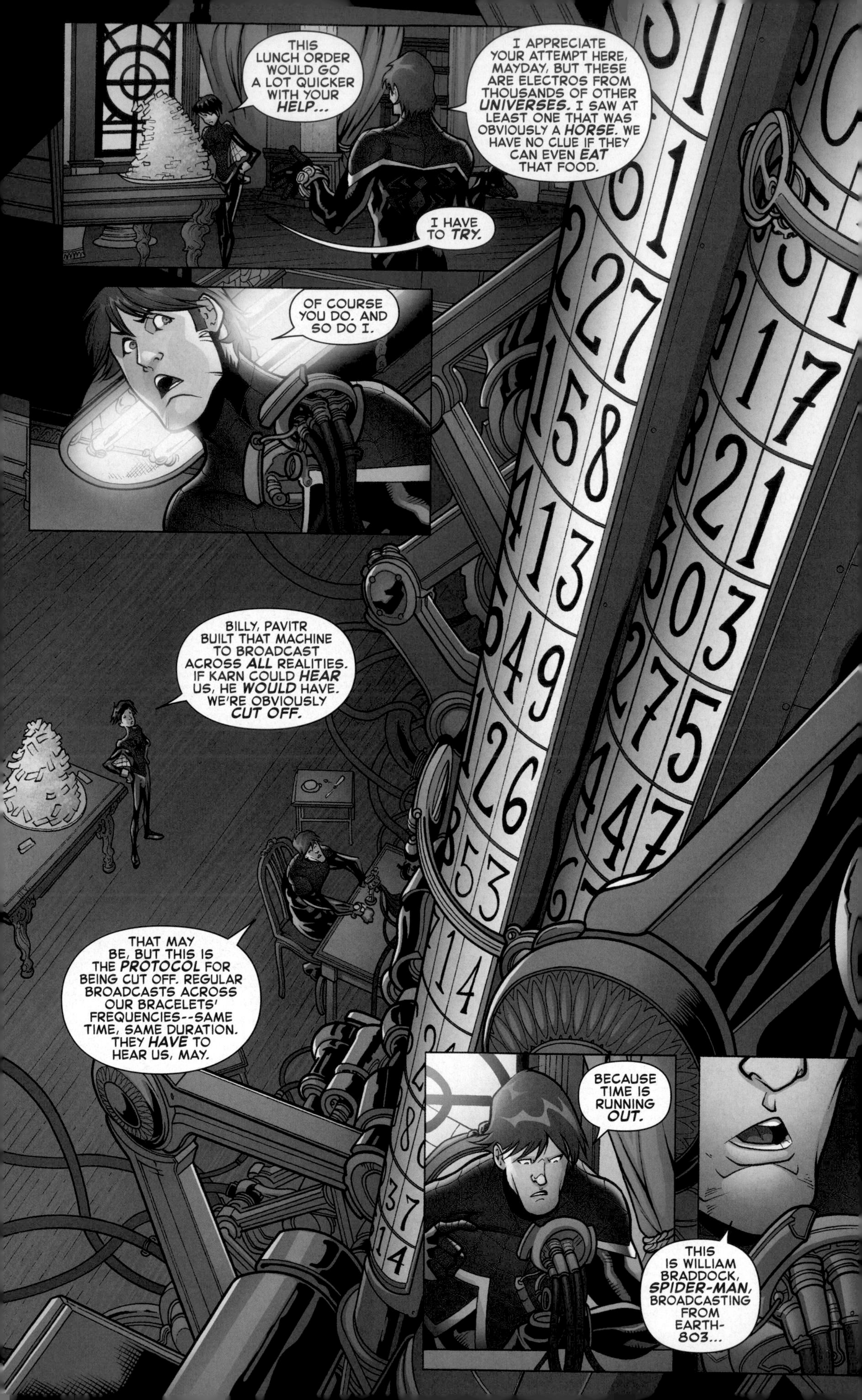
THIS LUNCH ORDER WOULD GO A LOT QUICKER WITH YOUR HELP...
I APPRECIATE YOUR ATTEMPT HERE, MAYDAY, BUT THESE ARE ELECTROS FROM THOUSANDS OF OTHER UNIVERSES. I SAW AT LEAST ONE THAT WAS OBVIOUSLY A HORSE. WE HAVE NO CLUE IF THEY CAN EVEN EAT THAT FOOD.
I HAVE TO TRY.
OF COURSE YOU DO. AND SO DO I.
BILLY, PAVITR BUILT THAT MACHINE TO BROADCAST ACROSS ALL REALITIES. IF KARN COULD HEAR US, HE WOULD HAVE. WE'RE OBVIOUSLY CUT OFF.
THAT MAY BE, BUT THIS IS THE PROTOCOL FOR BEING CUT OFF. REGULAR BROADCASTS ACROSS OUR BRACELETS' FREQUENCIES--SAME TIME, SAME DURATION. THEY HAVE TO HEAR US, MAY.
BECAUSE TIME IS RUNNING OUT.
THIS IS WILLIAM BRADDOCK, SPIDER-MAN, BROADCASTING FROM EARTH-803...

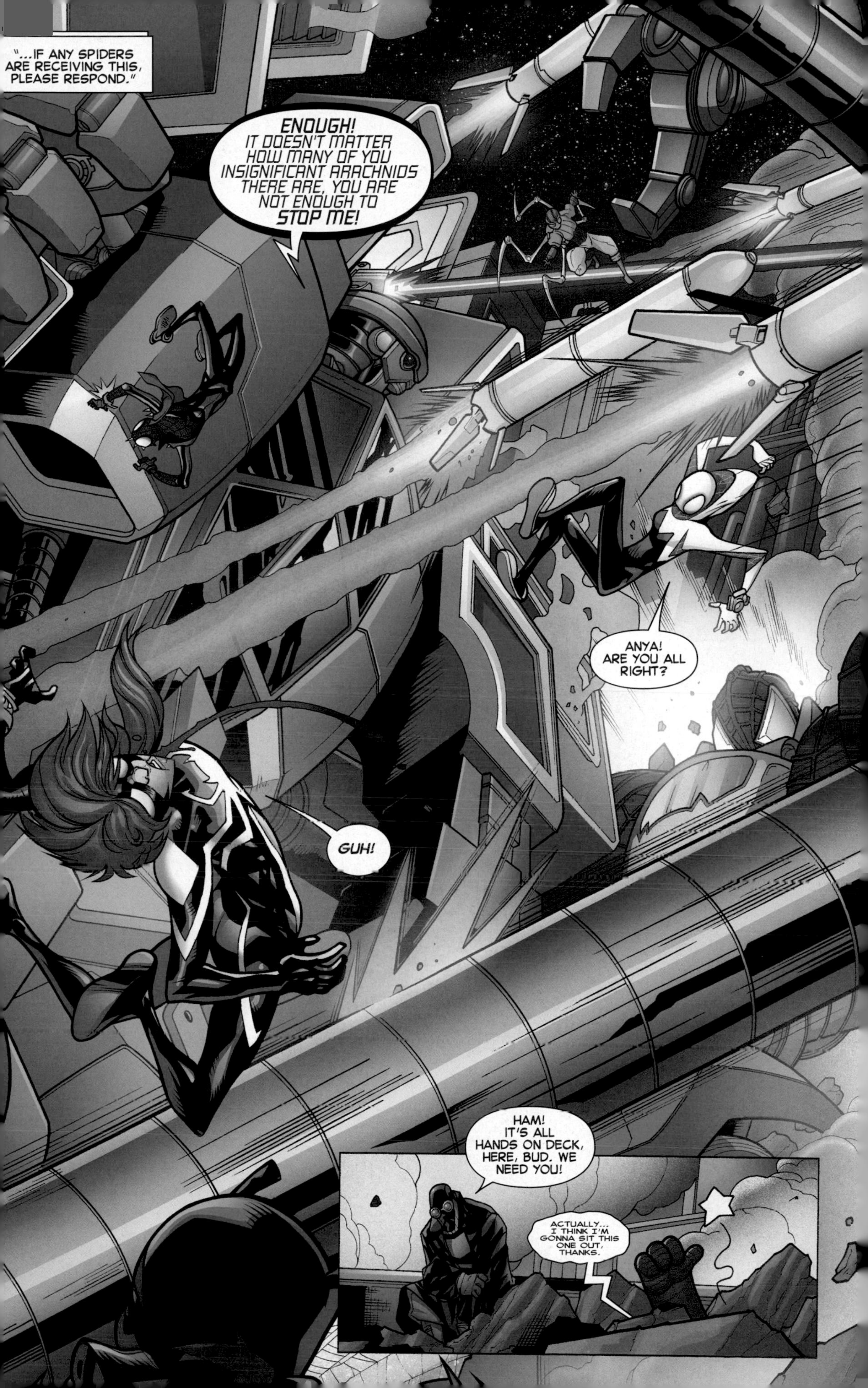
"...IF ANY SPIDERS ARE RECEIVING THIS, PLEASE RESPOND."
ENOUGH! IT DOESN'T MATTER HOW MANY OF YOU INSIGNIFICANT ARACHNIDS THERE ARE, YOU ARE NOT ENOUGH TO STOP ME!
ANYA! ARE YOU ALL RIGHT?
GUH!
HAM! IT'S ALL HANDS ON DECK, HERE, BUD. WE NEED YOU!
ACTUALLY... I THINK I'M GONNA SIT THIS ONE OUT, THANKS.

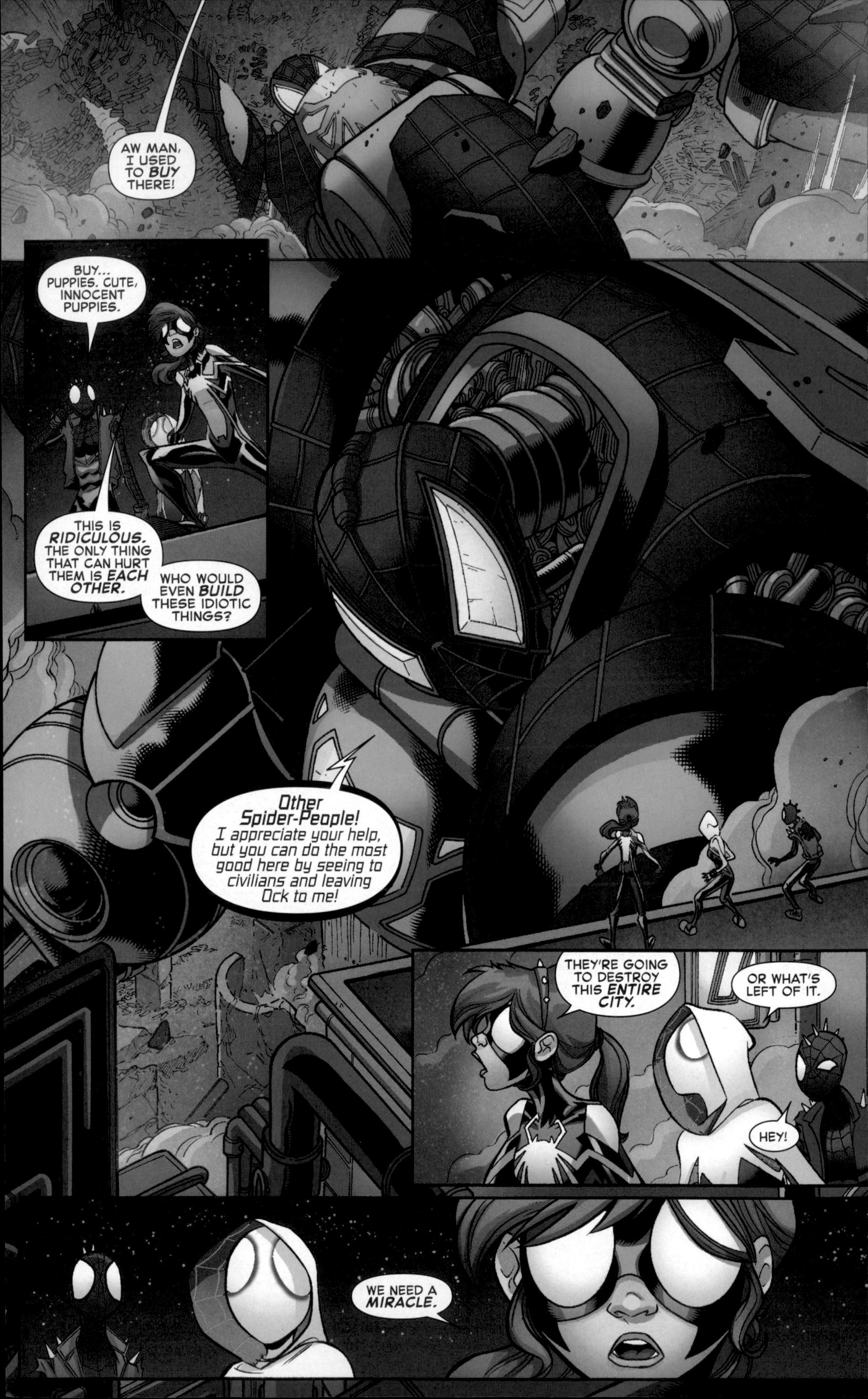
AW MAN, I USED TO BUY THERE!
BUY... PUPPIES. CUTE, INNOCENT PUPPIES.
THIS IS RIDICULOUS. THE ONLY THING THAT CAN HURT THEM IS EACH OTHER.
WHO WOULD EVEN BUILD THESE IDIOTIC THINGS?
Other Spider-People! I appreciate your help, but you can do the most good here by seeing to civilians and leaving Ock to me!
THEY'RE GOING TO DESTROY THIS ENTIRE CITY.
OR WHAT'S LEFT OF IT.
HEY!
WE NEED A MIRACLE.

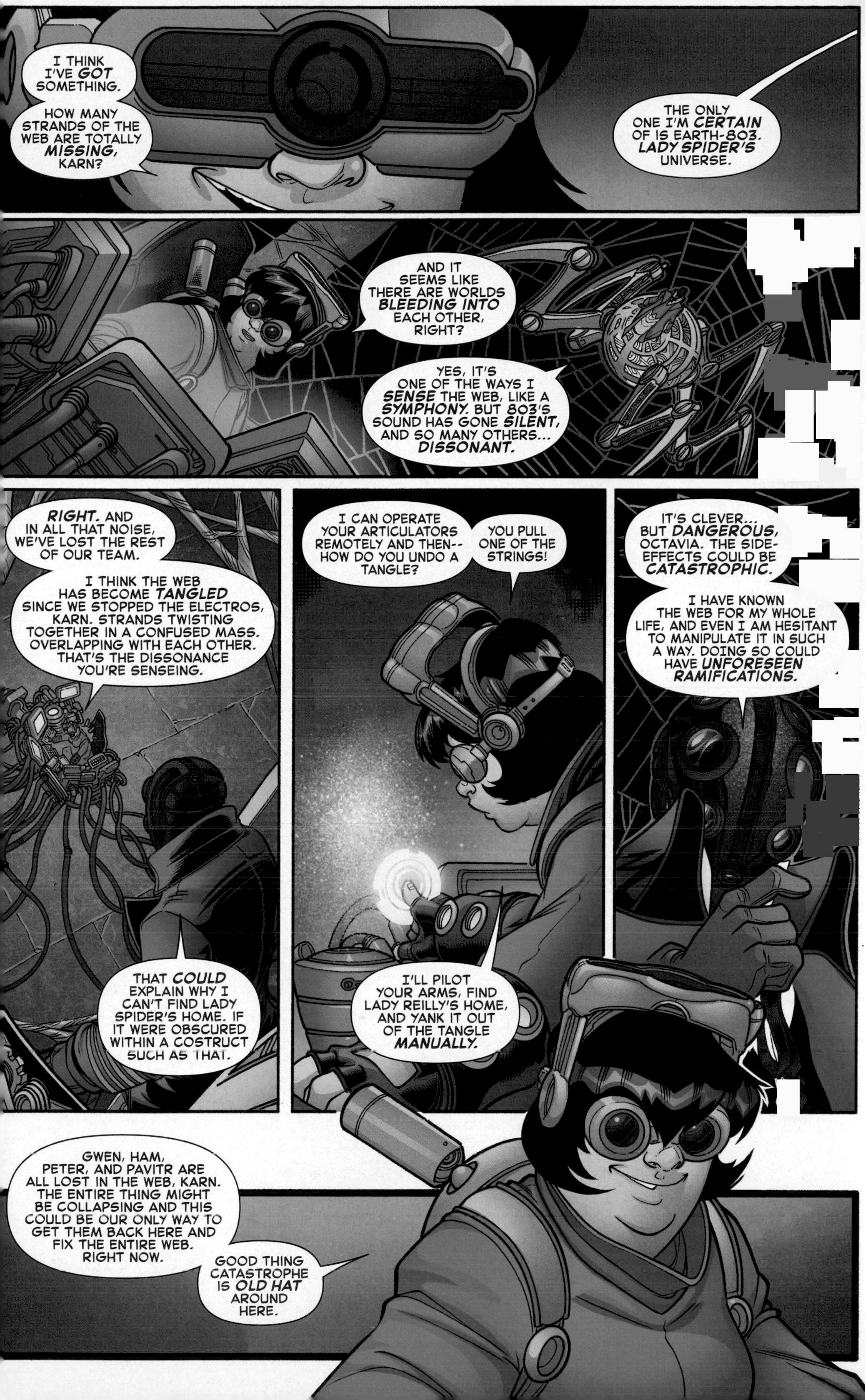
I THINK I'VE GOT SOMETHING.
HOW MANY STRANDS OF THE WEB ARE TOTALLY MISSING, KARN?
THE ONLY ONE I'M CERTAIN OF IS EARTH-803. LADY SPIDER'S UNIVERSE.
AND IT SEEMS LIKE THERE ARE WORLDS BLEEDING INTO EACH OTHER, RIGHT?
YES, IT'S ONE OF THE WAYS I SENSE THE WEB, LIKE A SYMPHONY. BUT 803'S SOUND HAS GONE SILENT, AND SO MANY OTHERS... DISSONANT.
RIGHT. AND IN ALL THAT NOISE, WE'VE LOST THE REST OF OUR TEAM.
I THINK THE WEB HAS BECOME TANGLED SINCE WE STOPPED THE ELECTROS, KARN. STRANDS TWISTING TOGETHER IN A CONFUSED MASS. OVERLAPPING WITH EACH OTHER. THAT'S THE DISSONANCE YOU'RE SENSEING.
THAT COULD EXPLAIN WHY I CAN'T FIND LADY SPIDER'S HOME. IF IT WERE OBSCURED WITHIN A COSTRUCT SUCH AS THAT.
I CAN OPERATE YOUR ARTICULATORS REMOTELY AND THEN-- HOW DO YOU UNDO A TANGLE?
YOU PULL ONE OF THE STRINGS!
I'LL PILOT YOUR ARMS, FIND LADY REILLY'S HOME, AND YANK IT OUT OF THE TANGLE MANUALLY.
IT'S CLEVER... BUT DANGEROUS, OCTAVIA. THE SIDE-EFFECTS COULD BE CATASTROPHIC.
I HAVE KNOWN THE WEB FOR MY WHOLE LIFE, AND EVEN I AM HESITANT TO MANIPULATE IT IN SUCH A WAY. DOING SO COULD HAVE UNFORESEEN RAMIFICATIONS.
GWEN, HAM, PETER, AND PAVITR ARE ALL LOST IN THE WEB, KARN. THE ENTIRE THING MIGHT BE COLLAPSING AND THIS COULD BE OUR ONLY WAY TO GET THEM BACK HERE AND FIX THE ENTIRE WEB. RIGHT NOW.
GOOD THING CATASTROPHE IS OLD HAT AROUND HERE.

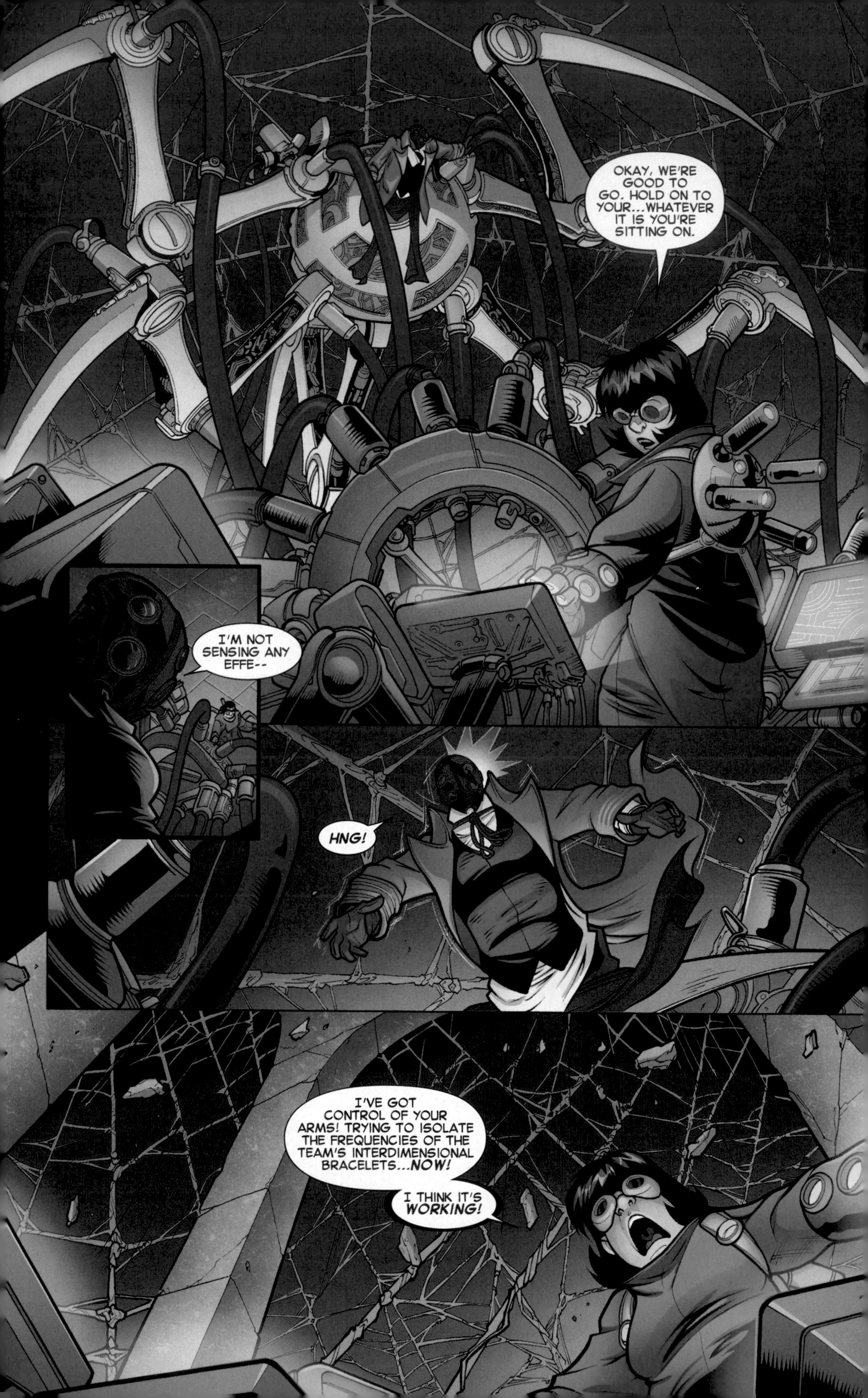
OKAY, WE'RE GOOD TO GO. HOLD ON TO YOUR...WHATEVER IT IS YOU'RE SITTING ON.
I'M NOT SENSING ANY EFFE--
HNG!
I'VE GOT CONTROL OF YOUR ARMS! TRYING TO ISOLATE THE FREQUENCIES OF THE TEAM'S INTERDIMENSIONAL BRACELETS...NOW!
I THINK IT'S WORKING!

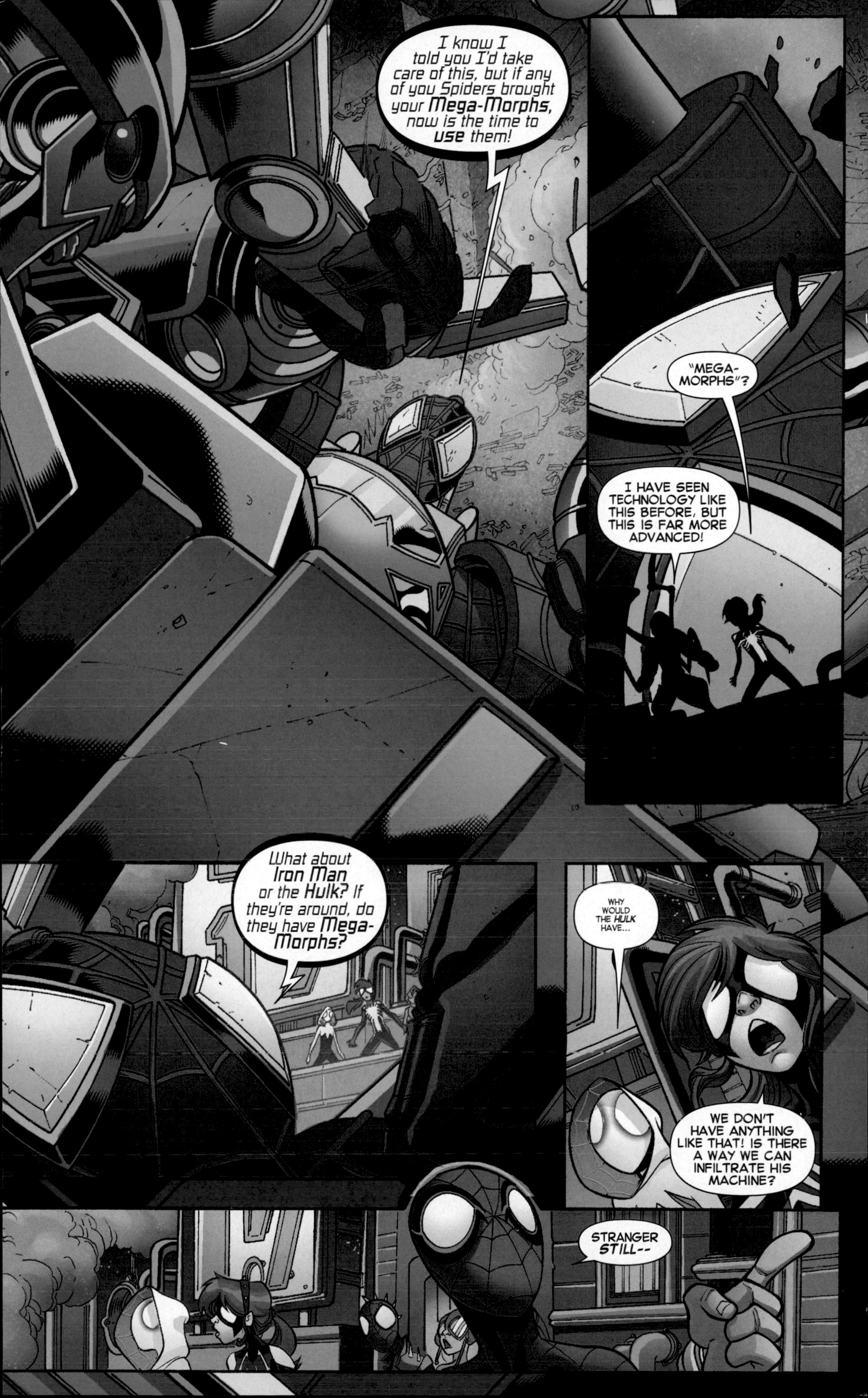
I know I told you I'd take care of this, but if any of you Spiders brought your Mega-Morphs, now is the time to use them!
"MEGA-MORPHS"?
I HAVE SEEN TECHNOLOGY LIKE THIS BEFORE, BUT THIS IS FAR MORE ADVANCED!
What about Iron Man or the Hulk? If they're around, do they have Mega-Morphs?
WHY WOULD THE HULK HAVE...
WE DON'T HAVE ANYTHING LIKE THAT! IS THERE A WAY WE CAN INFILTRATE HIS MACHINE?
STRANGER STILL--

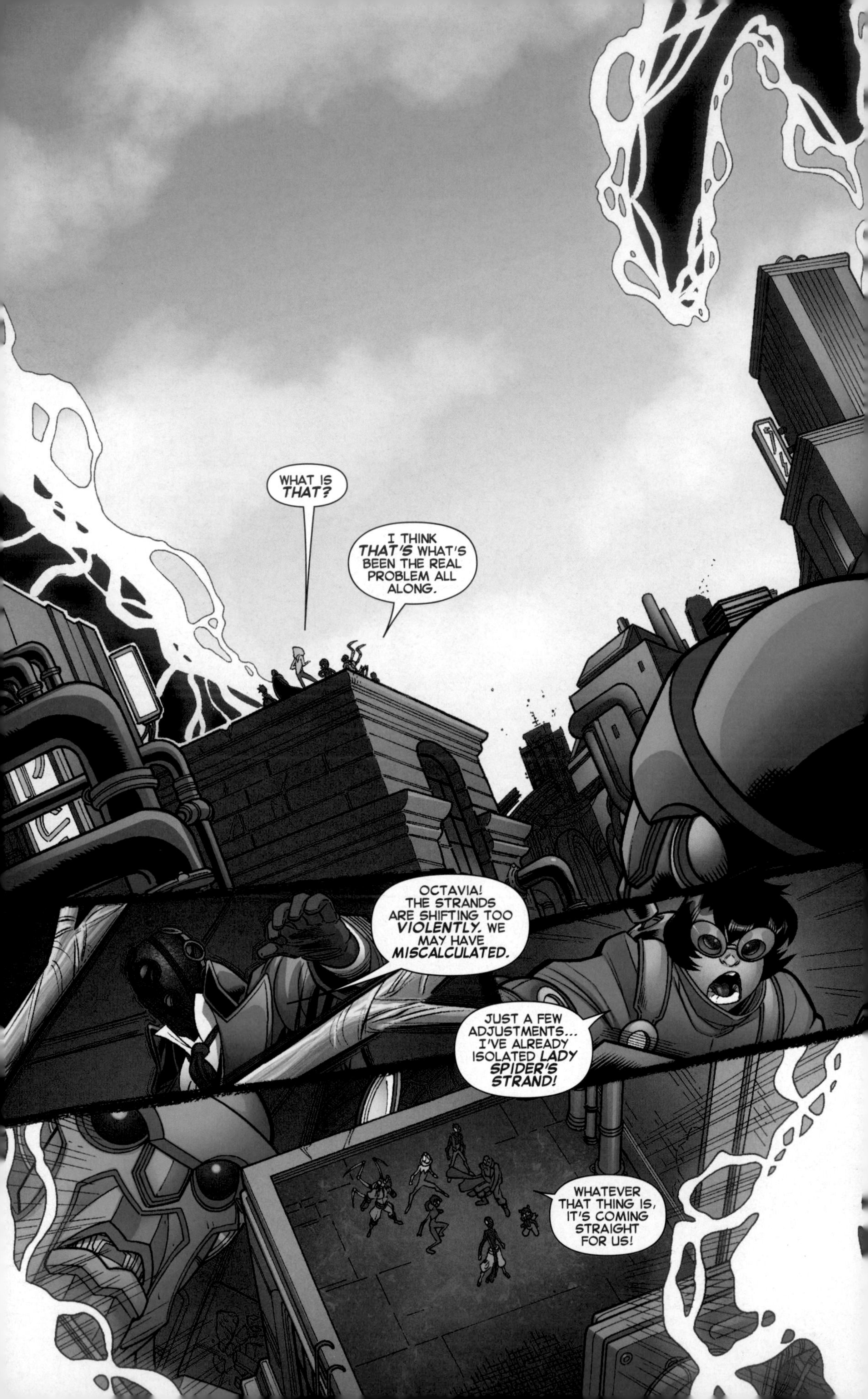
WHAT IS THAT?
I THINK THAT'S WHAT'S BEEN THE REAL PROBLEM ALL ALONG.
OCTAVIA! THE STRANDS ARE SHIFTING TOO VIOLENTLY. WE MAY HAVE MISCALCULATED.
JUST A FEW ADJUSTMENTS... I'VE ALREADY ISOLATED LADY SPIDER'S STRAND!
WHATEVER THAT THING IS, IT'S COMING STRAIGHT FOR US!

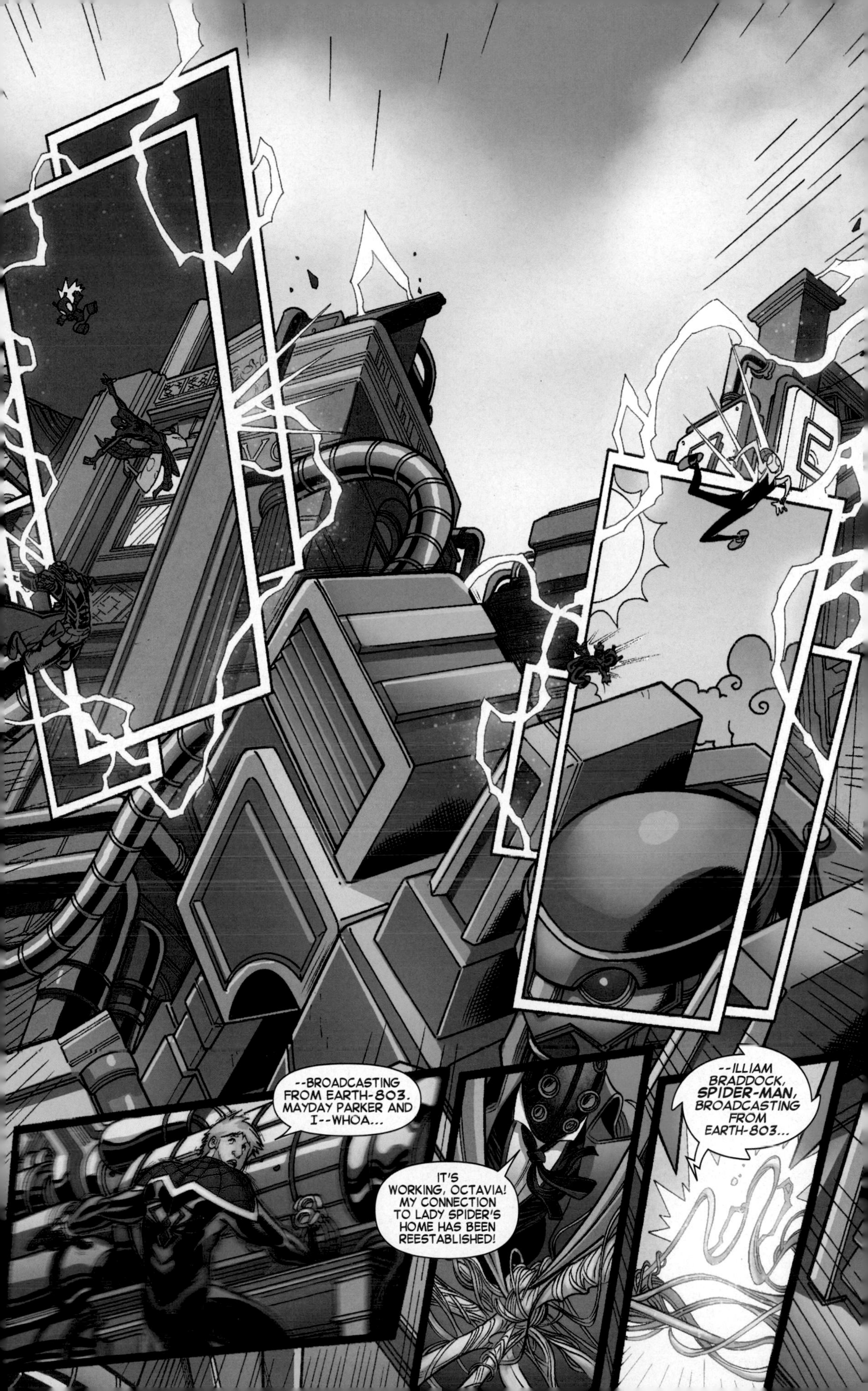
--BROADCASTING FROM EARTH-803. MAYDAY PARKER AND I--WHOA...
IT'S WORKING, OCTAVIA! MY CONNECTION TO LADY SPIDER'S HOME HAS BEEN REESTABLISHED!
--ILLIAM BRADDOCK, SPIDER-MAN, BROADCASTING FROM EARTH-803...

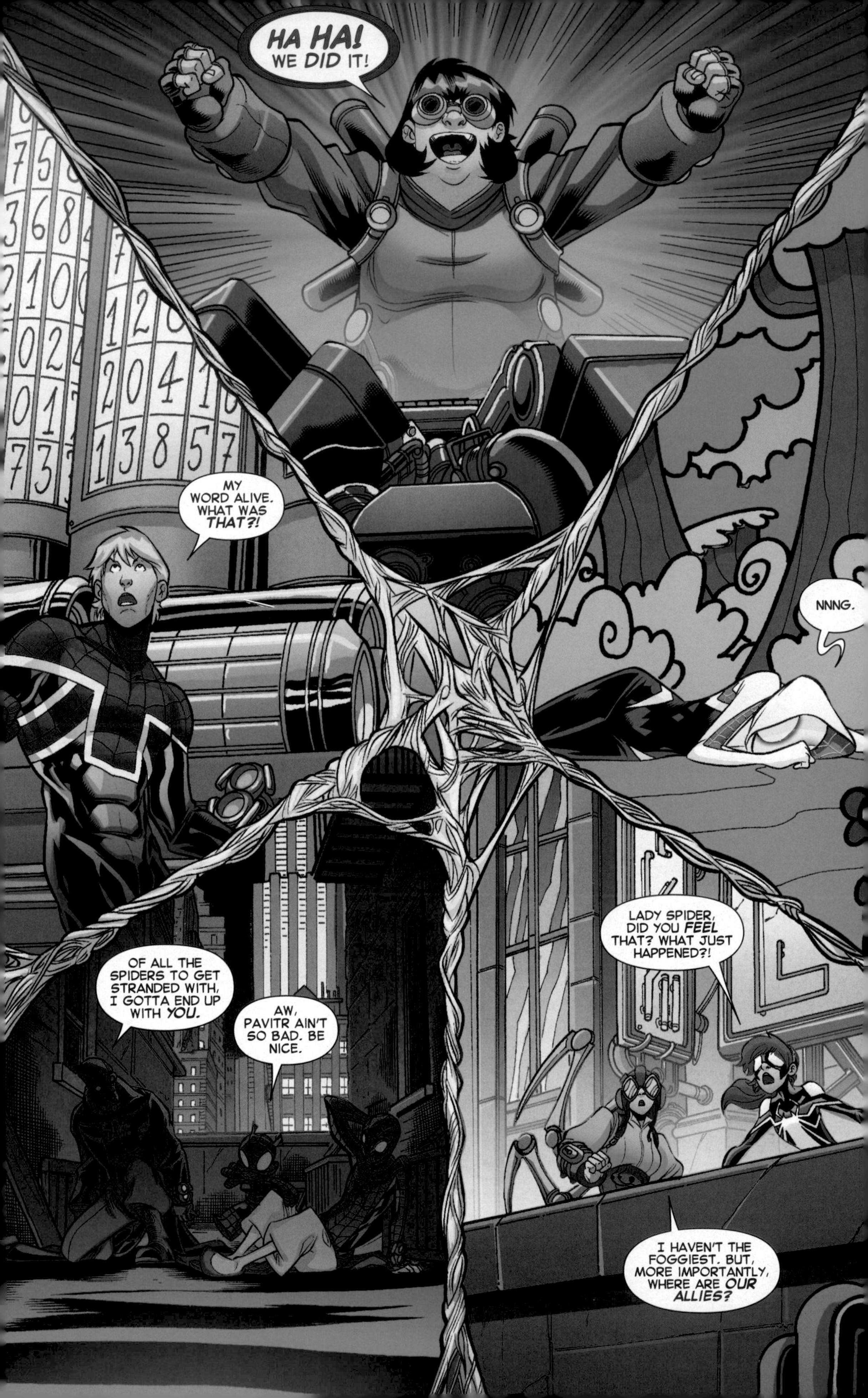
HA HA! WE DID IT!
MY WORD ALIVE. WHAT WAS THAT?!
NNNG.
OF ALL THE SPIDERS TO GET STRANDED WITH, I GOTTA END UP WITH YOU.
AW, PAVITR AIN'T SO BAD. BE NICE.
LADY SPIDER, DID YOU FEEL THAT? WHAT JUST HAPPENED?!
I HAVEN'T THE FOGGIEST. BUT, MORE IMPORTANTLY, WHERE ARE OUR ALLIES?

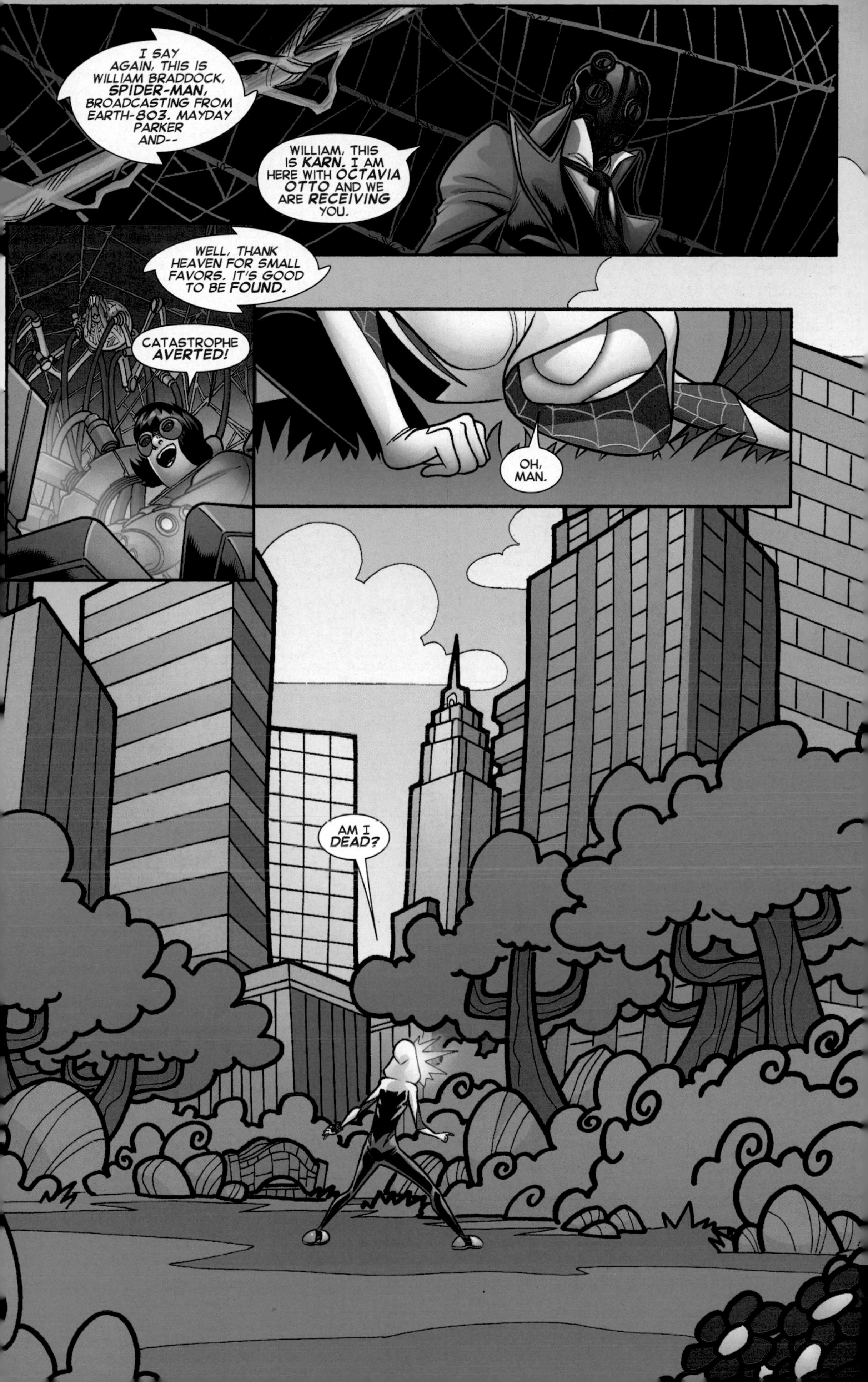
I SAY AGAIN, THIS IS WILLIAM BRADDOCK, SPIDER-MAN, BROADCASTING FROM EARTH-803. MAYDAY PARKER AND--
WILLIAM, THIS IS KARN. I AM HERE WITH OCTAVIA OTTO AND WE ARE RECEIVING YOU.
WELL, THANK HEAVEN FOR SMALL FAVORS. IT'S GOOD TO BE FOUND.
CATASTROPHE AVERTED!
OH, MAN.
AM I DEAD?

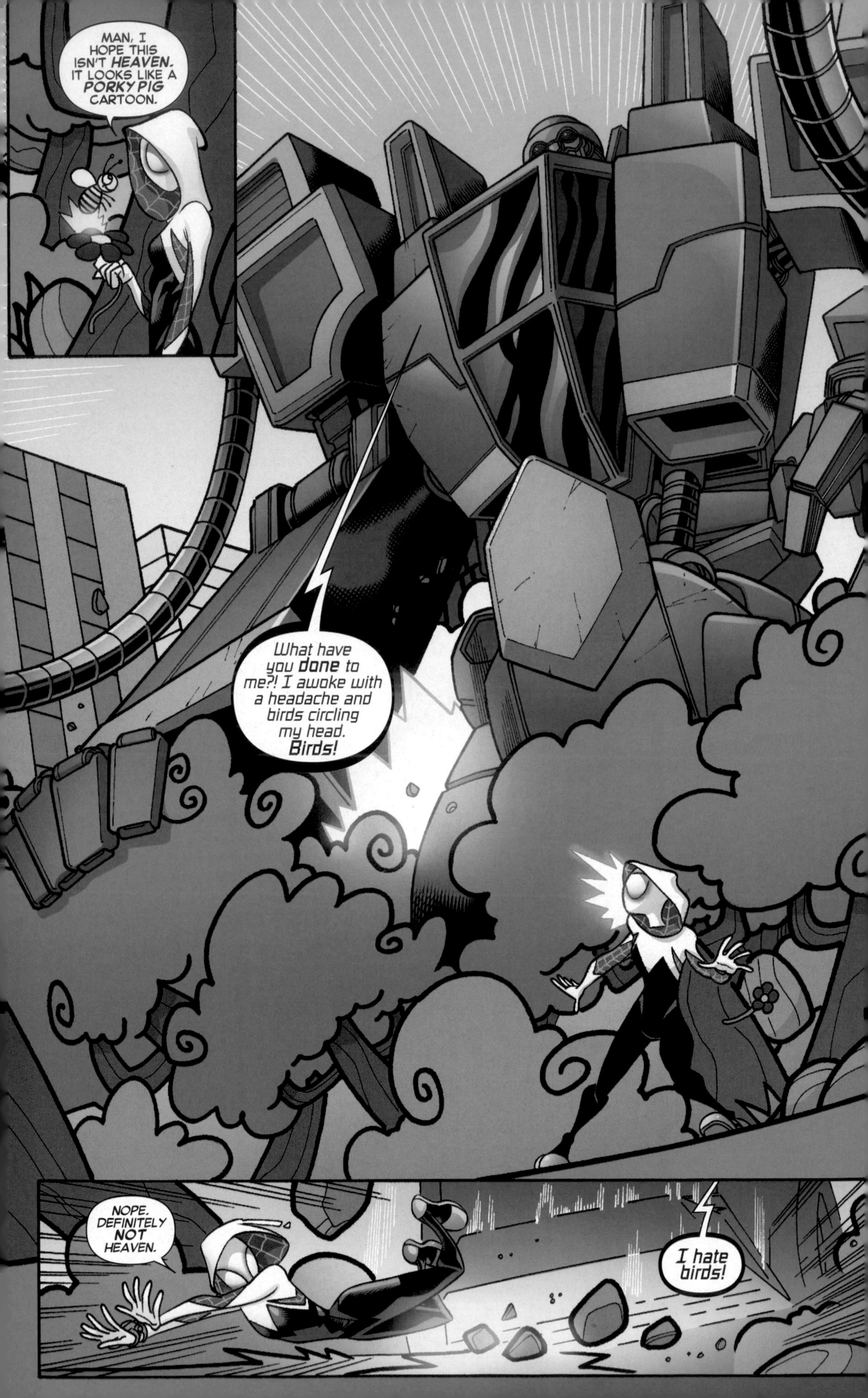

MAN, I HOPE THIS ISN'T HEAVEN. IT LOOKS LIKE A PORKY PIG CARTOON.
What have you done to me?! I awoke with a headache and birds circling my head. Birds!
NOPE. DEFINITELY NOT HEAVEN.
I hate birds!

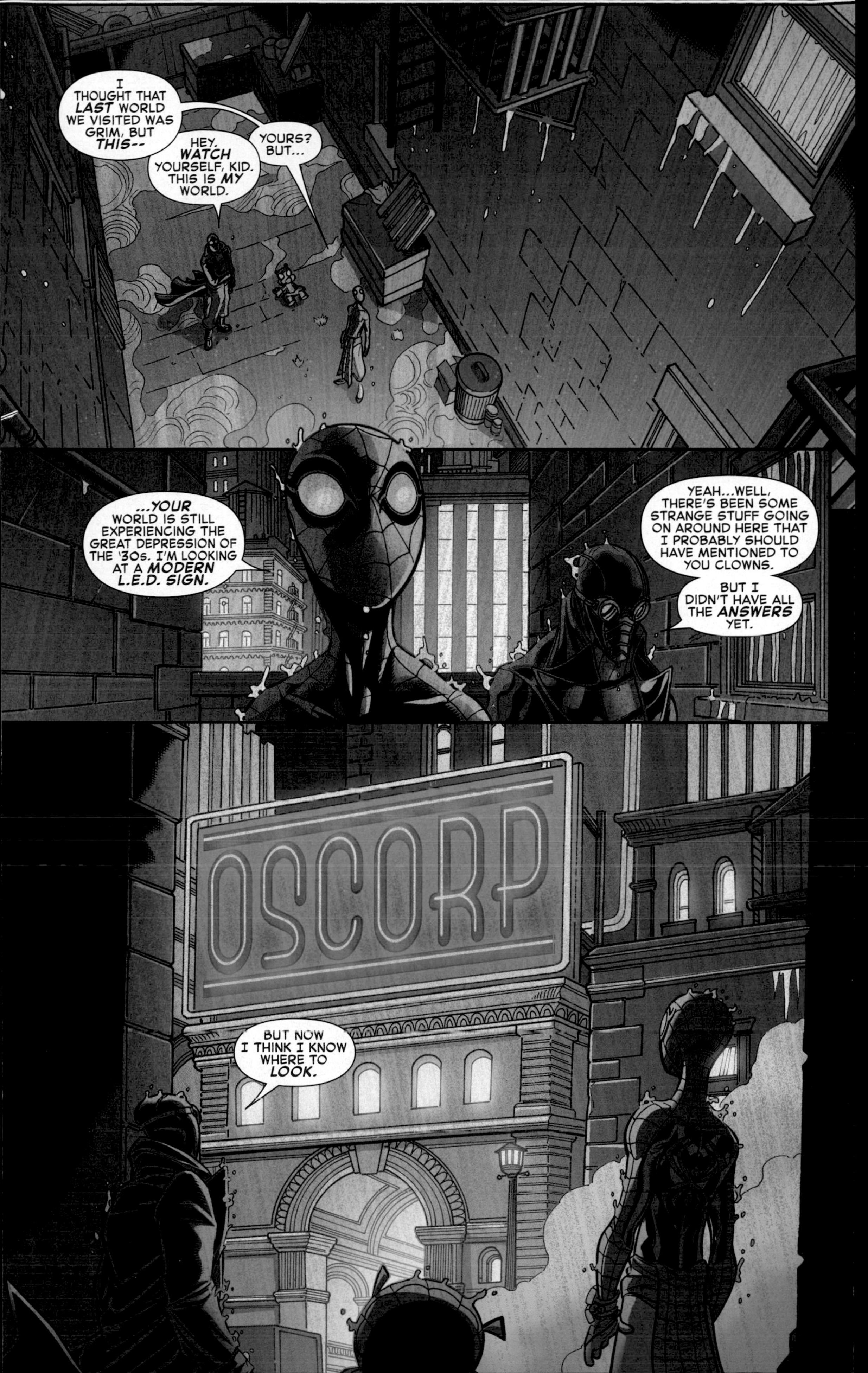
I THOUGHT THAT LAST WORLD WE VISITED WAS GRIM, BUT THIS--
HEY, WATCH YOURSELF, KID. THIS IS MY WORLD.
YOURS? BUT...
...YOUR WORLD IS STILL EXPERIENCING THE GREAT DEPRESSION OF THE '30s. I'M LOOKING AT A MODERN L.E.D. SIGN.
YEAH...WELL, THERE'S BEEN SOME STRANGE STUFF GOING ON AROUND HERE THAT I PROBABLY SHOULD HAVE MENTIONED TO YOU CLOWNS.
BUT I DIDN'T HAVE ALL THE ANSWERS YET.
OSCORP
BUT NOW I THINK I KNOW WHERE TO LOOK.

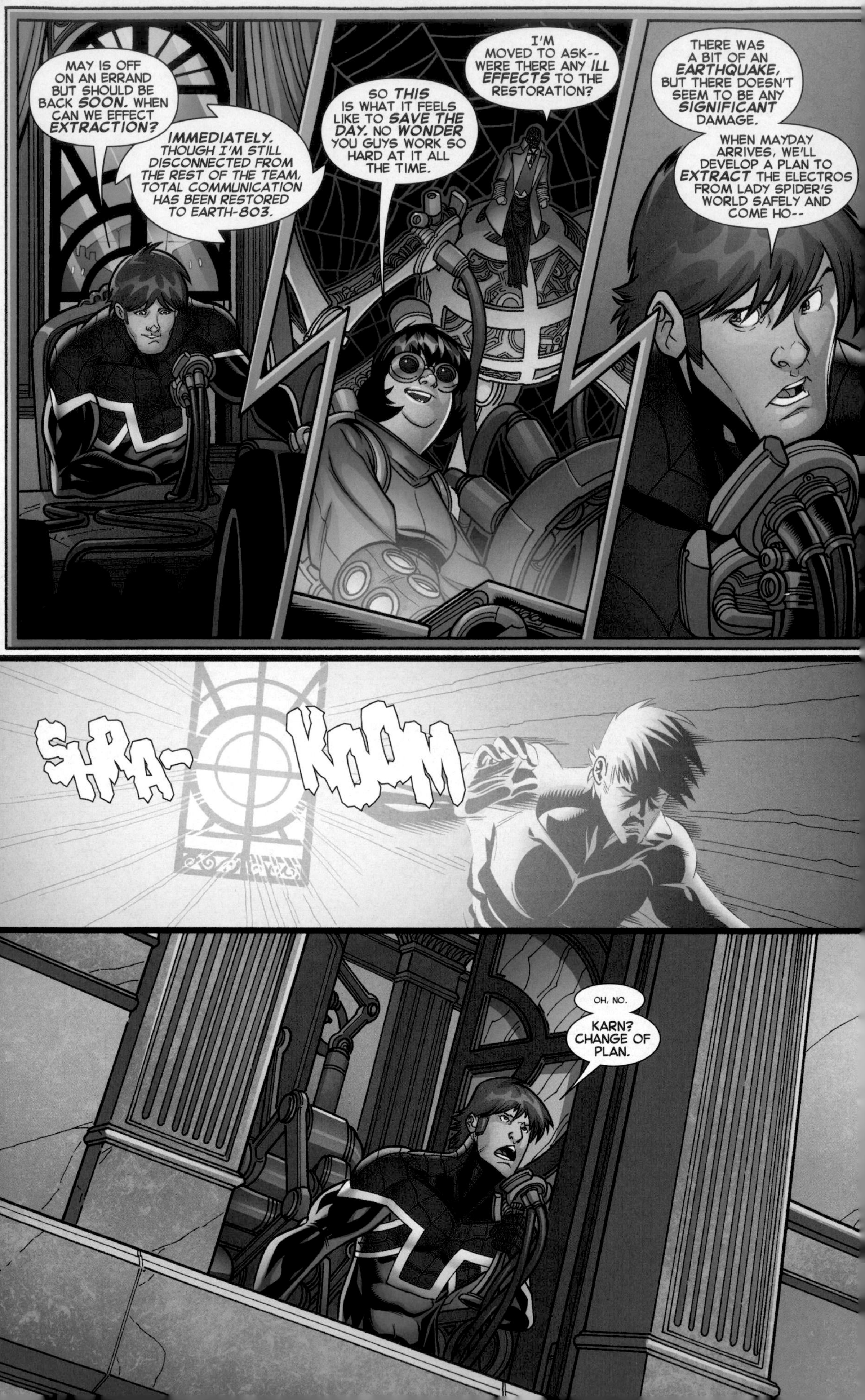
MAY IS OFF ON AN ERRAND BUT SHOULD BE BACK SOON. WHEN CAN WE EFFECT EXTRACTION?
IMMEDIATELY. THOUGH I'M STILL DISCONNECTED FROM THE REST OF THE TEAM, TOTAL COMMUNICATION HAS BEEN RESTORED TO EARTH-803.
SO THIS IS WHAT IT FEELS LIKE TO SAVE THE DAY. NO WONDER YOU GUYS WORK SO HARD AT IT ALL THE TIME.
I'M MOVED TO ASK-- WERE THERE ANY ILL EFFECTS TO THE RESTORATION?
THERE WAS A BIT OF AN EARTHQUAKE, BUT THERE DOESN'T SEEM TO BE ANY SIGNIFICANT DAMAGE.
WHEN MAYDAY ARRIVES, WE'LL DEVELOP A PLAN TO EXTRACT THE ELECTROS FROM LADY SPIDER'S WORLD SAFELY AND COME HO--
SHRA-KOOM
OH, NO.
KARN? CHANGE OF PLAN.

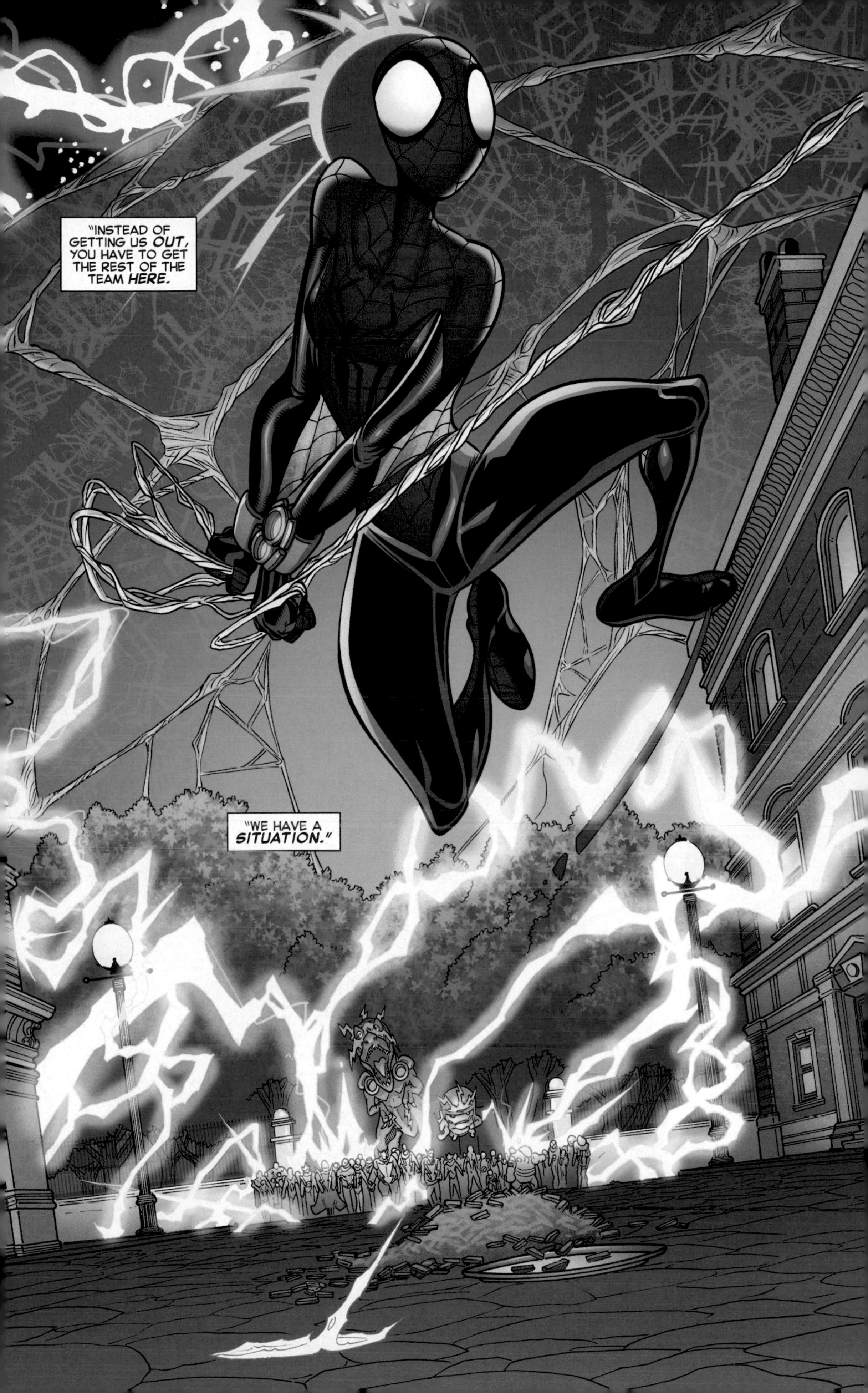
"INSTEAD OF GETTING US *OUT*, YOU HAVE TO GET THE REST OF THE TEAM *HERE*.
"WE HAVE A *SITUATION*."

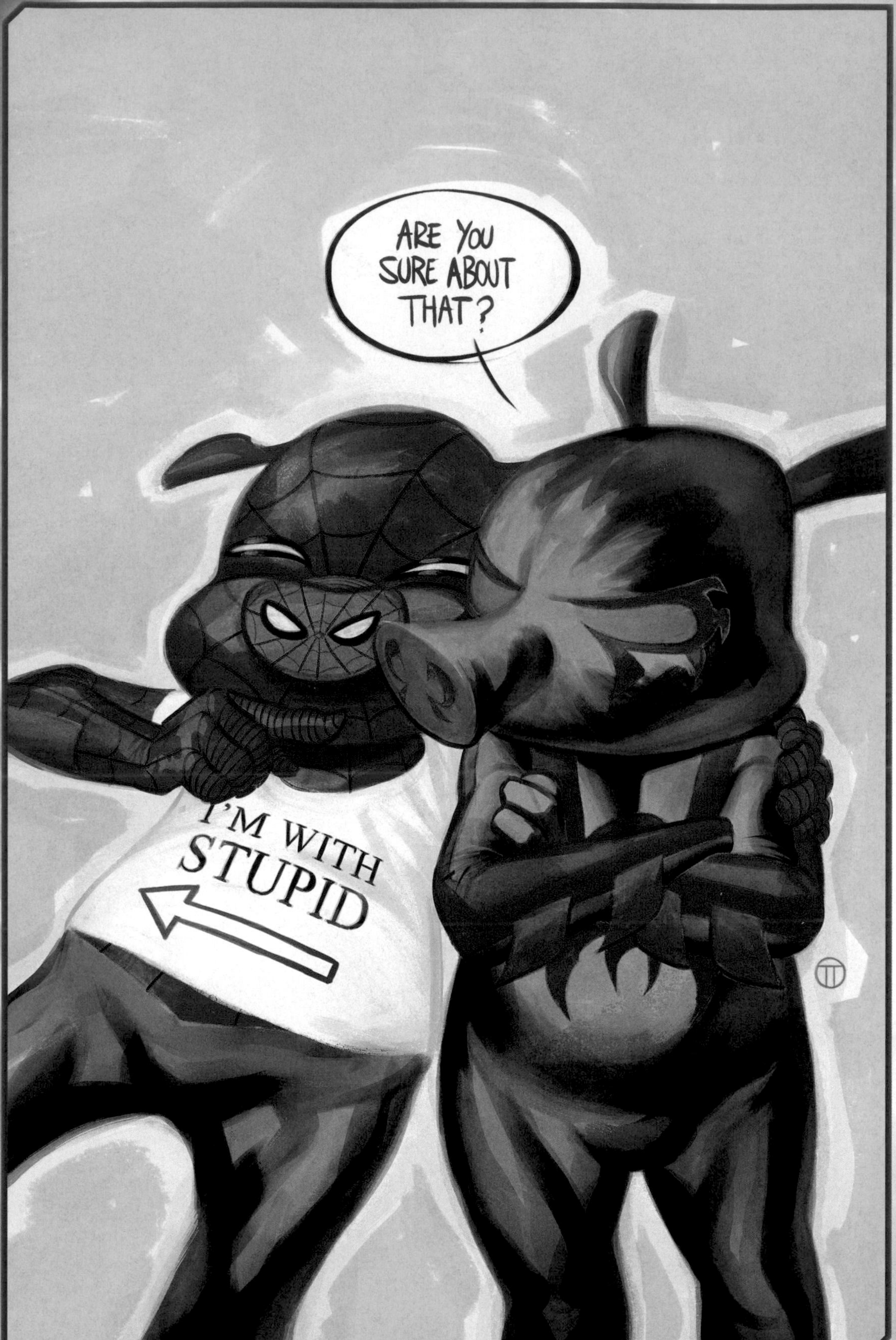
ARE YOU SURE ABOUT THAT?
I'M WITH STUPID

TANGLED STATES PART THREE : BRAVE NEW WORLD

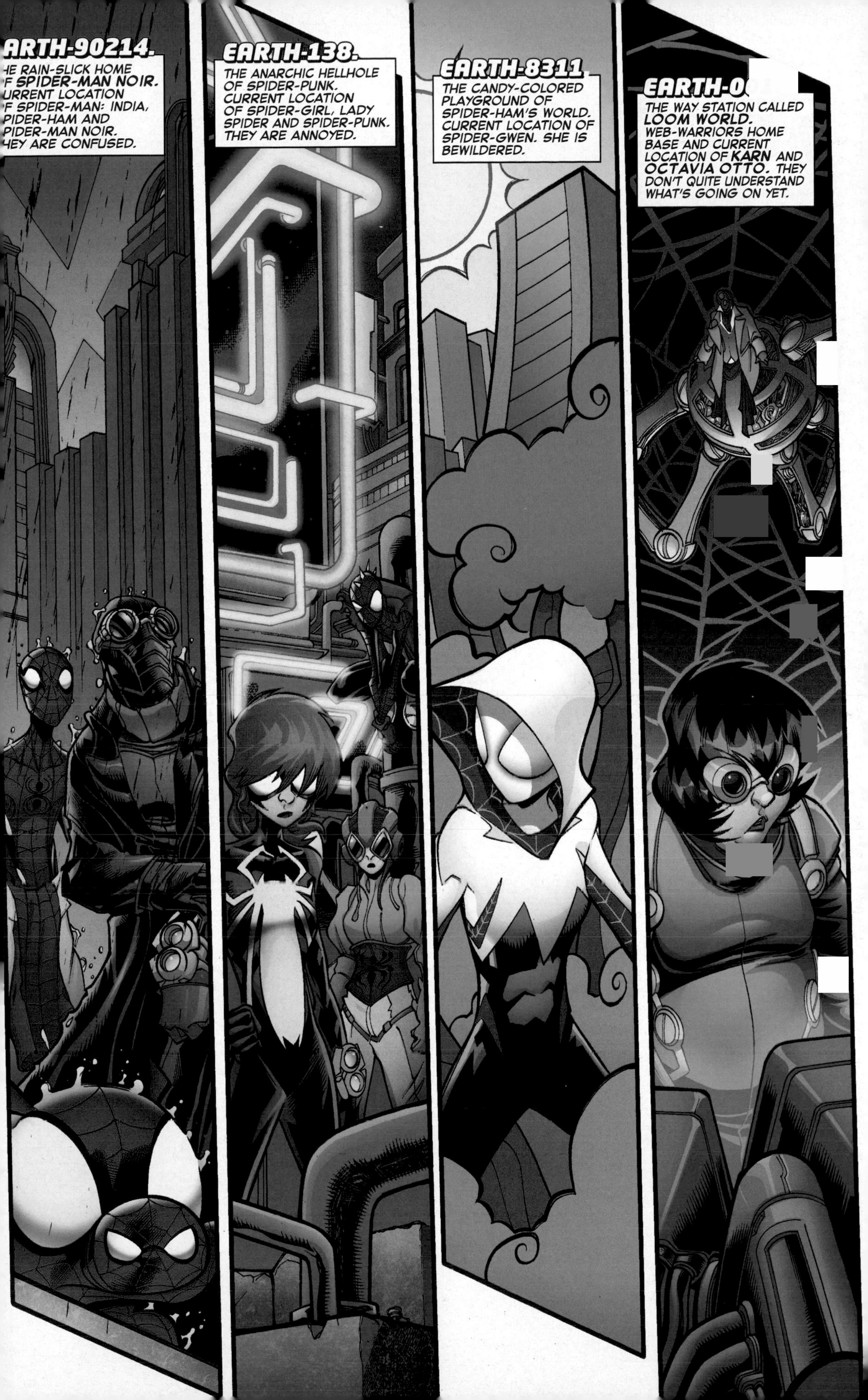
ARTH-90214.
HE RAIN-SLICK HOME
F SPIDER-MAN NOIR.
URRENT LOCATION
F SPIDER-MAN: INDIA,
PIDER-HAM AND
PIDER-MAN NOIR.
HEY ARE CONFUSED.
EARTH-138.
THE ANARCHIC HELLHOLE OF SPIDER-PUNK. CURRENT LOCATION OF SPIDER-GIRL, LADY SPIDER AND SPIDER-PUNK. THEY ARE ANNOYED.
EARTH-8311
THE CANDY-COLORED PLAYGROUND OF SPIDER-HAM'S WORLD. CURRENT LOCATION OF SPIDER-GWEN. SHE IS BEWILDERED.
EARTH-00
THE WAY STATION CALLED LOOM WORLD. WEB-WARRIORS HOME BASE AND CURRENT LOCATION OF KARN AND OCTAVIA OTTO. THEY DON'T QUITE UNDERSTAND WHAT'S GOING ON YET.

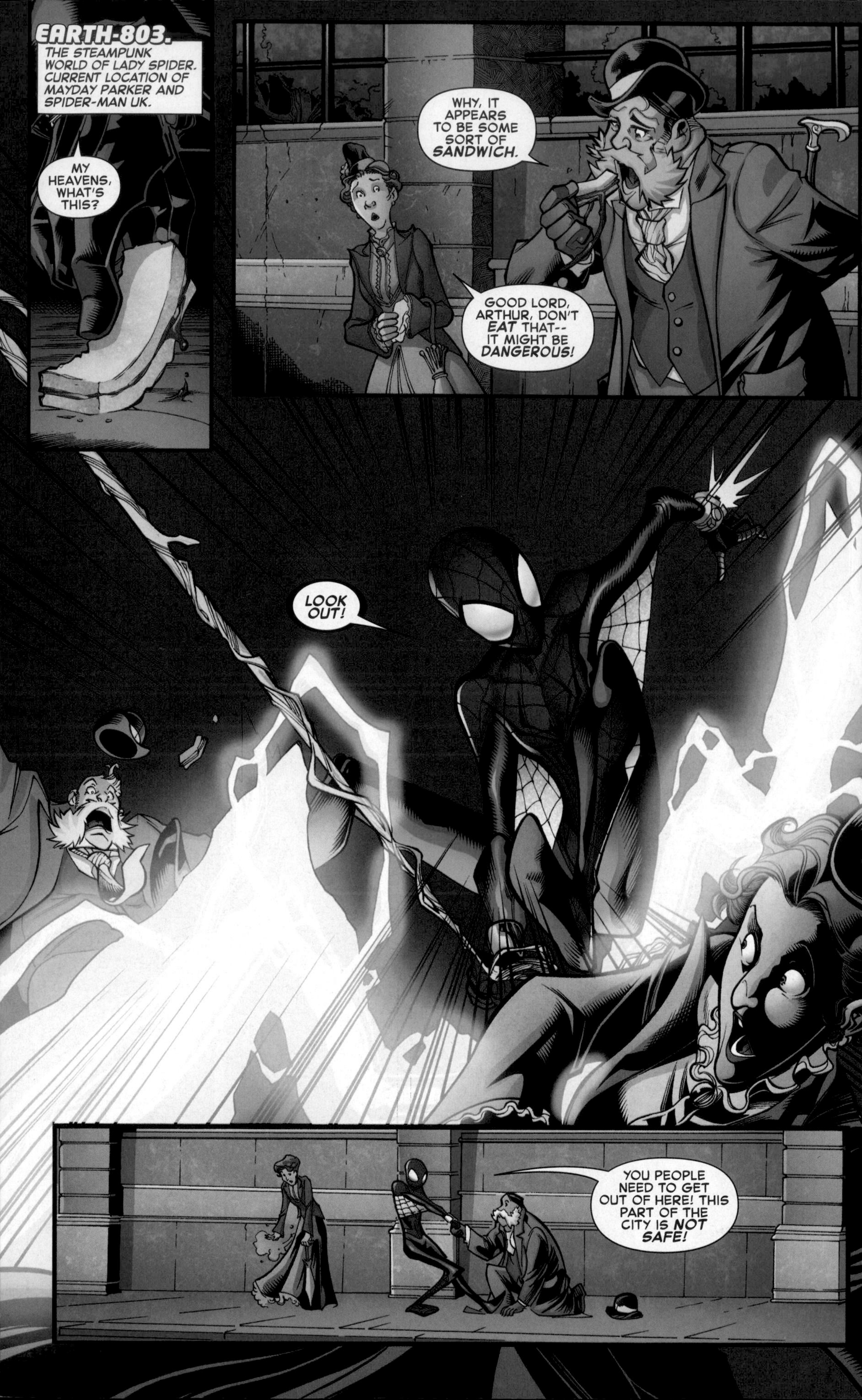
EARTH-803.
THE STEAMPUNK WORLD OF LADY SPIDER. CURRENT LOCATION OF MAYDAY PARKER AND SPIDER-MAN UK.
MY HEAVENS, WHAT'S THIS?
WHY, IT APPEARS TO BE SOME SORT OF SANDWICH.
GOOD LORD, ARTHUR, DON'T EAT THAT-- IT MIGHT BE DANGEROUS!
LOOK OUT!
YOU PEOPLE NEED TO GET OUT OF HERE! THIS PART OF THE CITY IS NOT SAFE!

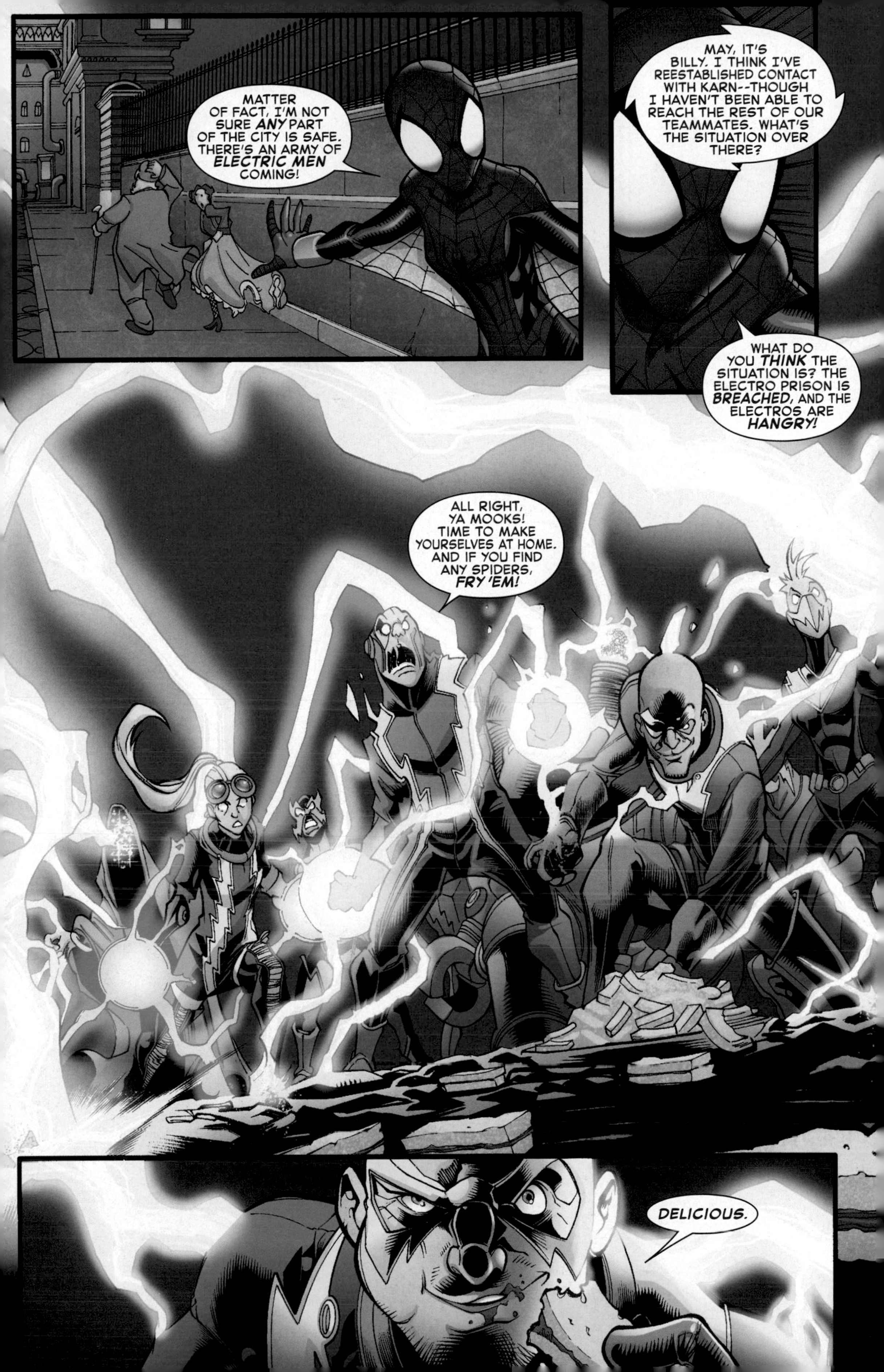
MATTER OF FACT, I'M NOT SURE ANY PART OF THE CITY IS SAFE. THERE'S AN ARMY OF ELECTRIC MEN COMING!
MAY, IT'S BILLY. I THINK I'VE REESTABLISHED CONTACT WITH KARN--THOUGH I HAVEN'T BEEN ABLE TO REACH THE REST OF OUR TEAMMATES. WHAT'S THE SITUATION OVER THERE?
WHAT DO YOU THINK THE SITUATION IS? THE ELECTRO PRISON IS BREACHED, AND THE ELECTROS ARE HANGRY!
ALL RIGHT, YA MOOKS! TIME TO MAKE YOURSELVES AT HOME. AND IF YOU FIND ANY SPIDERS, FRY 'EM!
DELICIOUS.

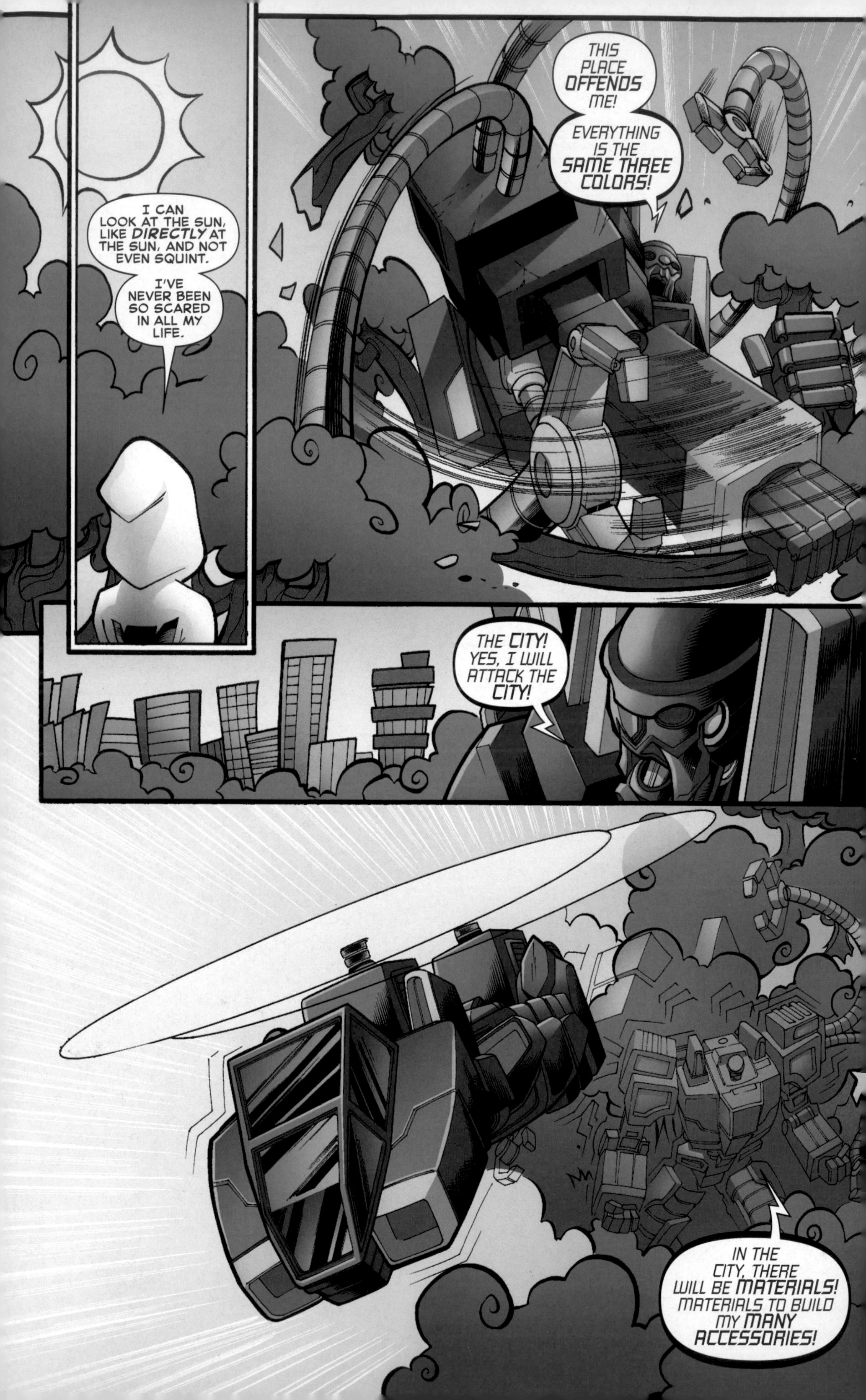
I CAN LOOK AT THE SUN, LIKE DIRECTLY AT THE SUN, AND NOT EVEN SQUINT.
I'VE NEVER BEEN SO SCARED IN ALL MY LIFE.
THIS PLACE OFFENDS ME!
EVERYTHING IS THE SAME THREE COLORS!
THE CITY! YES, I WILL ATTACK THE CITY!
IN THE CITY, THERE WILL BE MATERIALS! MATERIALS TO BUILD MY MANY ACCESSORIES!

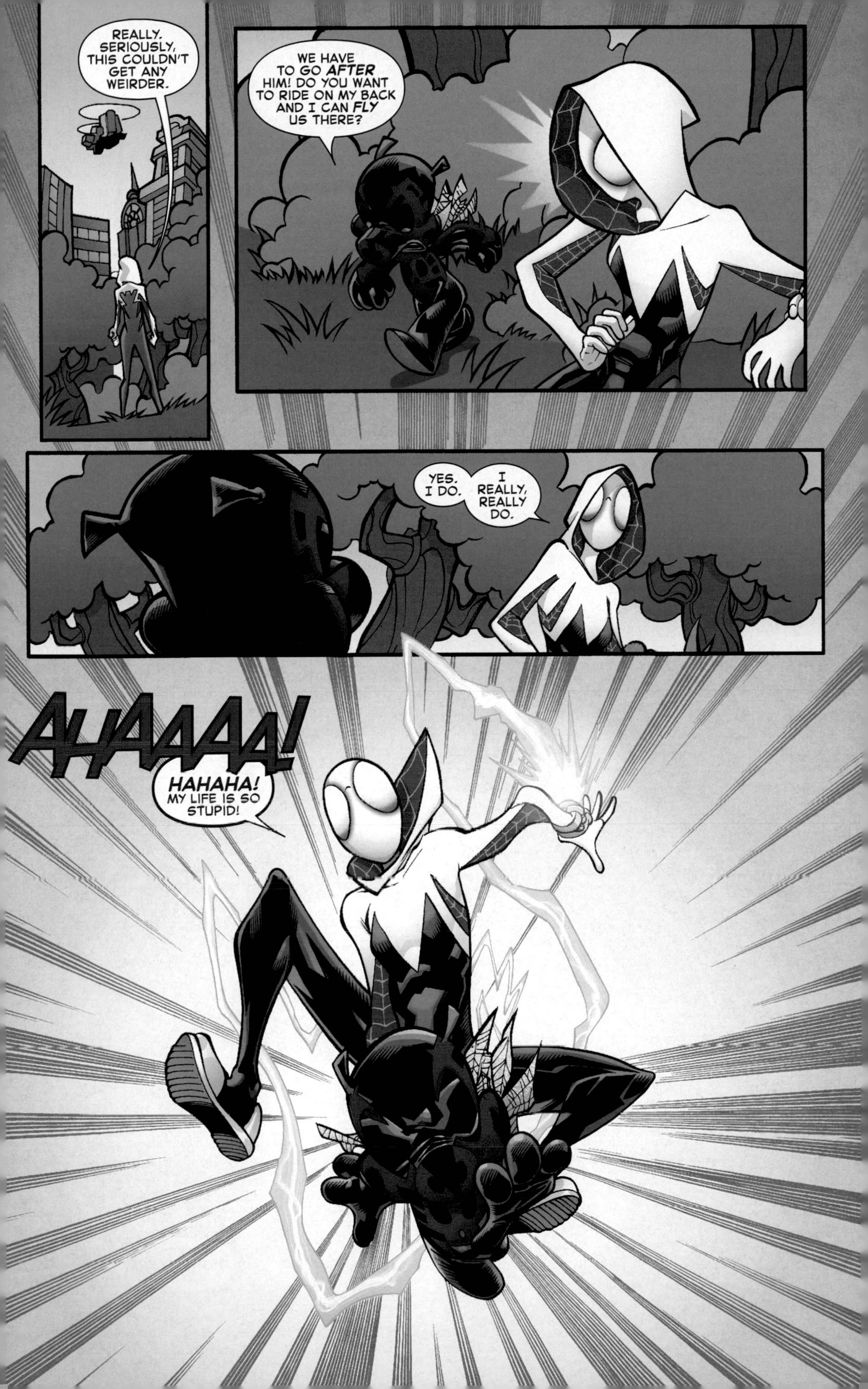
REALLY. SERIOUSLY, THIS COULDN'T GET ANY WEIRDER.
WE HAVE TO GO AFTER HIM! DO YOU WANT TO RIDE ON MY BACK AND I CAN FLY US THERE?
YES. I DO.
I REALLY, REALLY DO.
AHAAAA!
HAHAHA! MY LIFE IS SO STUPID!

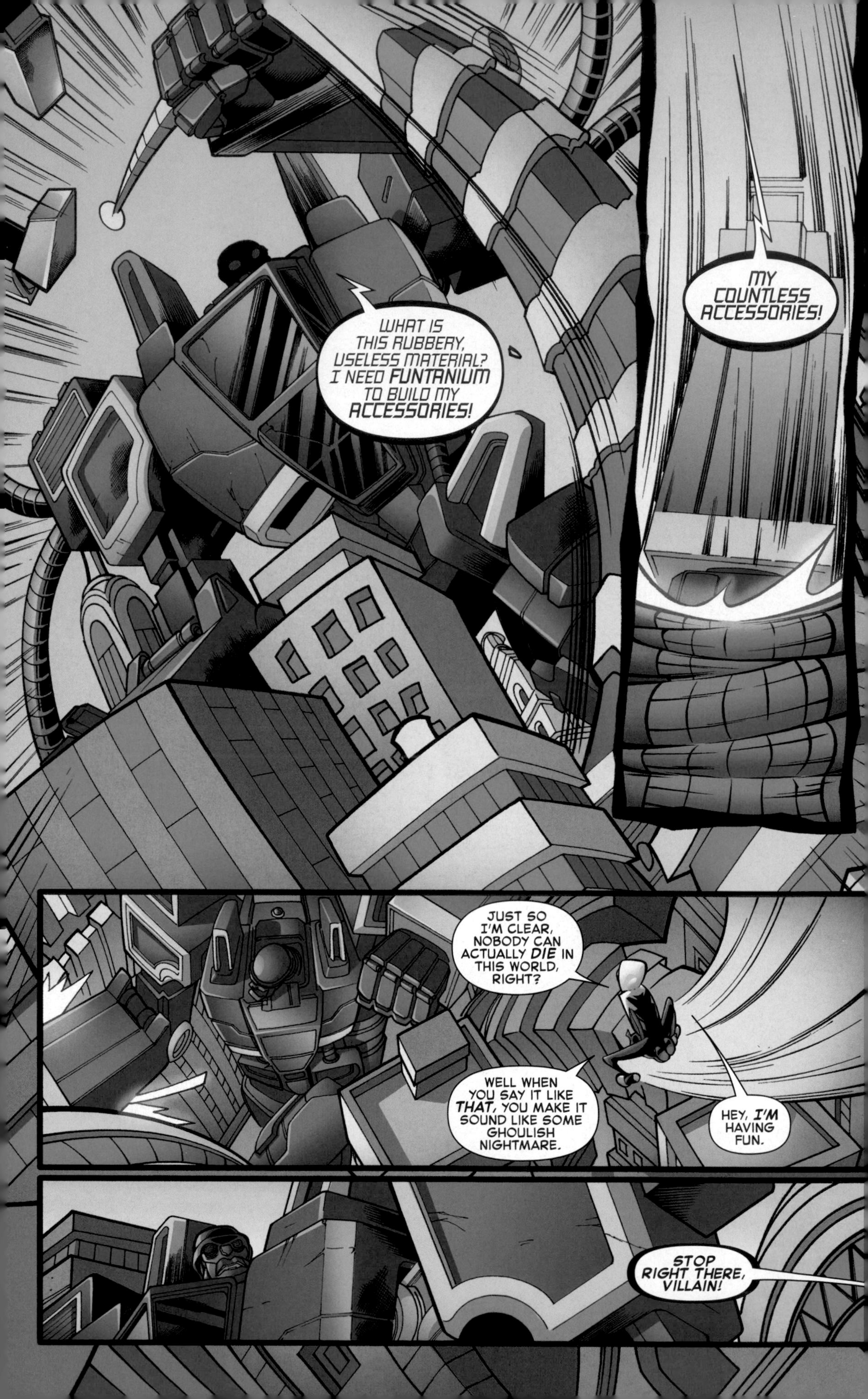
WHAT IS THIS RUBBERY, USELESS MATERIAL? I NEED FUNTANIUM TO BUILD MY ACCESSORIES!
MY COUNTLESS ACCESSORIES!
JUST SO I'M CLEAR, NOBODY CAN ACTUALLY DIE IN THIS WORLD, RIGHT?
WELL WHEN YOU SAY IT LIKE THAT, YOU MAKE IT SOUND LIKE SOME GHOULISH NIGHTMARE.
HEY, I'M HAVING FUN.
STOP RIGHT THERE, VILLAIN!

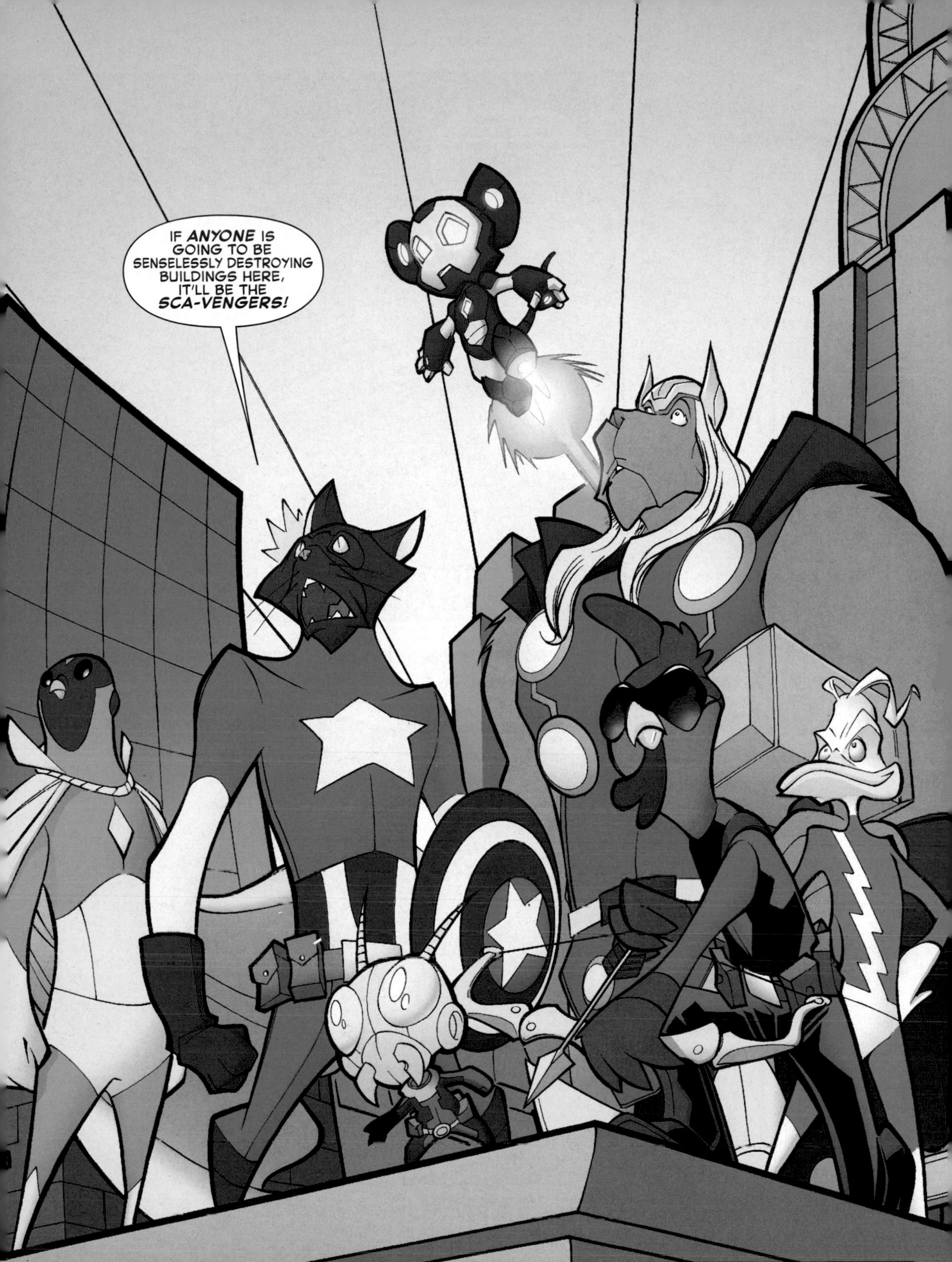
IF ANYONE IS GOING TO BE SENSELESSLY DESTROYING BUILDINGS HERE, IT'LL BE THE SCA-VENGERS!
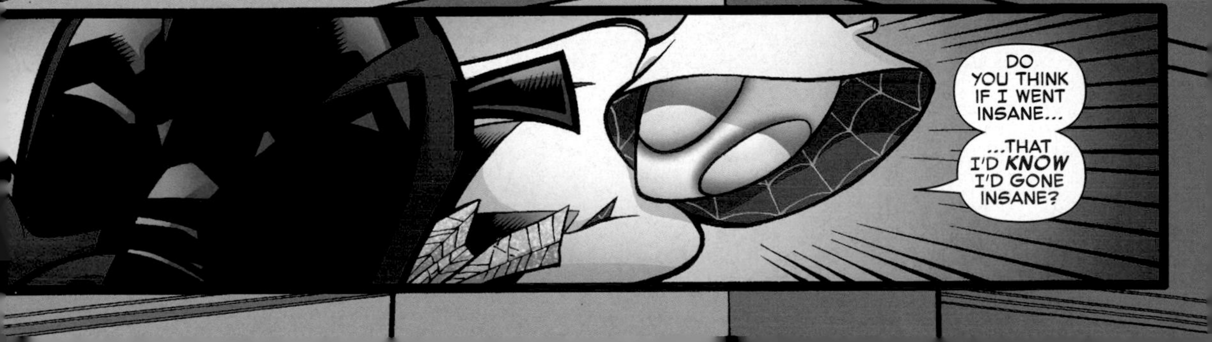
DO YOU THINK IF I WENT INSANE...
...THAT I'D KNOW I'D GONE INSANE?

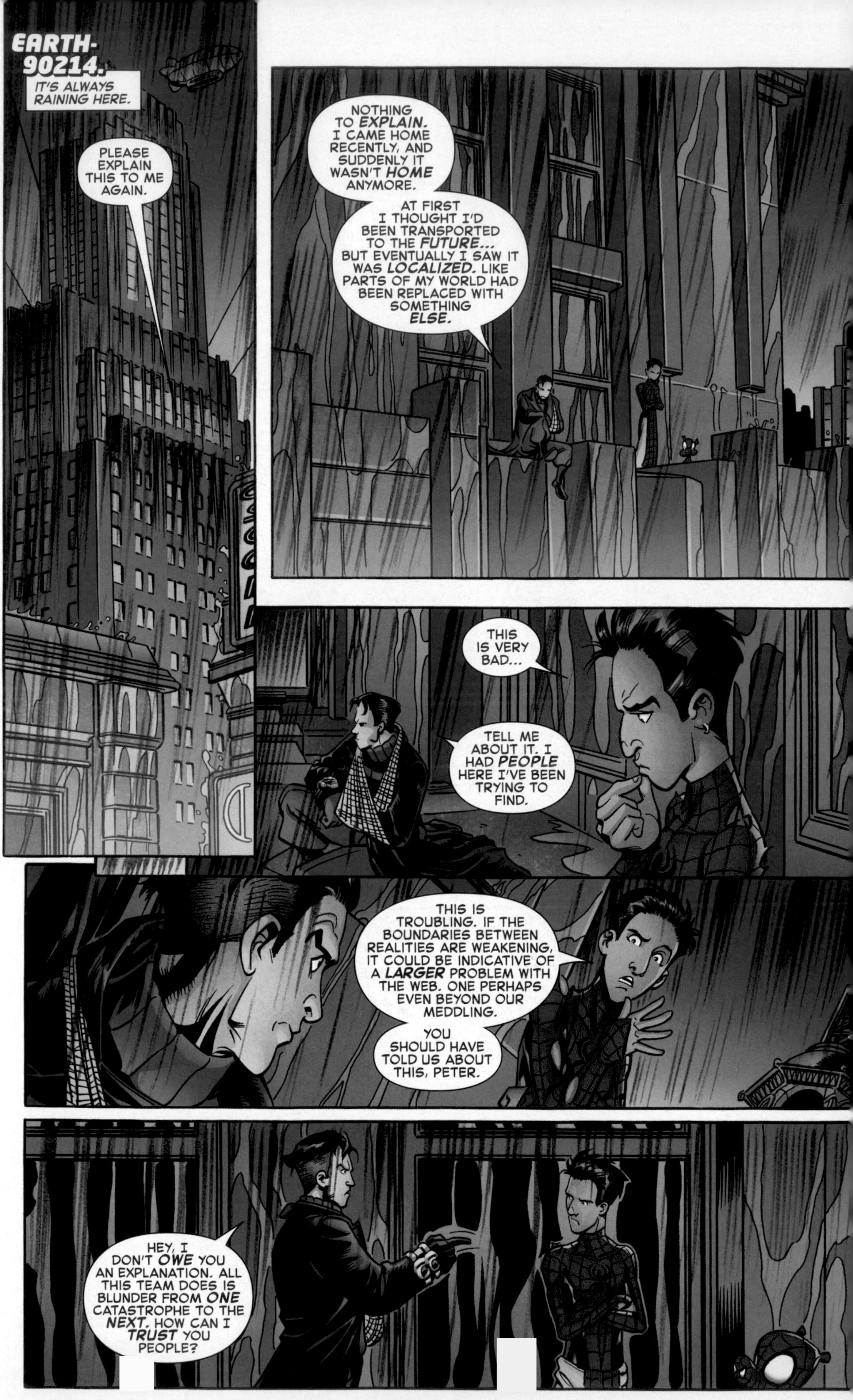
EARTH-90214.
IT'S ALWAYS RAINING HERE.
PLEASE EXPLAIN THIS TO ME AGAIN.
NOTHING TO EXPLAIN. I CAME HOME RECENTLY, AND SUDDENLY IT WASN'T HOME ANYMORE.
AT FIRST I THOUGHT I'D BEEN TRANSPORTED TO THE FUTURE... BUT EVENTUALLY I SAW IT WAS LOCALIZED. LIKE PARTS OF MY WORLD HAD BEEN REPLACED WITH SOMETHING ELSE.
THIS IS VERY BAD...
TELL ME ABOUT IT. I HAD PEOPLE HERE I'VE BEEN TRYING TO FIND.
THIS IS TROUBLING. IF THE BOUNDARIES BETWEEN REALITIES ARE WEAKENING, IT COULD BE INDICATIVE OF A LARGER PROBLEM WITH THE WEB. ONE PERHAPS EVEN BEYOND OUR MEDDLING.
YOU SHOULD HAVE TOLD US ABOUT THIS, PETER.
HEY, I DON'T OWE YOU AN EXPLANATION. ALL THIS TEAM DOES IS BLUNDER FROM ONE CATASTROPHE TO THE NEXT. HOW CAN I TRUST YOU PEOPLE?

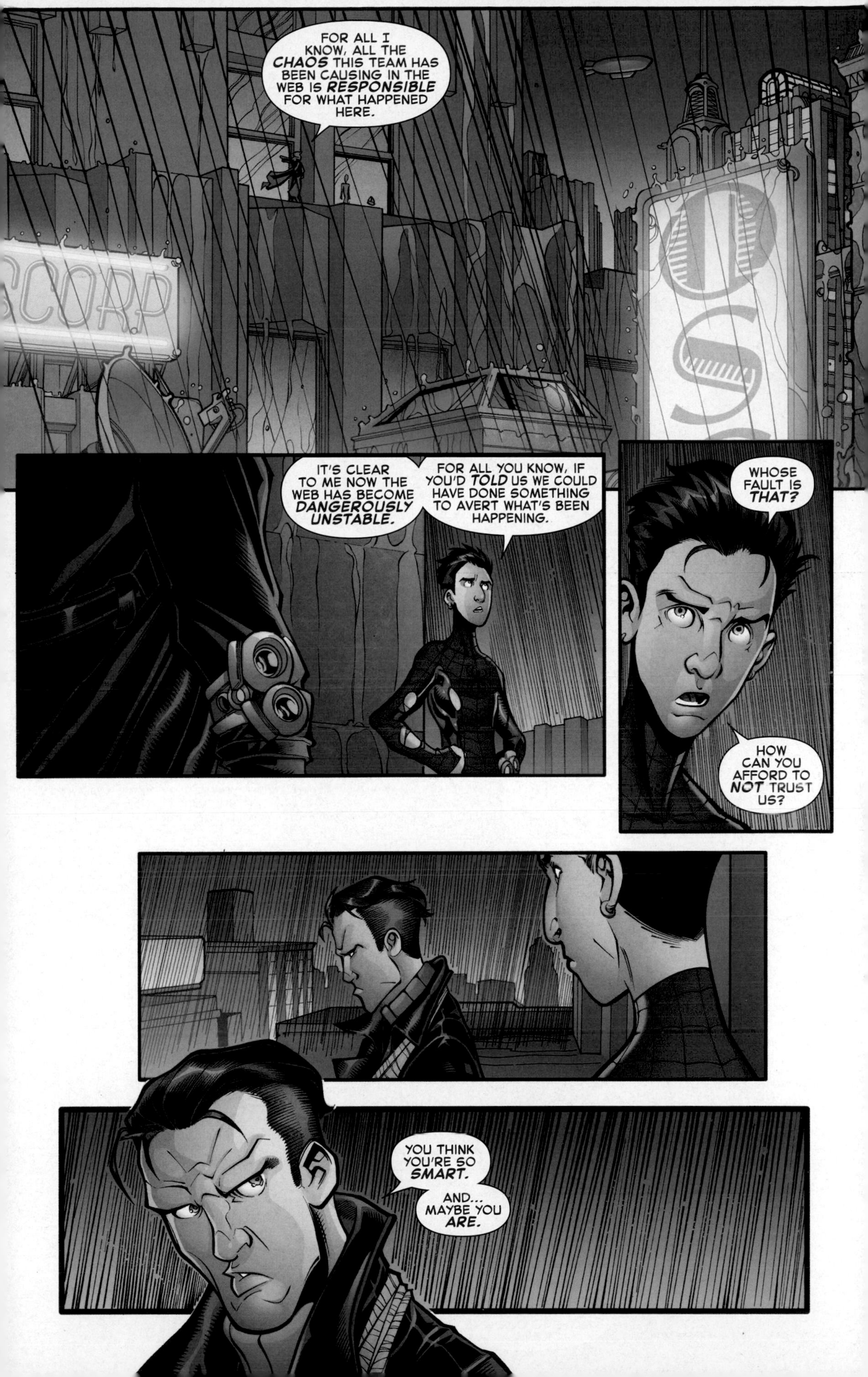
FOR ALL I KNOW, ALL THE CHAOS THIS TEAM HAS BEEN CAUSING IN THE WEB IS RESPONSIBLE FOR WHAT HAPPENED HERE.
SCORP
IT'S CLEAR TO ME NOW THE WEB HAS BECOME DANGEROUSLY UNSTABLE.
FOR ALL YOU KNOW, IF YOU'D TOLD US WE COULD HAVE DONE SOMETHING TO AVERT WHAT'S BEEN HAPPENING.
WHOSE FAULT IS THAT?
HOW CAN YOU AFFORD TO NOT TRUST US?
YOU THINK YOU'RE SO SMART.
AND... MAYBE YOU ARE.

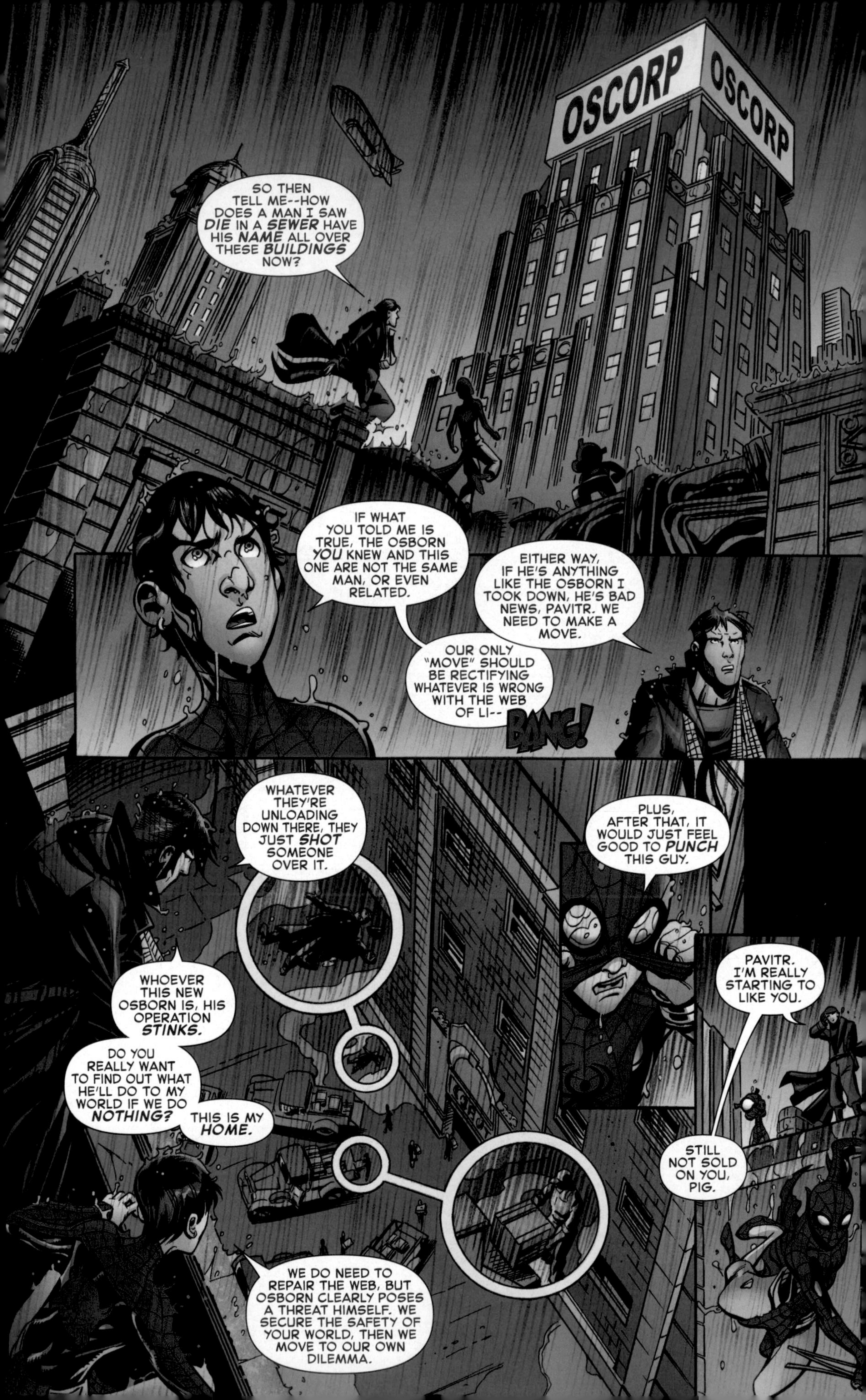
OSCORP
OSCORP
SO THEN TELL ME--HOW DOES A MAN I SAW DIE IN A SEWER HAVE HIS NAME ALL OVER THESE BUILDINGS NOW?
IF WHAT YOU TOLD ME IS TRUE, THE OSBORN YOU KNEW AND THIS ONE ARE NOT THE SAME MAN, OR EVEN RELATED.
EITHER WAY, IF HE'S ANYTHING LIKE THE OSBORN I TOOK DOWN, HE'S BAD NEWS, PAVITR. WE NEED TO MAKE A MOVE.
OUR ONLY "MOVE" SHOULD BE RECTIFYING WHATEVER IS WRONG WITH THE WEB OF LI--
BANG!
WHATEVER THEY'RE UNLOADING DOWN THERE, THEY JUST SHOT SOMEONE OVER IT.
WHOEVER THIS NEW OSBORN IS, HIS OPERATION STINKS.
DO YOU REALLY WANT TO FIND OUT WHAT HE'LL DO TO MY WORLD IF WE DO NOTHING?
THIS IS MY HOME.
WE DO NEED TO REPAIR THE WEB, BUT OSBORN CLEARLY POSES A THREAT HIMSELF. WE SECURE THE SAFETY OF YOUR WORLD, THEN WE MOVE TO OUR OWN DILEMMA.
PLUS, AFTER THAT, IT WOULD JUST FEEL GOOD TO PUNCH THIS GUY.
PAVITR. I'M REALLY STARTING TO LIKE YOU.
STILL NOT SOLD ON YOU, PIG.

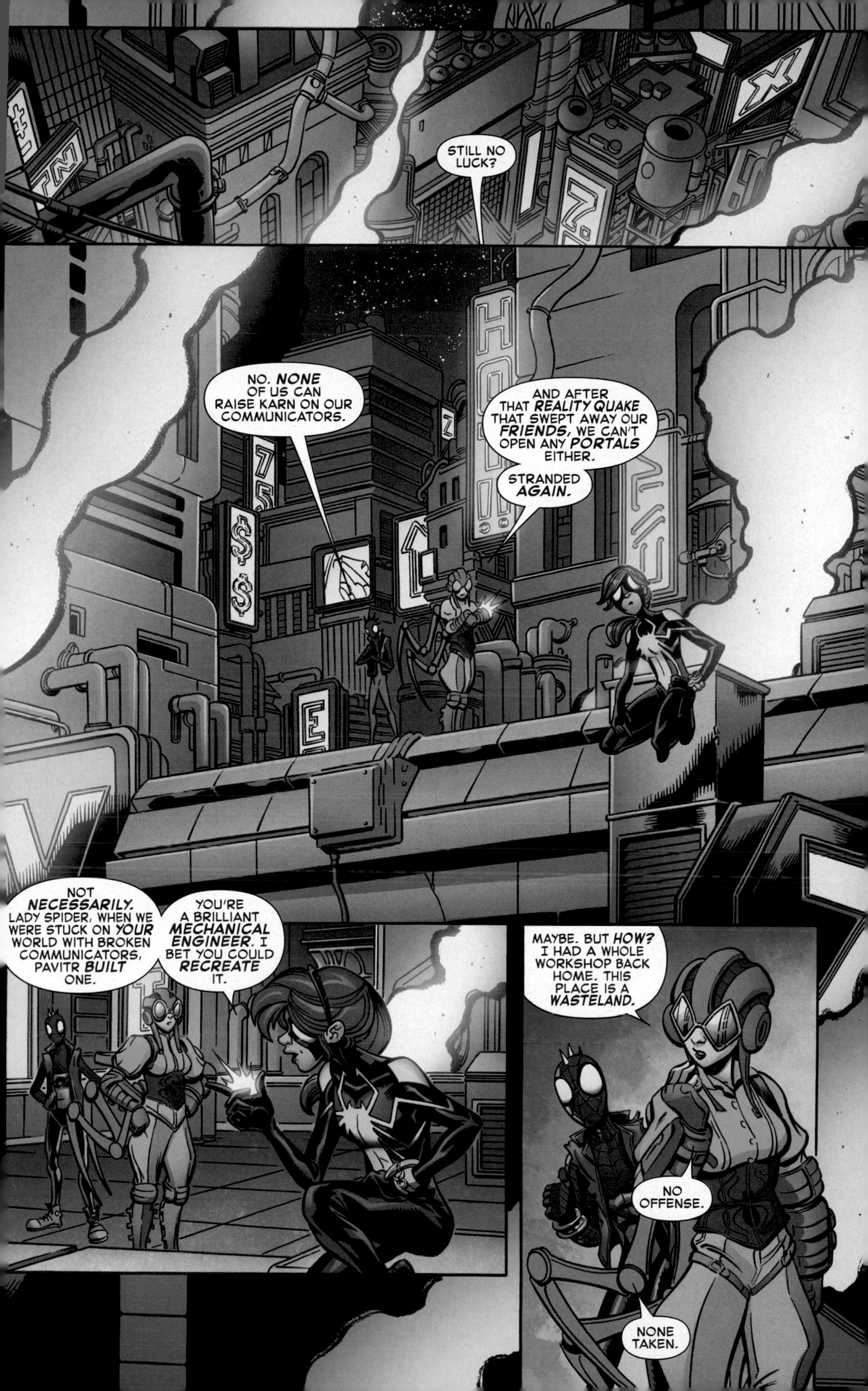
STILL NO LUCK?
NO. NONE OF US CAN RAISE KARN ON OUR COMMUNICATORS.
AND AFTER THAT REALITY QUAKE THAT SWEPT AWAY OUR FRIENDS, WE CAN'T OPEN ANY PORTALS EITHER.
STRANDED AGAIN.
NOT NECESSARILY. LADY SPIDER, WHEN WE WERE STUCK ON YOUR WORLD WITH BROKEN COMMUNICATORS, PAVITR BUILT ONE.
YOU'RE A BRILLIANT MECHANICAL ENGINEER. I BET YOU COULD RECREATE IT.
MAYBE. BUT HOW? I HAD A WHOLE WORKSHOP BACK HOME. THIS PLACE IS A WASTELAND.
NO OFFENSE.
NONE TAKEN.

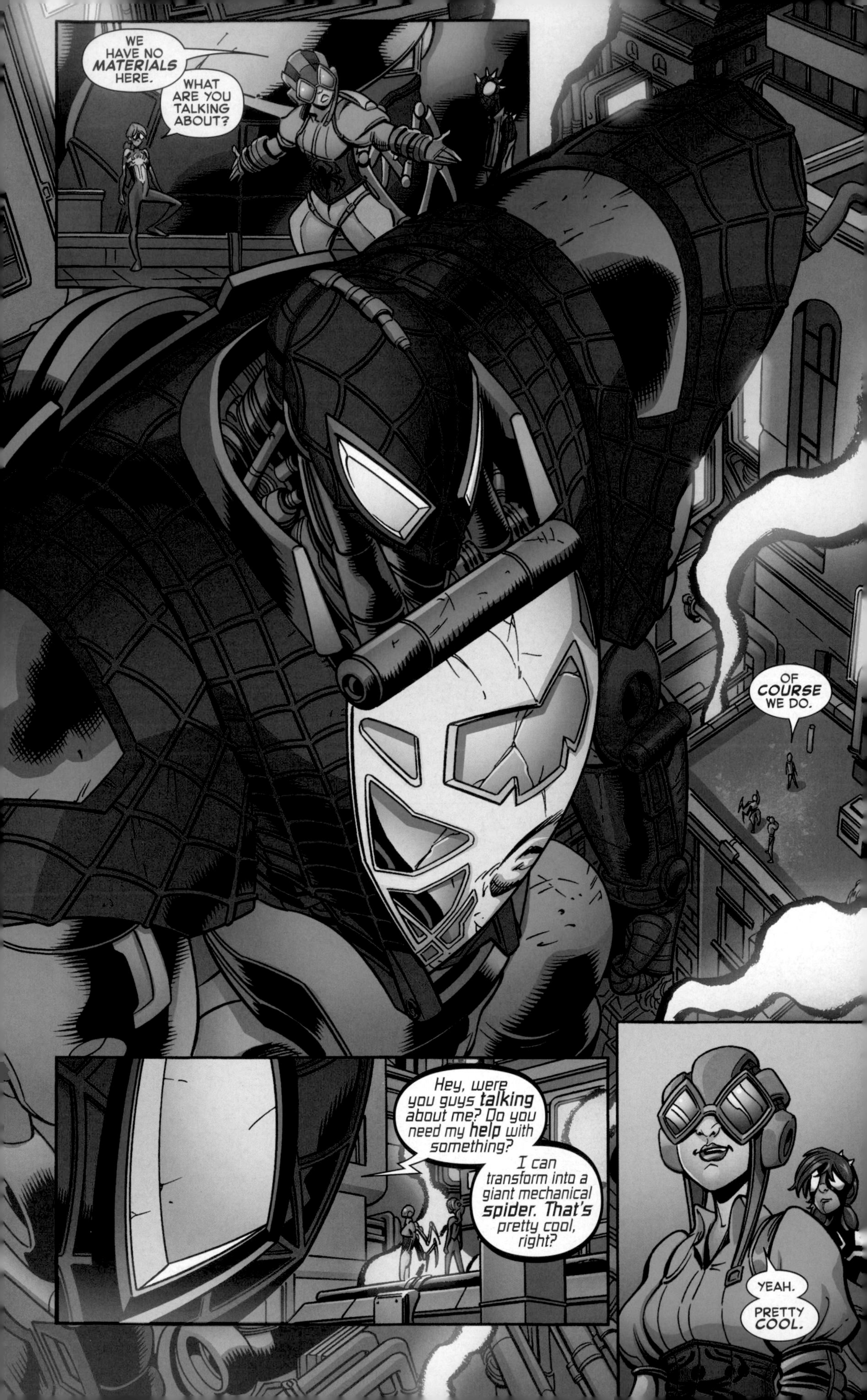

WE HAVE NO MATERIALS HERE.
WHAT ARE YOU TALKING ABOUT?
OF COURSE WE DO.
Hey, were you guys talking about me? Do you need my help with something?
I can transform into a giant mechanical spider. That's pretty cool, right?
YEAH.
PRETTY COOL.

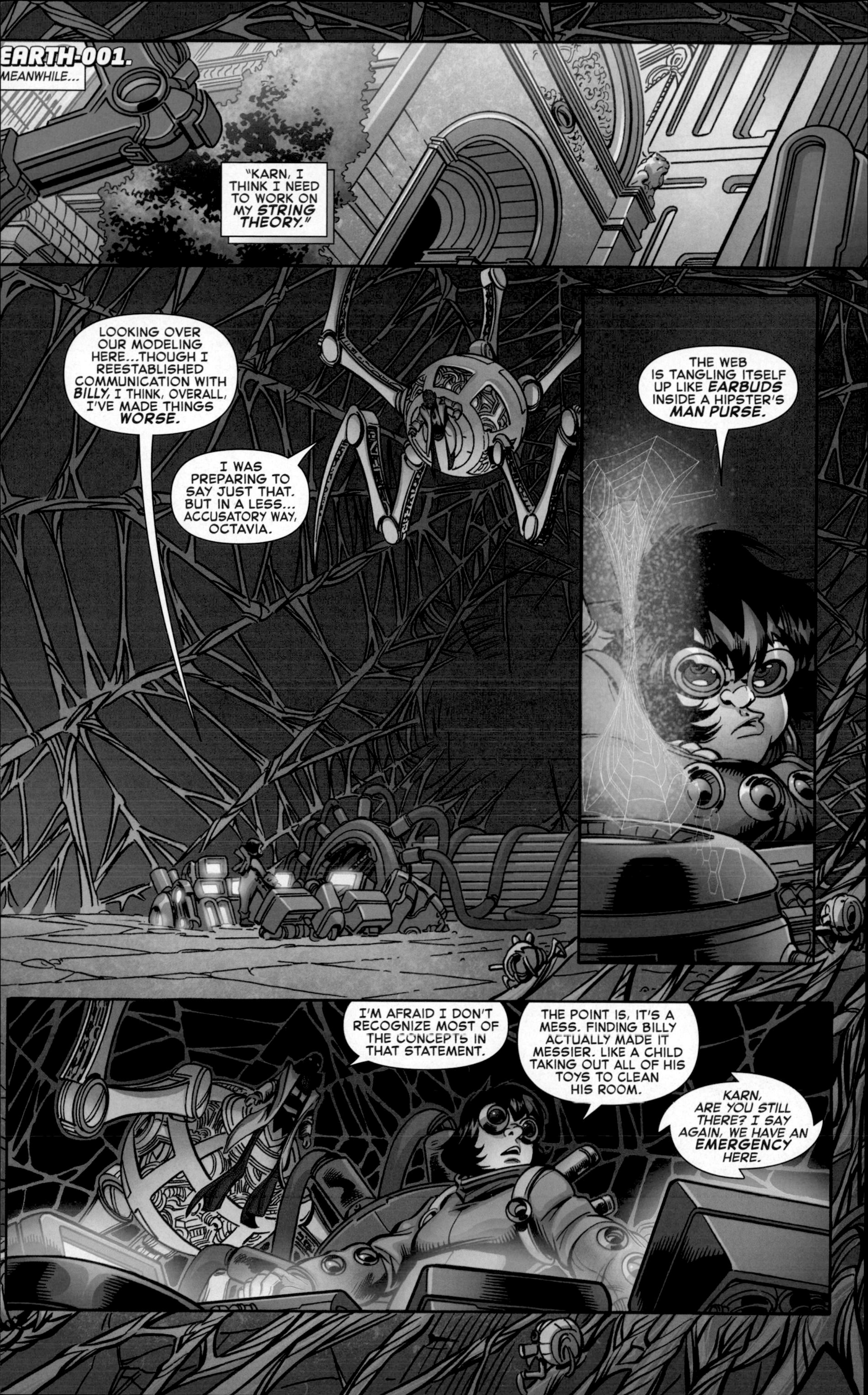
EARTH-001.
MEANWHILE...
"KARN, I THINK I NEED TO WORK ON MY STRING THEORY."
LOOKING OVER OUR MODELING HERE...THOUGH I REESTABLISHED COMMUNICATION WITH BILLY, I THINK, OVERALL, I'VE MADE THINGS WORSE.
I WAS PREPARING TO SAY JUST THAT. BUT IN A LESS... ACCUSATORY WAY, OCTAVIA.
THE WEB IS TANGLING ITSELF UP LIKE EARBUDS INSIDE A HIPSTER'S MAN PURSE.
I'M AFRAID I DON'T RECOGNIZE MOST OF THE CONCEPTS IN THAT STATEMENT.
THE POINT IS, IT'S A MESS. FINDING BILLY ACTUALLY MADE IT MESSIER. LIKE A CHILD TAKING OUT ALL OF HIS TOYS TO CLEAN HIS ROOM.
KARN, ARE YOU STILL THERE? I SAY AGAIN, WE HAVE AN EMERGENCY HERE.

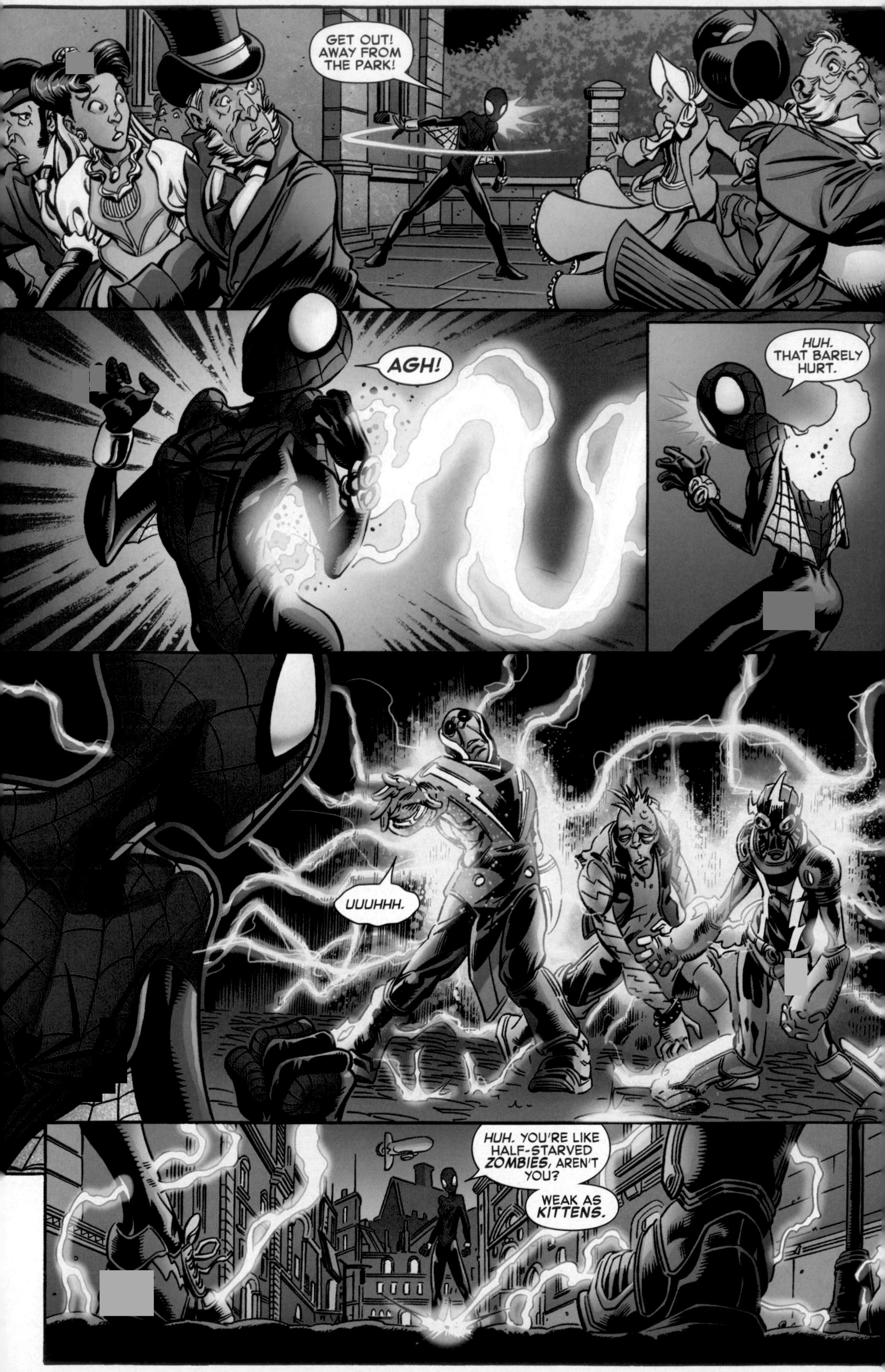
GET OUT! AWAY FROM THE PARK!
AGH!
HUH. THAT BARELY HURT.
UUUHHH.
HUH. YOU'RE LIKE HALF-STARVED ZOMBIES, AREN'T YOU?
WEAK AS KITTENS.

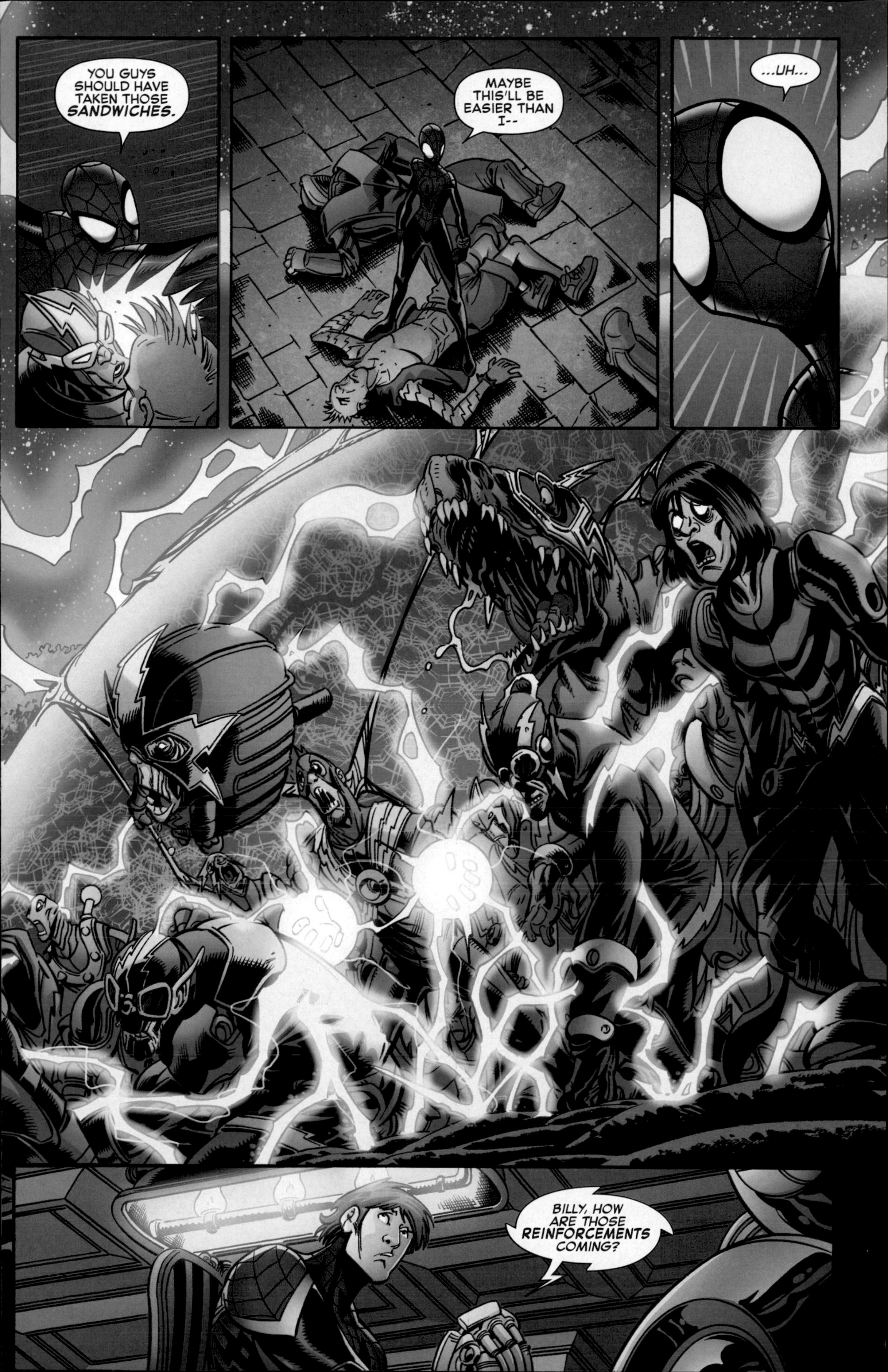
YOU GUYS SHOULD HAVE TAKEN THOSE SANDWICHES.
MAYBE THIS'LL BE EASIER THAN I--
...UH...
BILLY, HOW ARE THOSE REINFORCEMENTS COMING?

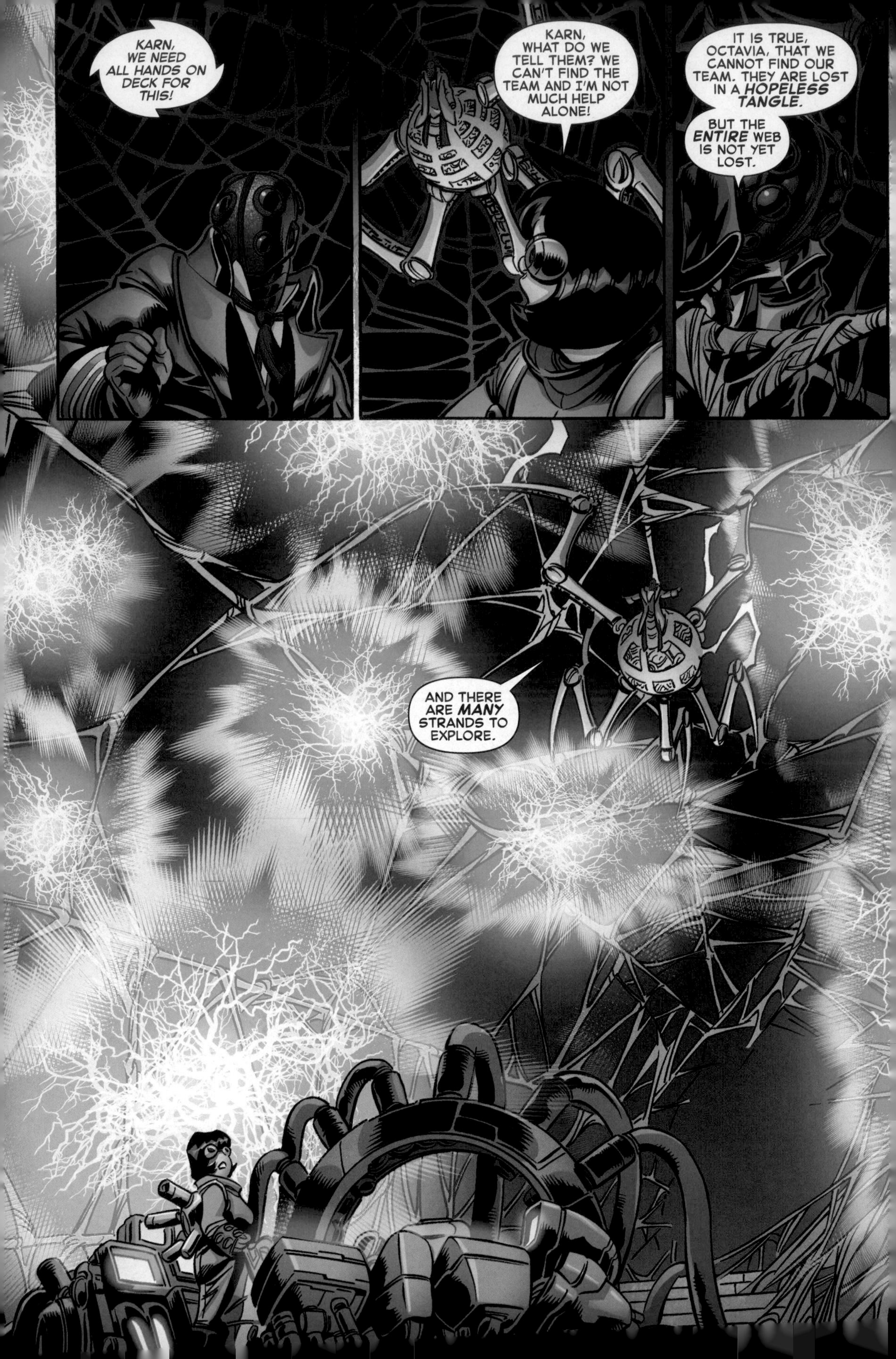

KARN, WE NEED ALL HANDS ON DECK FOR THIS!
KARN, WHAT DO WE TELL THEM? WE CAN'T FIND THE TEAM AND I'M NOT MUCH HELP ALONE!
IT IS TRUE, OCTAVIA, THAT WE CANNOT FIND OUR TEAM. THEY ARE LOST IN A ***HOPELESS TANGLE.***
BUT THE ***ENTIRE*** WEB IS NOT YET LOST.
AND THERE ARE ***MANY*** STRANDS TO EXPLORE.

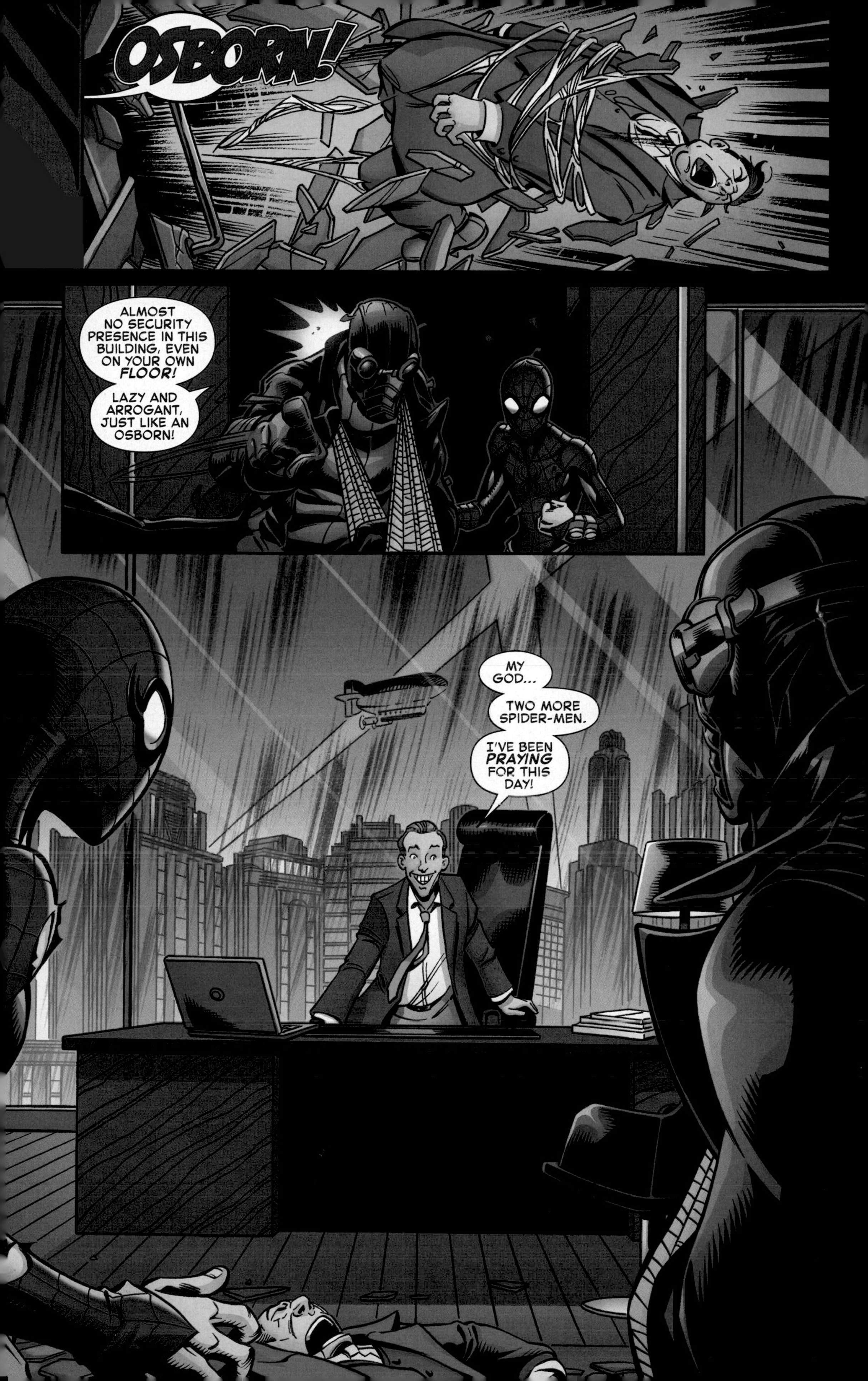
OSBORN!
ALMOST NO SECURITY PRESENCE IN THIS BUILDING, EVEN ON YOUR OWN FLOOR!
LAZY AND ARROGANT, JUST LIKE AN OSBORN!
MY GOD...
TWO MORE SPIDER-MEN.
I'VE BEEN PRAYING FOR THIS DAY!

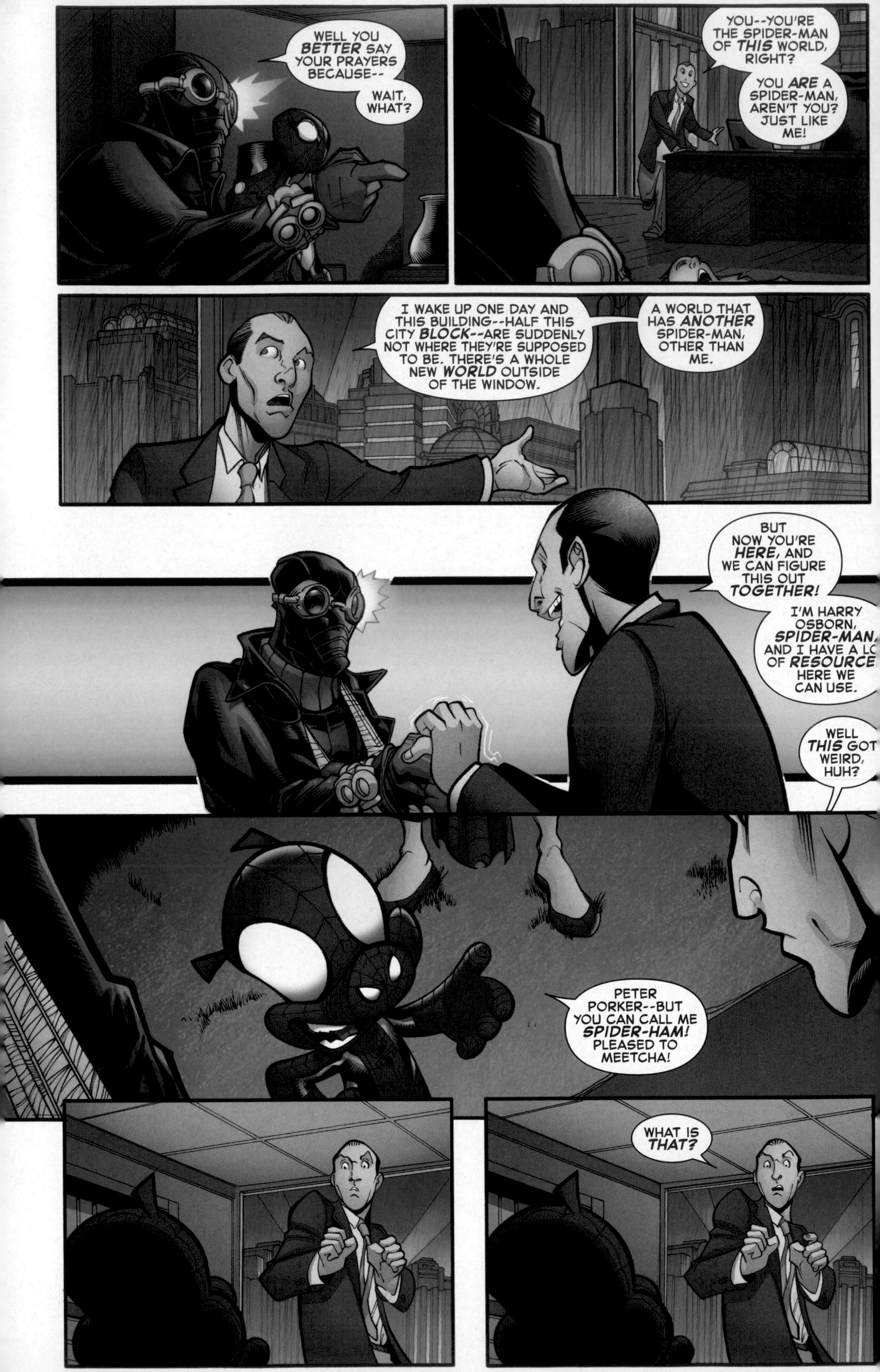
WELL YOU BETTER SAY YOUR PRAYERS BECAUSE--
WAIT, WHAT?
YOU--YOU'RE THE SPIDER-MAN OF THIS WORLD, RIGHT?
YOU ARE A SPIDER-MAN, AREN'T YOU? JUST LIKE ME!
I WAKE UP ONE DAY AND THIS BUILDING--HALF THIS CITY BLOCK--ARE SUDDENLY NOT WHERE THEY'RE SUPPOSED TO BE. THERE'S A WHOLE NEW WORLD OUTSIDE OF THE WINDOW.
A WORLD THAT HAS ANOTHER SPIDER-MAN, OTHER THAN ME.
BUT NOW YOU'RE HERE, AND WE CAN FIGURE THIS OUT TOGETHER!
I'M HARRY OSBORN, SPIDER-MAN, AND I HAVE A LO OF RESOURCE HERE WE CAN USE.
WELL THIS GOT WEIRD, HUH?
PETER PORKER--BUT YOU CAN CALL ME SPIDER-HAM! PLEASED TO MEETCHA!
WHAT IS THAT?

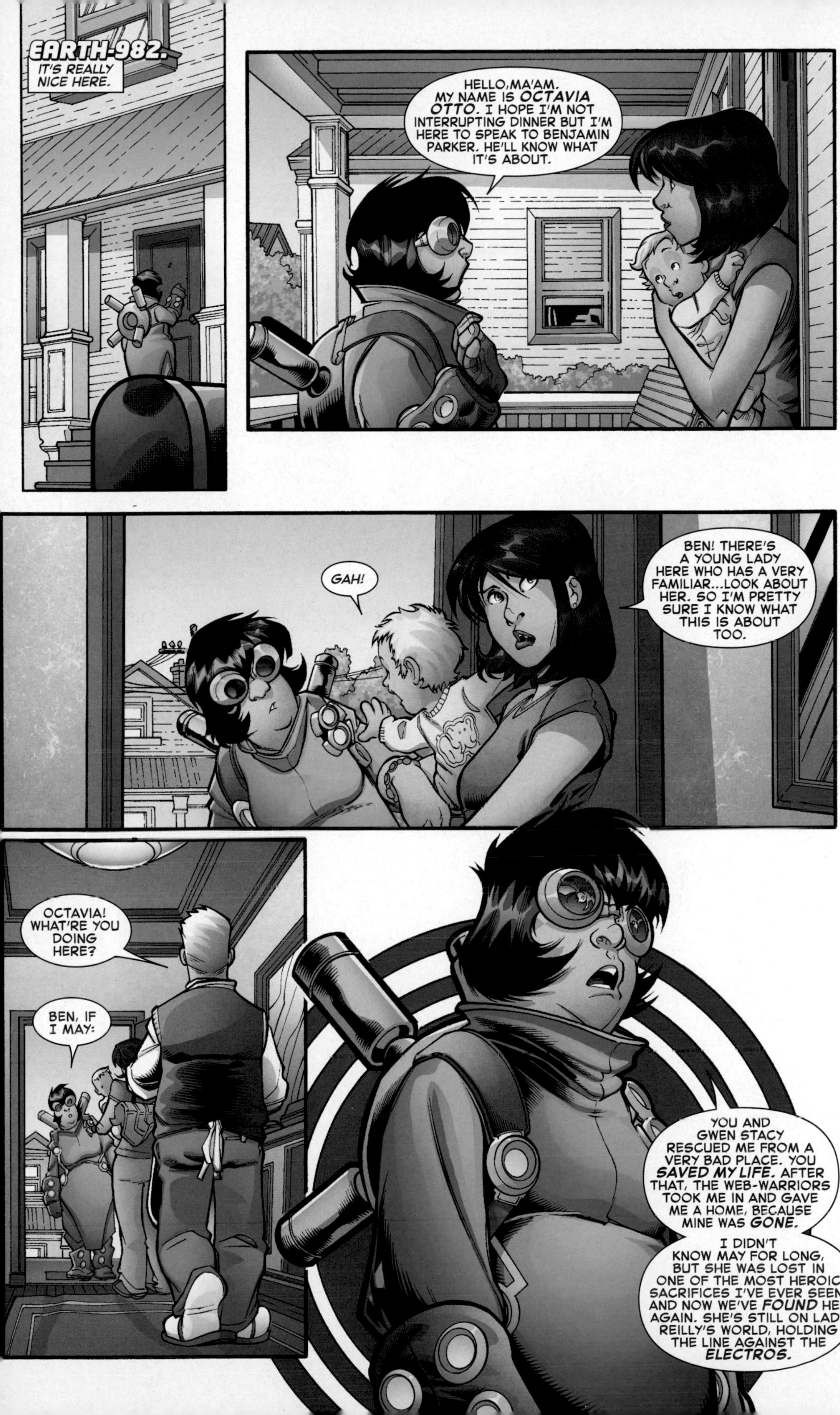
EARTH-982.
IT'S REALLY NICE HERE.
HELLO, MA'AM. MY NAME IS OCTAVIA OTTO. I HOPE I'M NOT INTERRUPTING DINNER BUT I'M HERE TO SPEAK TO BENJAMIN PARKER. HE'LL KNOW WHAT IT'S ABOUT.
GAH!
BEN! THERE'S A YOUNG LADY HERE WHO HAS A VERY FAMILIAR...LOOK ABOUT HER. SO I'M PRETTY SURE I KNOW WHAT THIS IS ABOUT TOO.
OCTAVIA! WHAT'RE YOU DOING HERE?
BEN, IF I MAY:
YOU AND GWEN STACY RESCUED ME FROM A VERY BAD PLACE. YOU SAVED MY LIFE. AFTER THAT, THE WEB-WARRIORS TOOK ME IN AND GAVE ME A HOME, BECAUSE MINE WAS GONE.
I DIDN'T KNOW MAY FOR LONG, BUT SHE WAS LOST IN ONE OF THE MOST HEROIC SACRIFICES I'VE EVER SEEN. AND NOW WE'VE FOUND HER AGAIN. SHE'S STILL ON LADY REILLY'S WORLD, HOLDING THE LINE AGAINST THE ELECTROS.

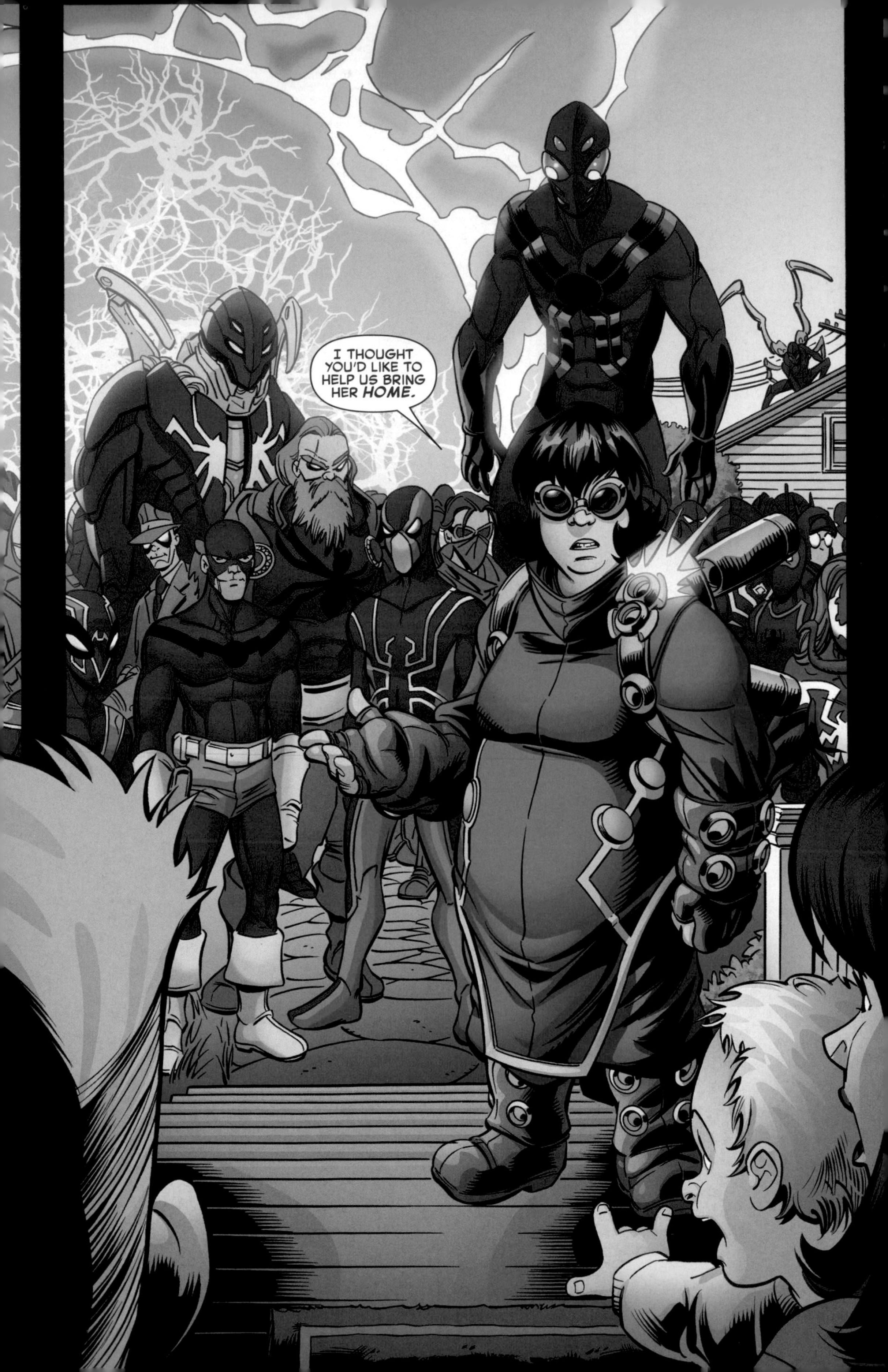
I THOUGHT YOU'D LIKE TO HELP US BRING HER *HOME.*

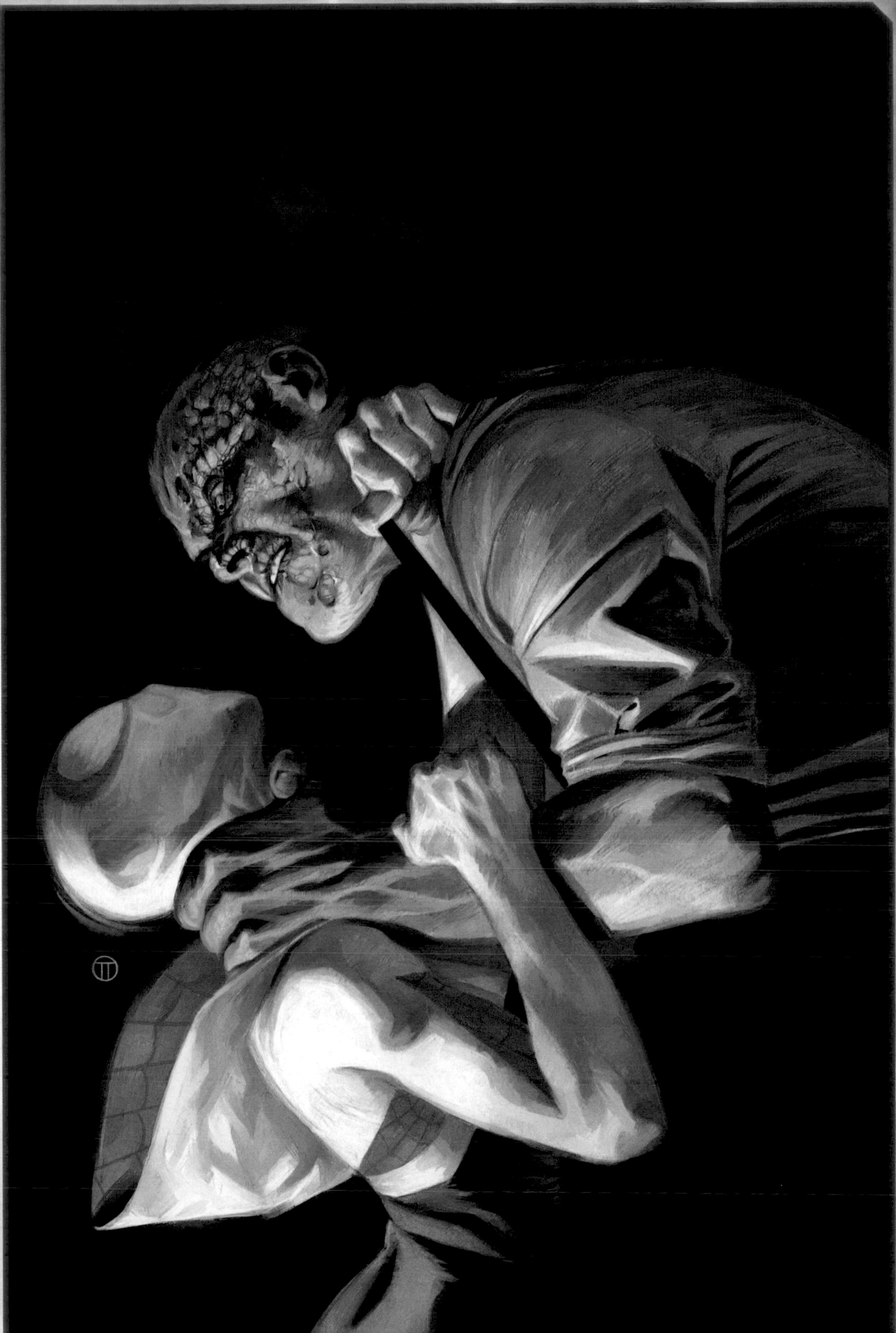

TANGLED STATES PART FOUR : MONARCHY

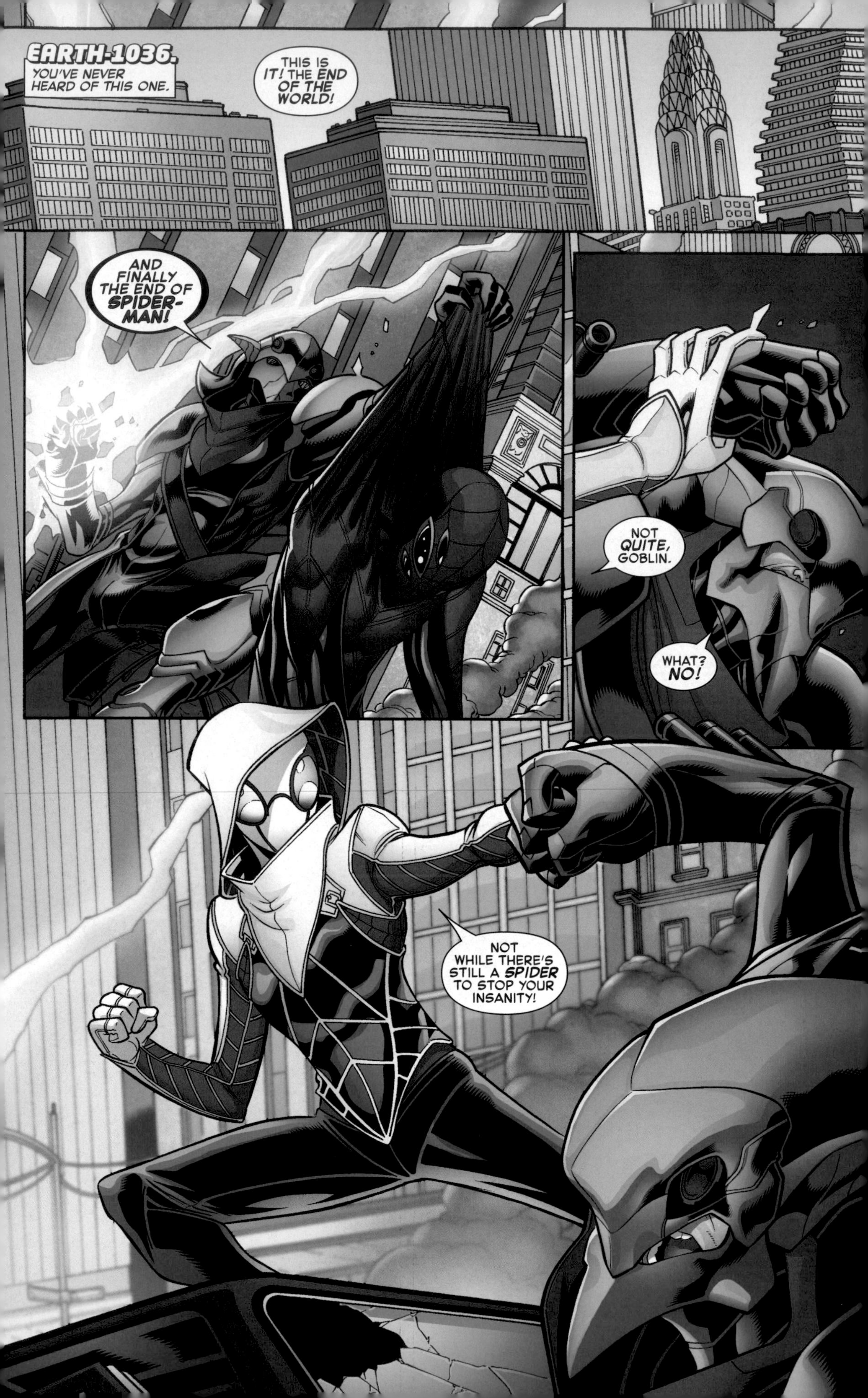
EARTH-1036.
YOU'VE NEVER HEARD OF THIS ONE.
THIS IS IT! THE END OF THE WORLD!
AND FINALLY THE END OF SPIDER-MAN!
NOT QUITE, GOBLIN.
WHAT? NO!
NOT WHILE THERE'S STILL A SPIDER TO STOP YOUR INSANITY!

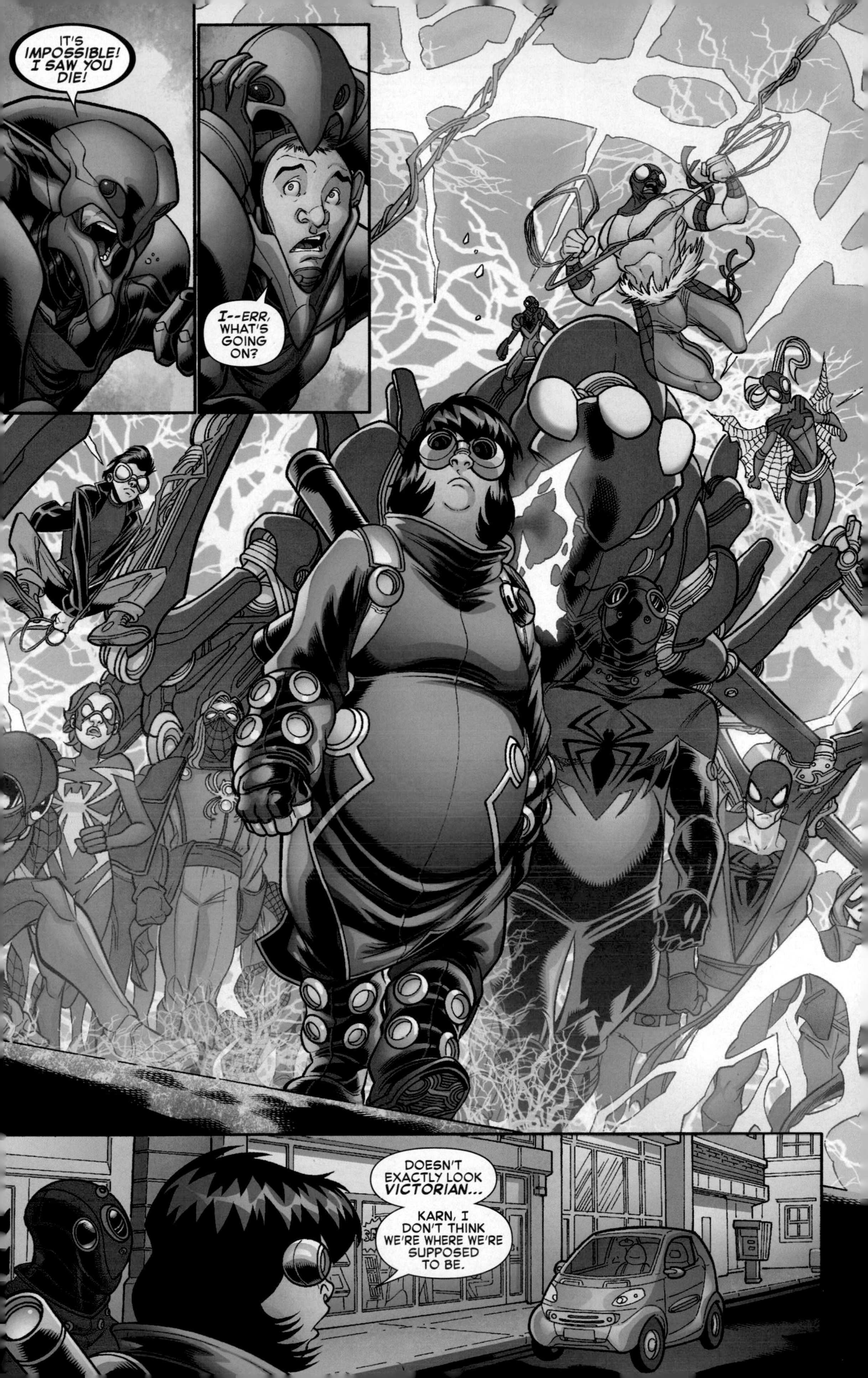
IT'S IMPOSSIBLE! I SAW YOU DIE!
I--ERR, WHAT'S GOING ON?
DOESN'T EXACTLY LOOK VICTORIAN...
KARN, I DON'T THINK WE'RE WHERE WE'RE SUPPOSED TO BE.

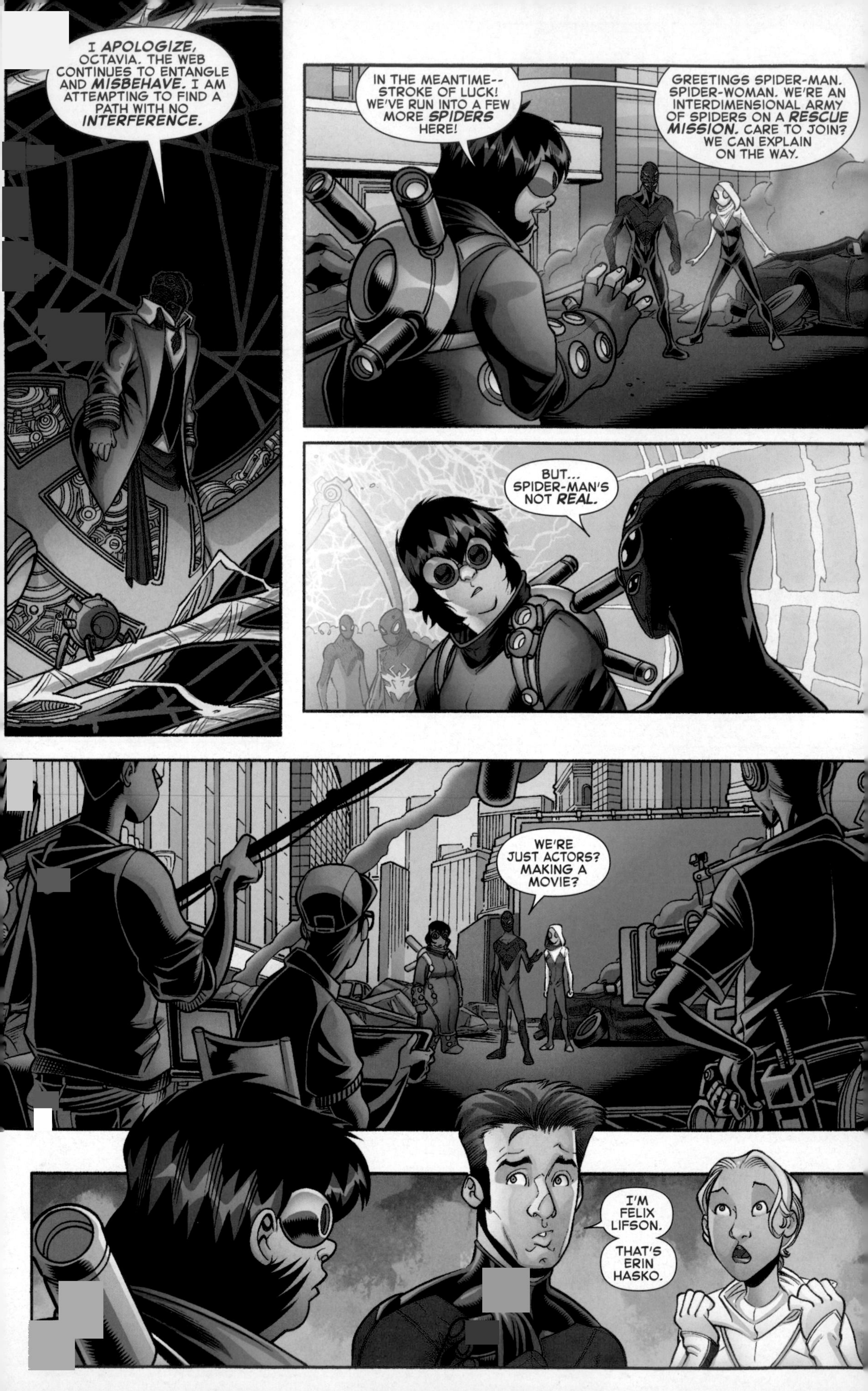
I APOLOGIZE, OCTAVIA. THE WEB CONTINUES TO ENTANGLE AND MISBEHAVE. I AM ATTEMPTING TO FIND A PATH WITH NO INTERFERENCE.
IN THE MEANTIME-- STROKE OF LUCK! WE'VE RUN INTO A FEW MORE SPIDERS HERE!
GREETINGS SPIDER-MAN. SPIDER-WOMAN. WE'RE AN INTERDIMENSIONAL ARMY OF SPIDERS ON A RESCUE MISSION. CARE TO JOIN? WE CAN EXPLAIN ON THE WAY.
BUT... SPIDER-MAN'S NOT REAL.
WE'RE JUST ACTORS? MAKING A MOVIE?
I'M FELIX LIFSON.
THAT'S ERIN HASKO.

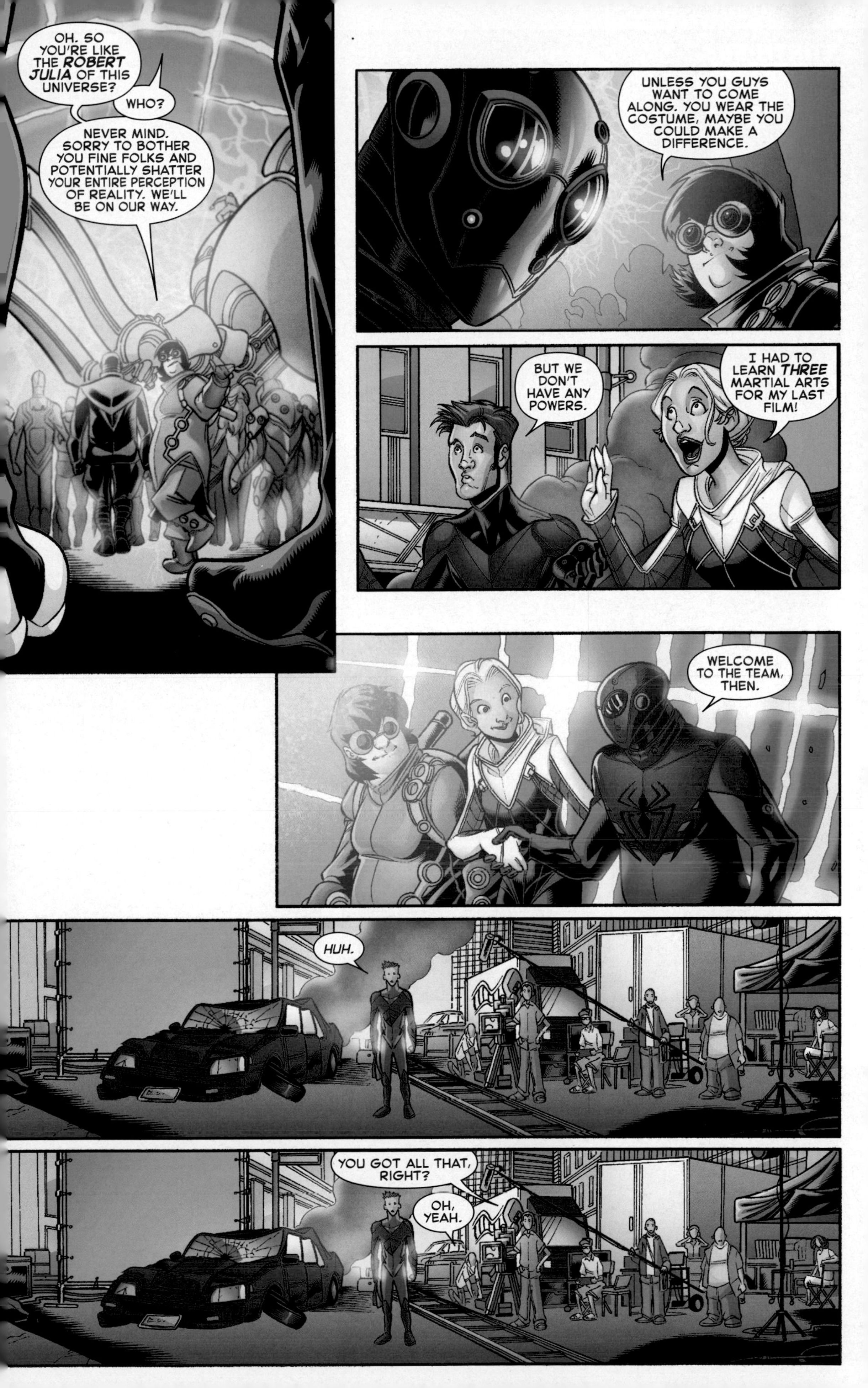
OH. SO YOU'RE LIKE THE ROBERT JULIA OF THIS UNIVERSE?
WHO?
NEVER MIND. SORRY TO BOTHER YOU FINE FOLKS AND POTENTIALLY SHATTER YOUR ENTIRE PERCEPTION OF REALITY. WE'LL BE ON OUR WAY.
UNLESS YOU GUYS WANT TO COME ALONG. YOU WEAR THE COSTUME, MAYBE YOU COULD MAKE A DIFFERENCE.
BUT WE DON'T HAVE ANY POWERS.
I HAD TO LEARN THREE MARTIAL ARTS FOR MY LAST FILM!
WELCOME TO THE TEAM, THEN.
HUH.
YOU GOT ALL THAT, RIGHT?
OH, YEAH.

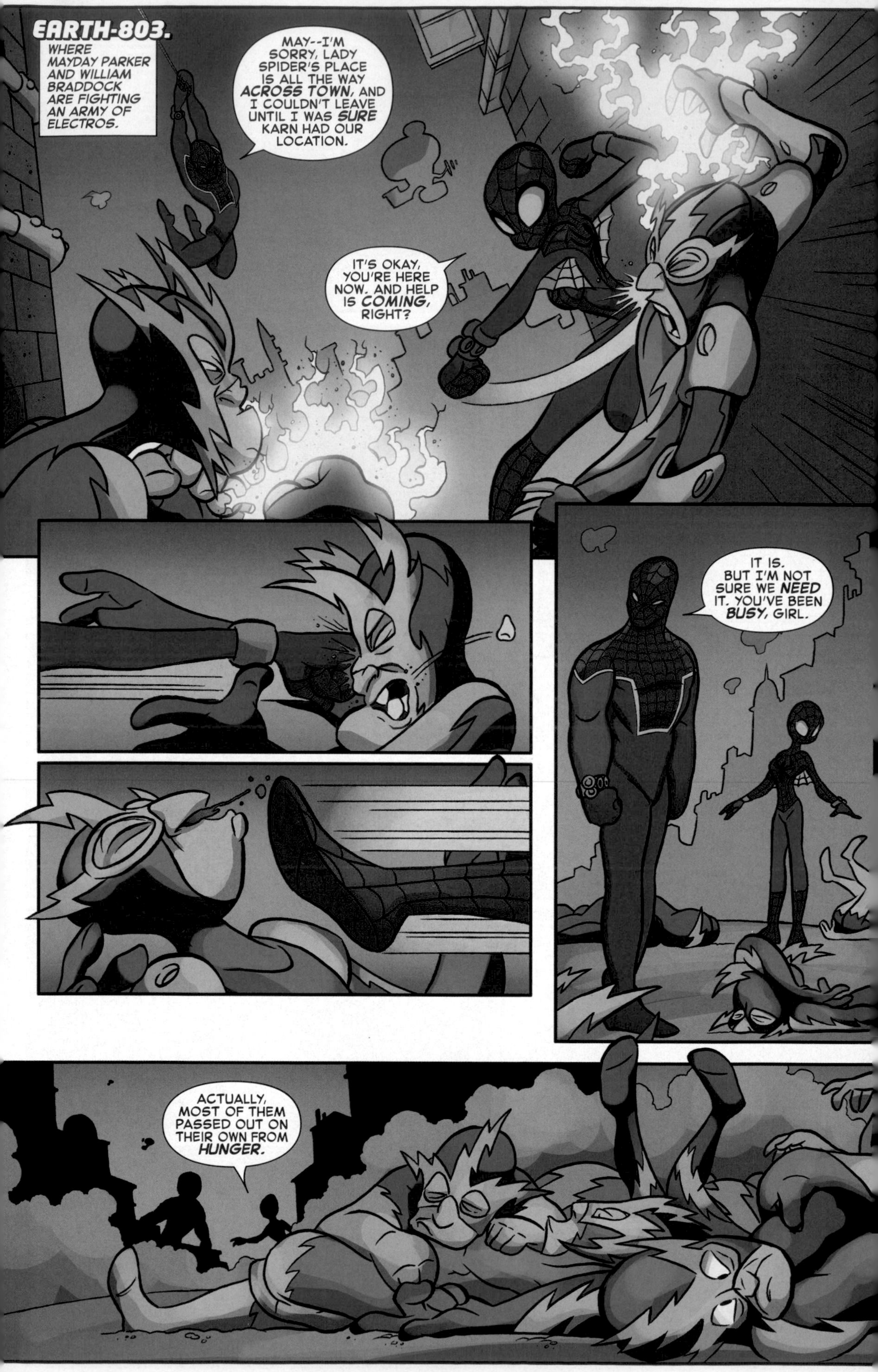
EARTH-803.
WHERE MAYDAY PARKER AND WILLIAM BRADDOCK ARE FIGHTING AN ARMY OF ELECTROS.
MAY--I'M SORRY, LADY SPIDER'S PLACE IS ALL THE WAY ACROSS TOWN, AND I COULDN'T LEAVE UNTIL I WAS SURE KARN HAD OUR LOCATION.
IT'S OKAY, YOU'RE HERE NOW. AND HELP IS COMING, RIGHT?
IT IS. BUT I'M NOT SURE WE NEED IT. YOU'VE BEEN BUSY, GIRL.
ACTUALLY, MOST OF THEM PASSED OUT ON THEIR OWN FROM HUNGER.

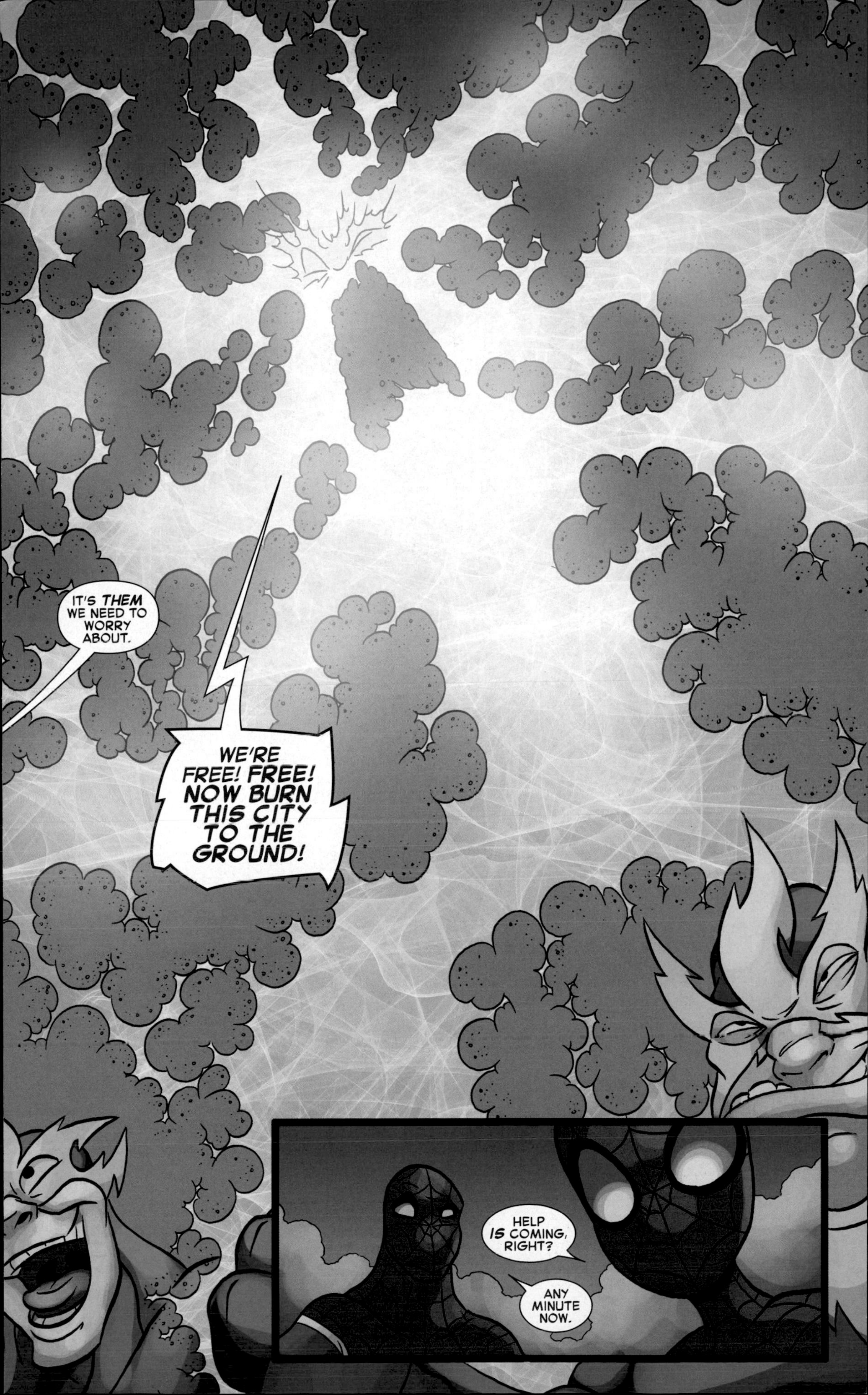
IT'S THEM WE NEED TO WORRY ABOUT.
WE'RE FREE! FREE! NOW BURN THIS CITY TO THE GROUND!
HELP IS COMING, RIGHT?
ANY MINUTE NOW.

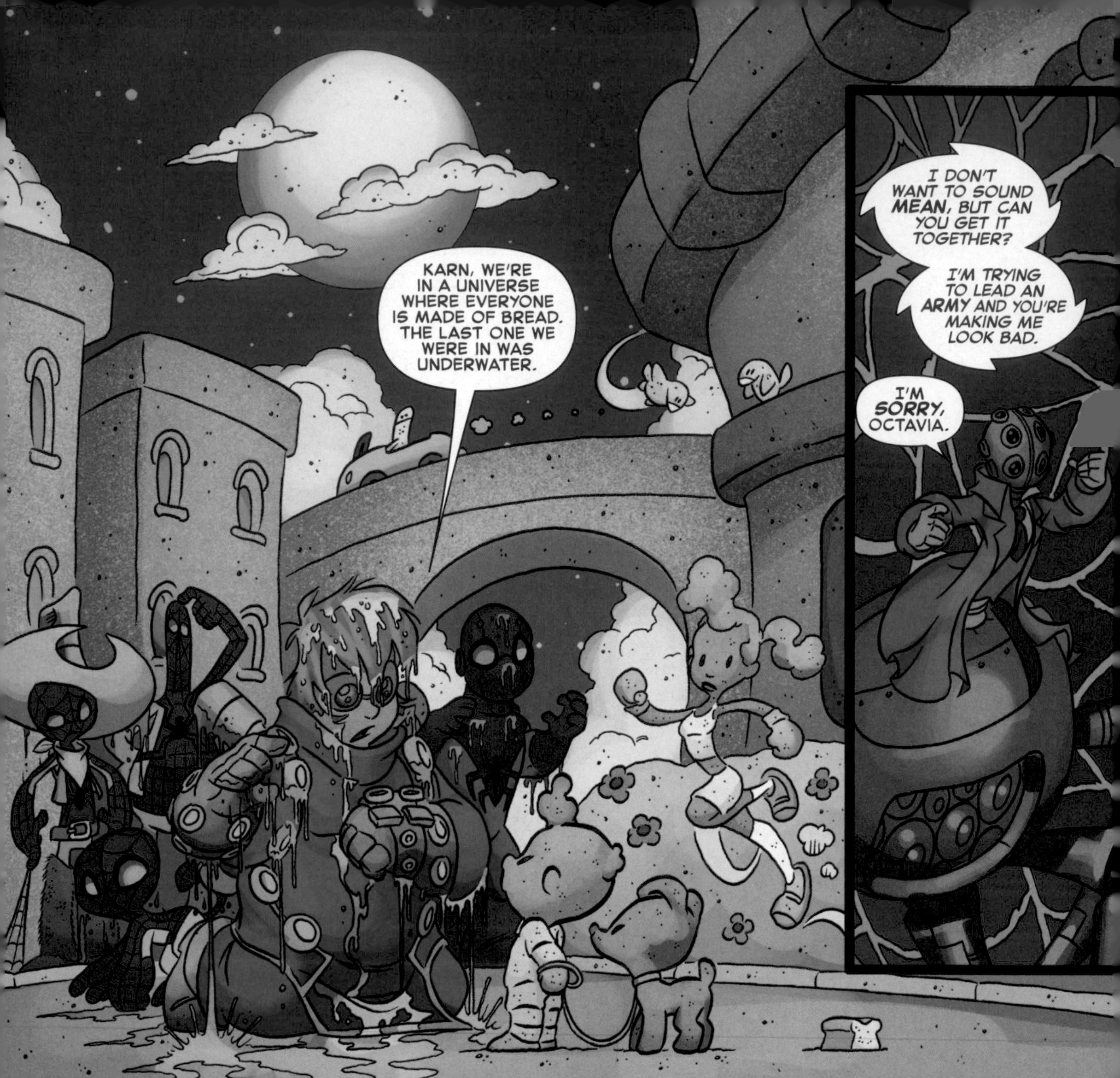
KARN, WE'RE IN A UNIVERSE WHERE EVERYONE IS MADE OF BREAD. THE LAST ONE WE WERE IN WAS UNDERWATER.
I DON'T WANT TO SOUND MEAN, BUT CAN YOU GET IT TOGETHER?
I'M TRYING TO LEAD AN ARMY AND YOU'RE MAKING ME LOOK BAD.
I'M SORRY, OCTAVIA.

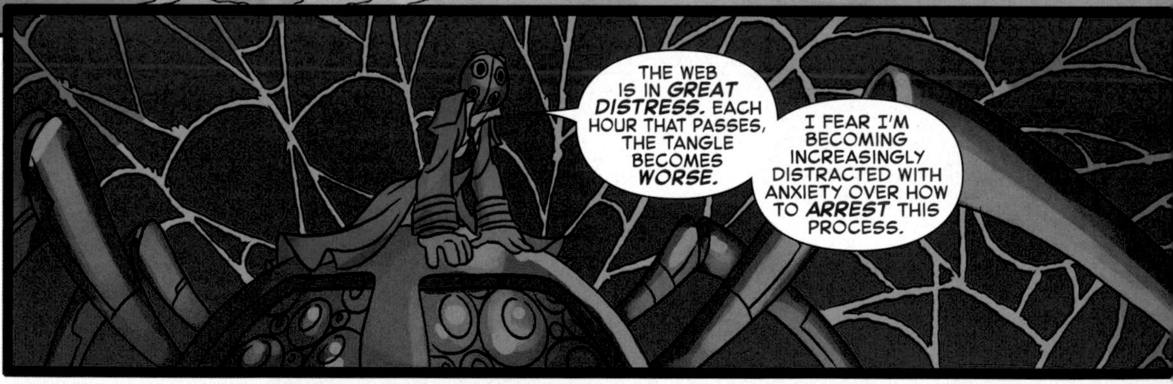
THE WEB IS IN GREAT DISTRESS. EACH HOUR THAT PASSES, THE TANGLE BECOMES WORSE.
I FEAR I'M BECOMING INCREASINGLY DISTRACTED WITH ANXIETY OVER HOW TO ARREST THIS PROCESS.

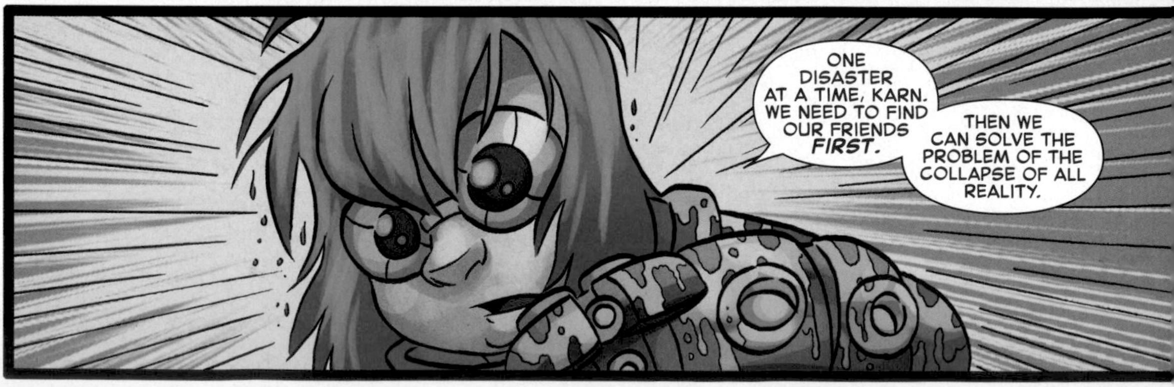
ONE DISASTER AT A TIME, KARN. WE NEED TO FIND OUR FRIENDS FIRST.
THEN WE CAN SOLVE THE PROBLEM OF THE COLLAPSE OF ALL REALITY.

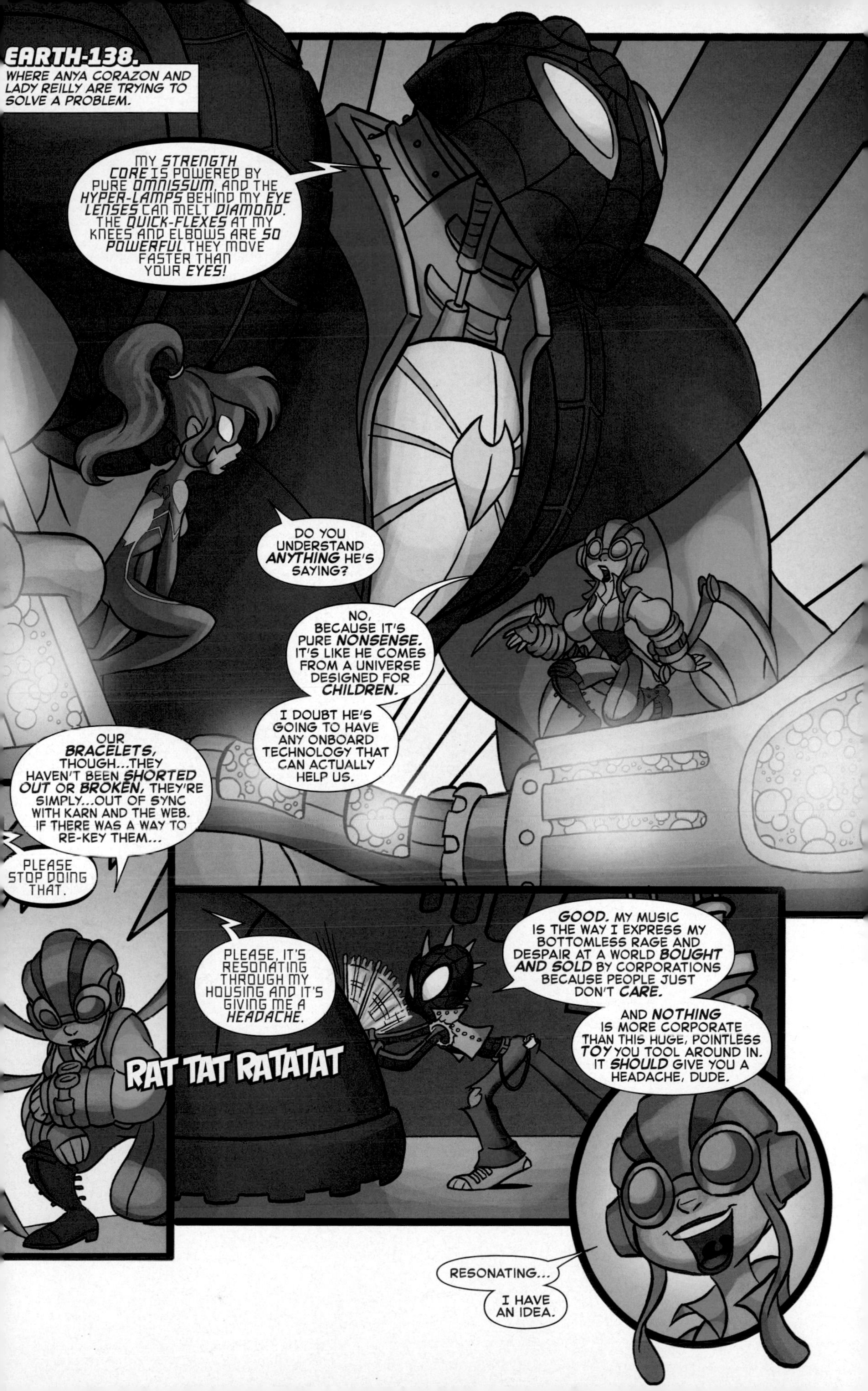
EARTH-138.
WHERE ANYA CORAZON AND LADY REILLY ARE TRYING TO SOLVE A PROBLEM.
MY STRENGTH CORE IS POWERED BY PURE OMNISSUM, AND THE HYPER-LAMPS BEHIND MY EYE LENSES CAN MELT DIAMOND. THE QUICK-FLEXES AT MY KNEES AND ELBOWS ARE SO POWERFUL THEY MOVE FASTER THAN YOUR EYES!
DO YOU UNDERSTAND ANYTHING HE'S SAYING?
NO, BECAUSE IT'S PURE NONSENSE. IT'S LIKE HE COMES FROM A UNIVERSE DESIGNED FOR CHILDREN.
I DOUBT HE'S GOING TO HAVE ANY ONBOARD TECHNOLOGY THAT CAN ACTUALLY HELP US.
OUR BRACELETS, THOUGH...THEY HAVEN'T BEEN SHORTED OUT OR BROKEN, THEY'RE SIMPLY...OUT OF SYNC WITH KARN AND THE WEB. IF THERE WAS A WAY TO RE-KEY THEM...
PLEASE STOP DOING THAT.
RAT TAT RATATAT
PLEASE, IT'S RESONATING THROUGH MY HOUSING AND IT'S GIVING ME A HEADACHE.
GOOD. MY MUSIC IS THE WAY I EXPRESS MY BOTTOMLESS RAGE AND DESPAIR AT A WORLD BOUGHT AND SOLD BY CORPORATIONS BECAUSE PEOPLE JUST DON'T CARE.
AND NOTHING IS MORE CORPORATE THAN THIS HUGE, POINTLESS TOY YOU TOOL AROUND IN. IT SHOULD GIVE YOU A HEADACHE, DUDE.
RESONATING...
I HAVE AN IDEA.

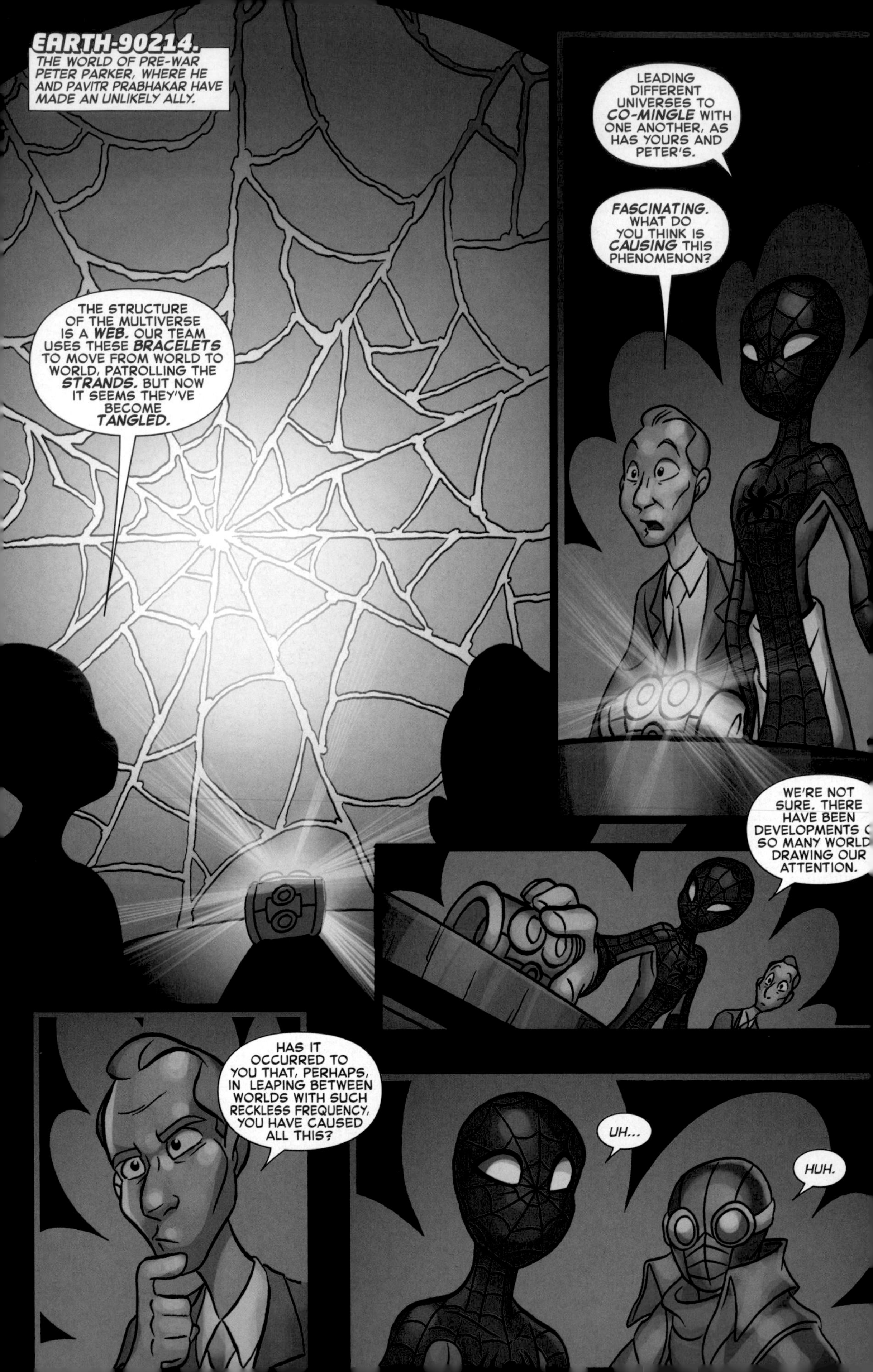
EARTH-90214.
THE WORLD OF PRE-WAR PETER PARKER, WHERE HE AND PAVITR PRABHAKAR HAVE MADE AN UNLIKELY ALLY.
THE STRUCTURE OF THE MULTIVERSE IS A WEB. OUR TEAM USES THESE BRACELETS TO MOVE FROM WORLD TO WORLD, PATROLLING THE STRANDS. BUT NOW IT SEEMS THEY'VE BECOME TANGLED.
LEADING DIFFERENT UNIVERSES TO CO-MINGLE WITH ONE ANOTHER, AS HAS YOURS AND PETER'S.
FASCINATING. WHAT DO YOU THINK IS CAUSING THIS PHENOMENON?
WE'RE NOT SURE. THERE HAVE BEEN DEVELOPMENTS ON SO MANY WORLDS DRAWING OUR ATTENTION.
HAS IT OCCURRED TO YOU THAT, PERHAPS, IN LEAPING BETWEEN WORLDS WITH SUCH RECKLESS FREQUENCY, YOU HAVE CAUSED ALL THIS?
UH...
HUH.

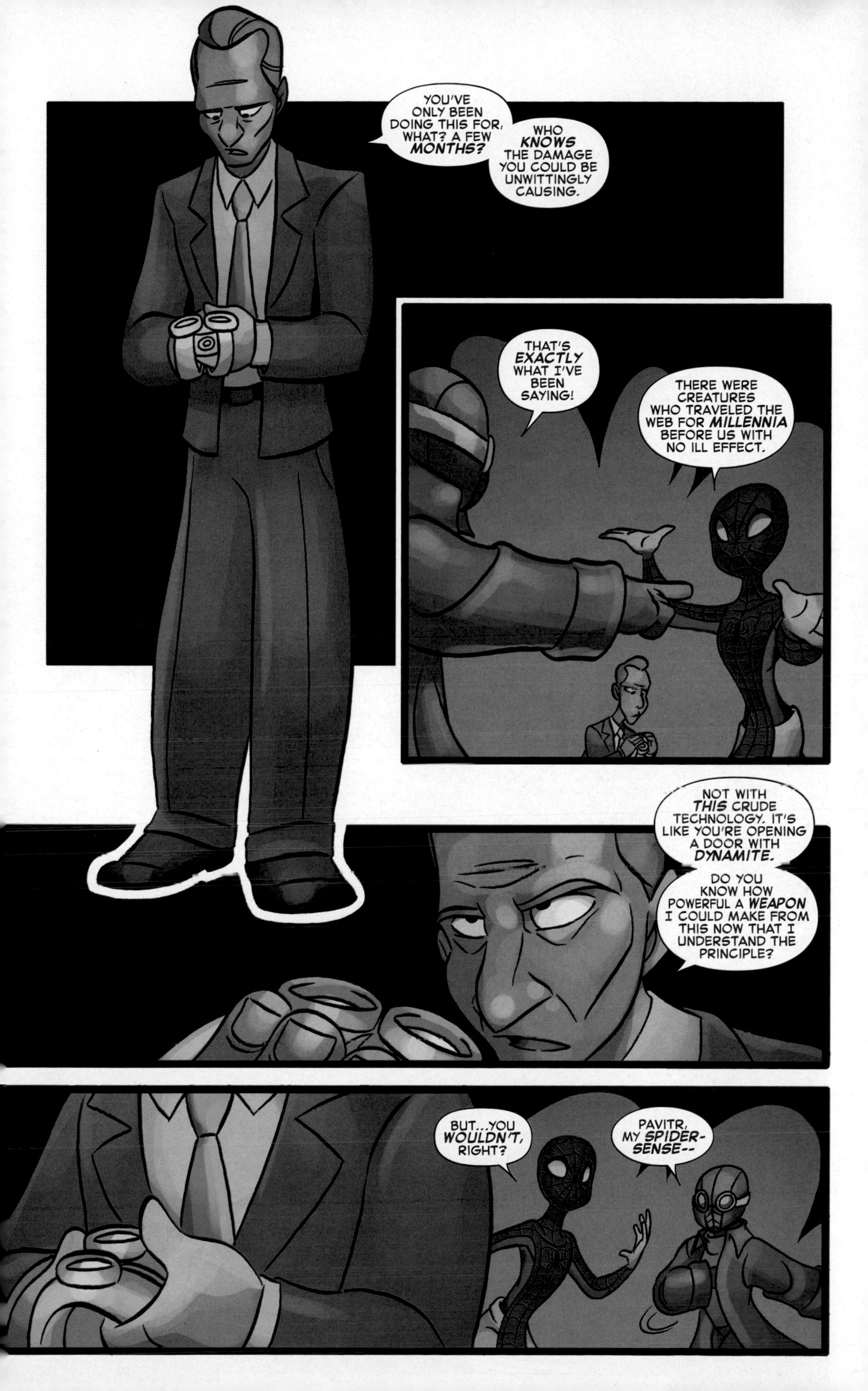
YOU'VE ONLY BEEN DOING THIS FOR, WHAT? A FEW MONTHS?
WHO KNOWS THE DAMAGE YOU COULD BE UNWITTINGLY CAUSING.
THAT'S EXACTLY WHAT I'VE BEEN SAYING!
THERE WERE CREATURES WHO TRAVELED THE WEB FOR MILLENNIA BEFORE US WITH NO ILL EFFECT.
NOT WITH THIS CRUDE TECHNOLOGY. IT'S LIKE YOU'RE OPENING A DOOR WITH DYNAMITE.
DO YOU KNOW HOW POWERFUL A WEAPON I COULD MAKE FROM THIS NOW THAT I UNDERSTAND THE PRINCIPLE?
BUT...YOU WOULDN'T, RIGHT?
PAVITR, MY SPIDER-SENSE--

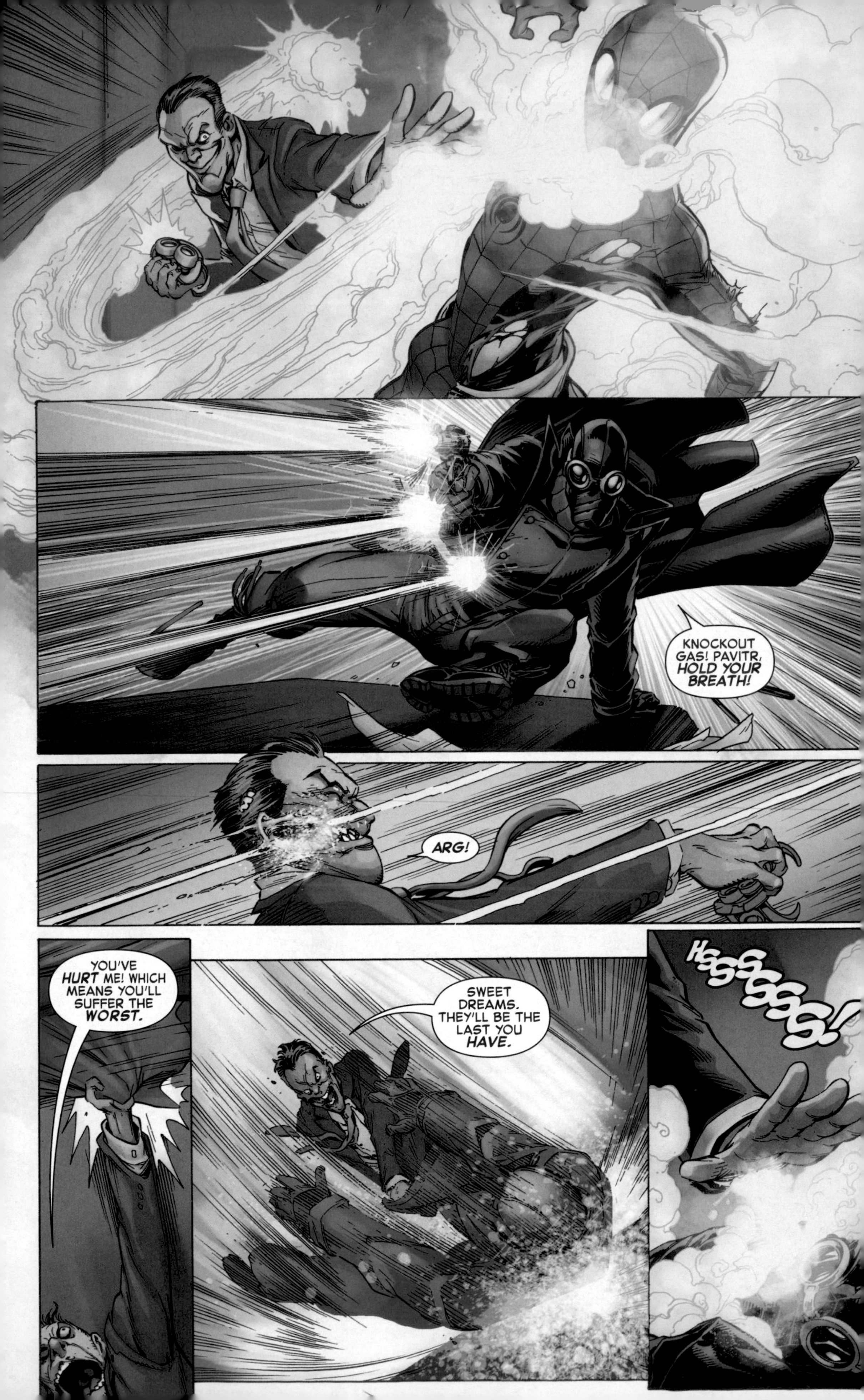
KNOCKOUT GAS! PAVITR, HOLD YOUR BREATH!
ARG!
YOU'VE HURT ME! WHICH MEANS YOU'LL SUFFER THE WORST.
SWEET DREAMS. THEY'LL BE THE LAST YOU HAVE.
HSSSSSSS!

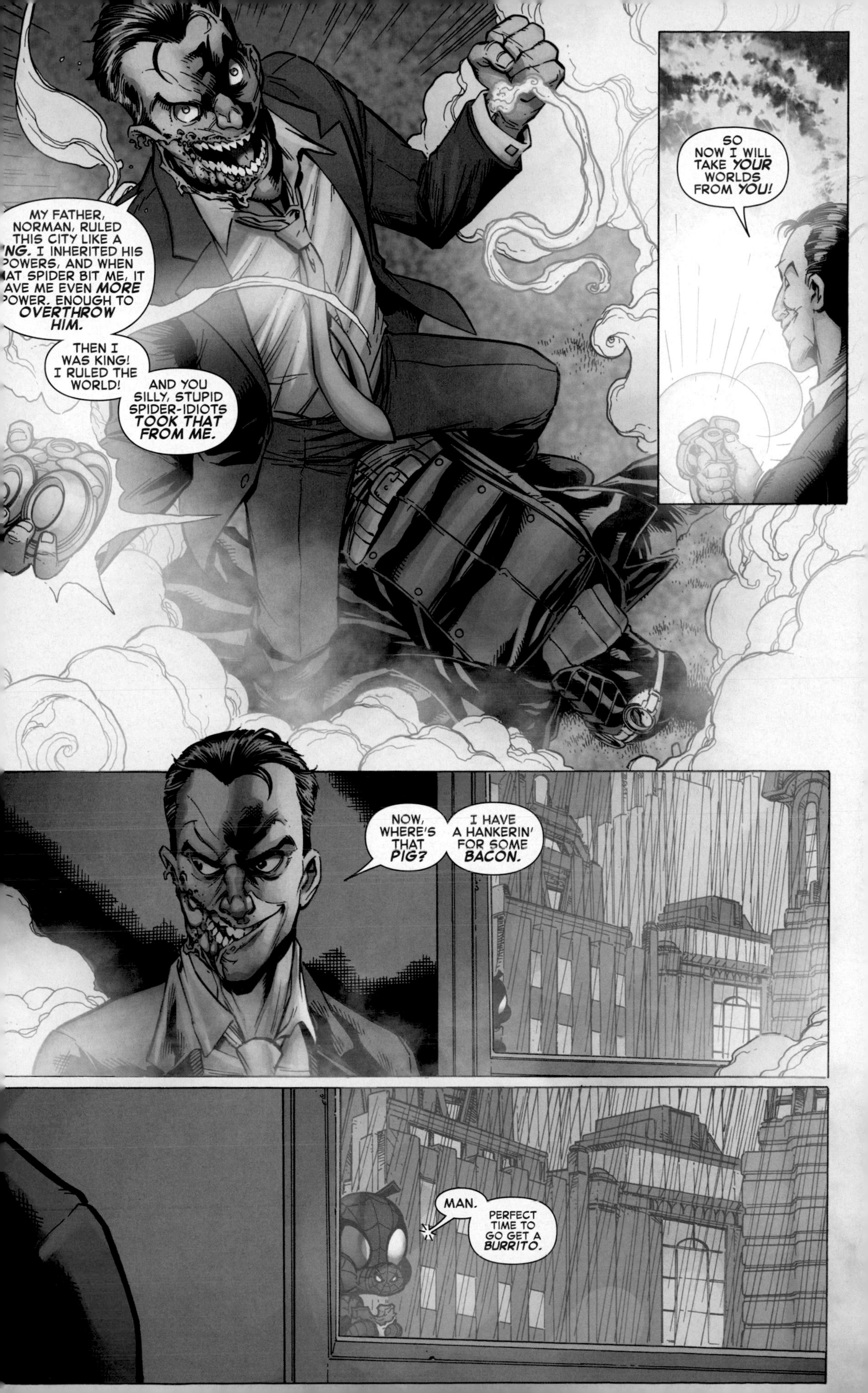

MY FATHER, NORMAN, RULED THIS CITY LIKE A KING. I INHERITED HIS POWERS, AND WHEN THAT SPIDER BIT ME, IT GAVE ME EVEN MORE POWER. ENOUGH TO OVERTHROW HIM.
THEN I WAS KING! I RULED THE WORLD!
AND YOU SILLY, STUPID SPIDER-IDIOTS TOOK THAT FROM ME.
SO NOW I WILL TAKE YOUR WORLDS FROM YOU!
NOW, WHERE'S THAT PIG?
I HAVE A HANKERIN' FOR SOME BACON.
MAN.
PERFECT TIME TO GO GET A BURRITO.

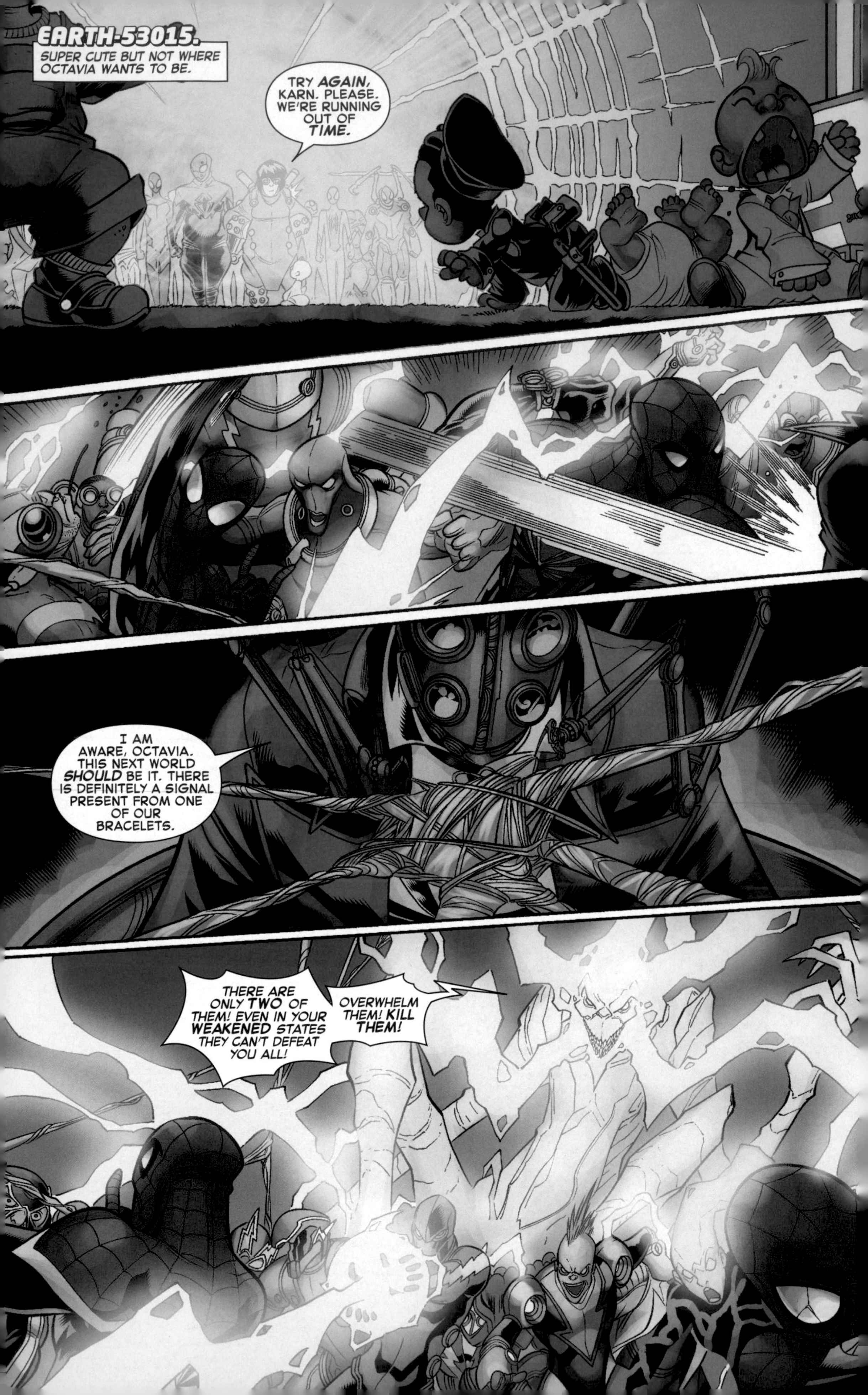
EARTH-53015.
SUPER CUTE BUT NOT WHERE OCTAVIA WANTS TO BE.
TRY AGAIN, KARN. PLEASE. WE'RE RUNNING OUT OF TIME.
I AM AWARE, OCTAVIA. THIS NEXT WORLD SHOULD BE IT. THERE IS DEFINITELY A SIGNAL PRESENT FROM ONE OF OUR BRACELETS.
THERE ARE ONLY TWO OF THEM! EVEN IN YOUR WEAKENED STATES THEY CAN'T DEFEAT YOU ALL!
OVERWHELM THEM! KILL THEM!

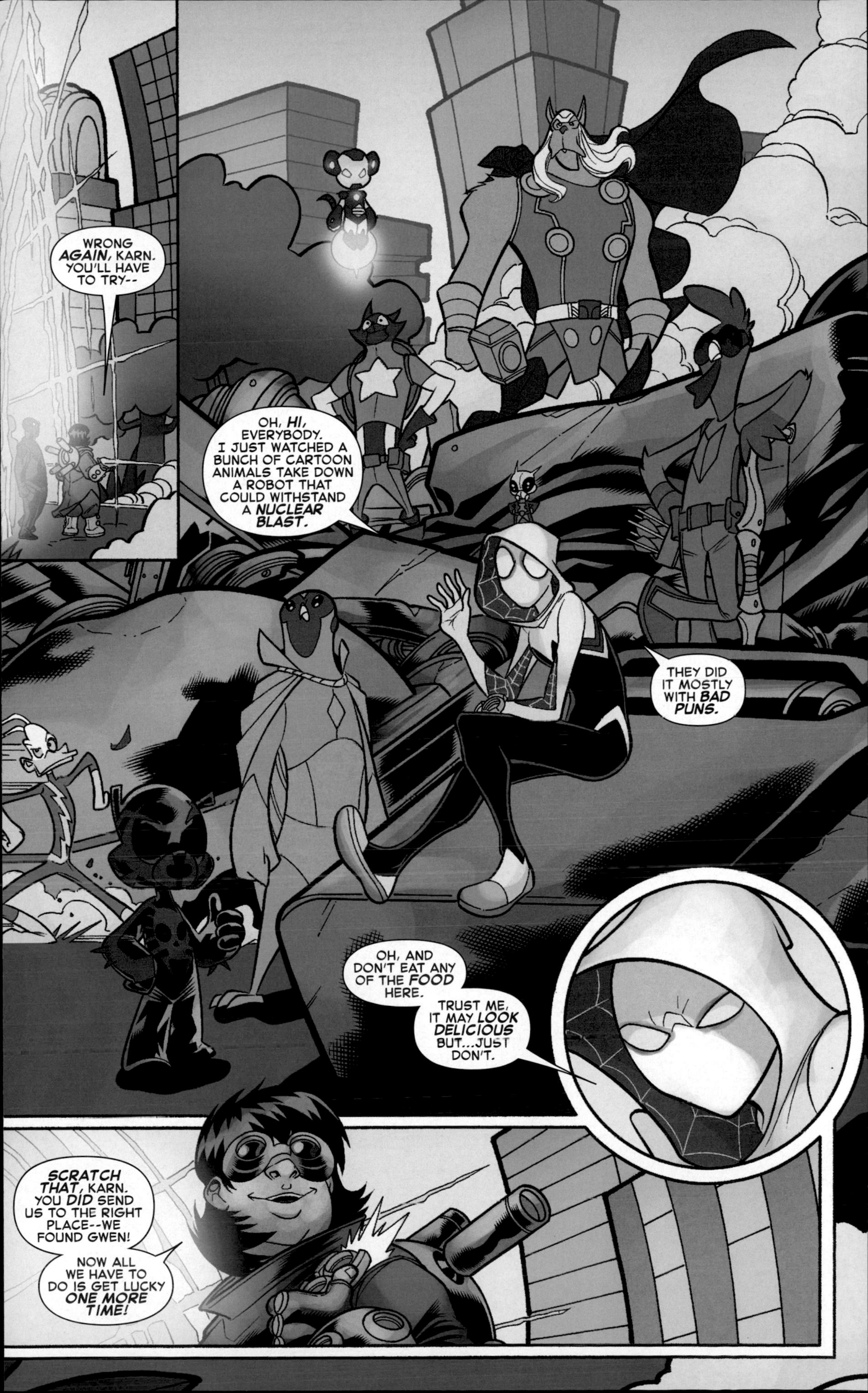
WRONG AGAIN, KARN. YOU'LL HAVE TO TRY--
OH, HI, EVERYBODY. I JUST WATCHED A BUNCH OF CARTOON ANIMALS TAKE DOWN A ROBOT THAT COULD WITHSTAND A NUCLEAR BLAST.
THEY DID IT MOSTLY WITH BAD PUNS.
OH, AND DON'T EAT ANY OF THE FOOD HERE.
TRUST ME, IT MAY LOOK DELICIOUS BUT...JUST DON'T.
SCRATCH THAT, KARN. YOU DID SEND US TO THE RIGHT PLACE--WE FOUND GWEN!
NOW ALL WE HAVE TO DO IS GET LUCKY ONE MORE TIME!

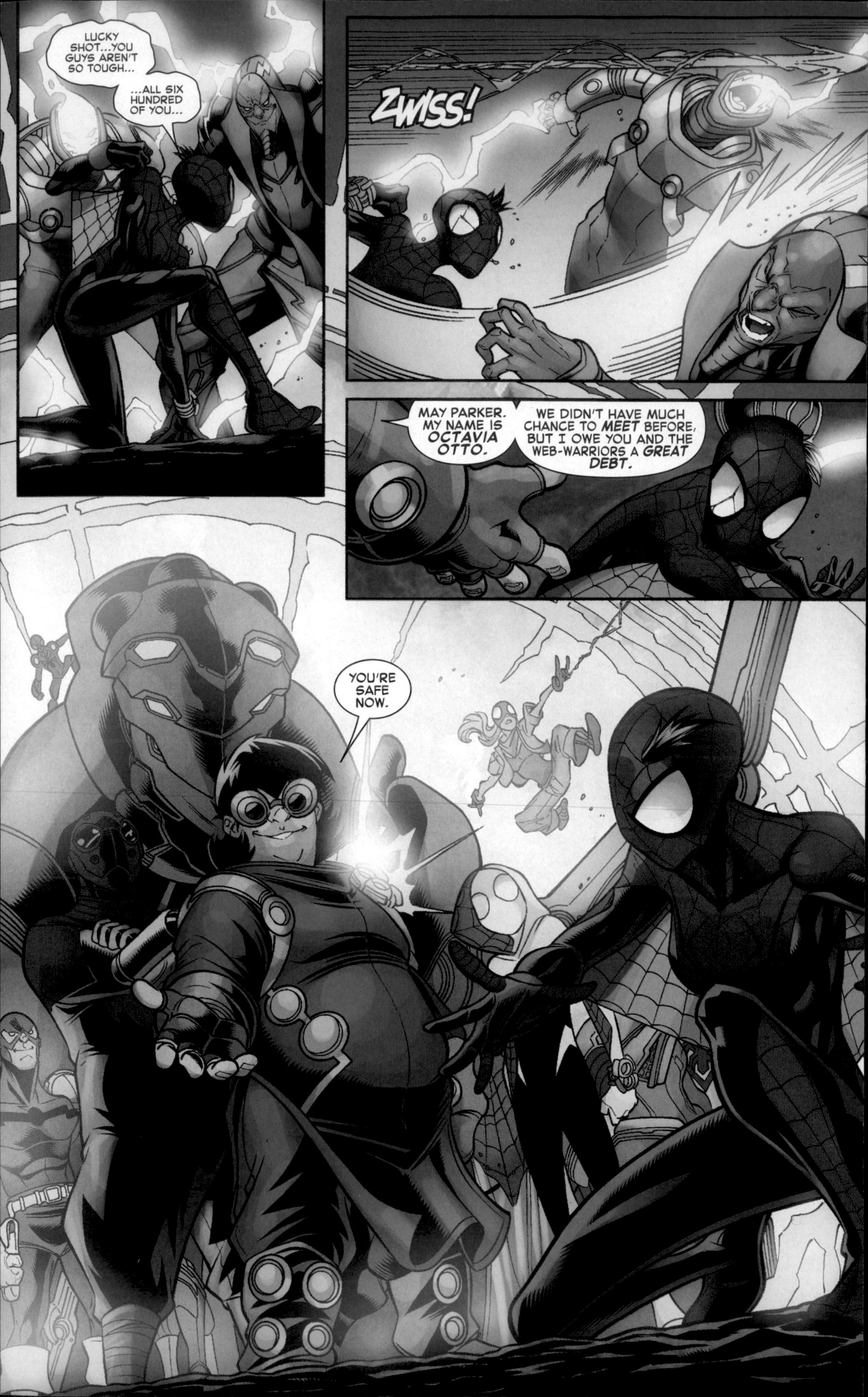
LUCKY SHOT...YOU GUYS AREN'T SO TOUGH...
...ALL SIX HUNDRED OF YOU...
ZWISS!
MAY PARKER. MY NAME IS OCTAVIA OTTO.
WE DIDN'T HAVE MUCH CHANCE TO MEET BEFORE, BUT I OWE YOU AND THE WEB-WARRIORS A GREAT DEBT.
YOU'RE SAFE NOW.

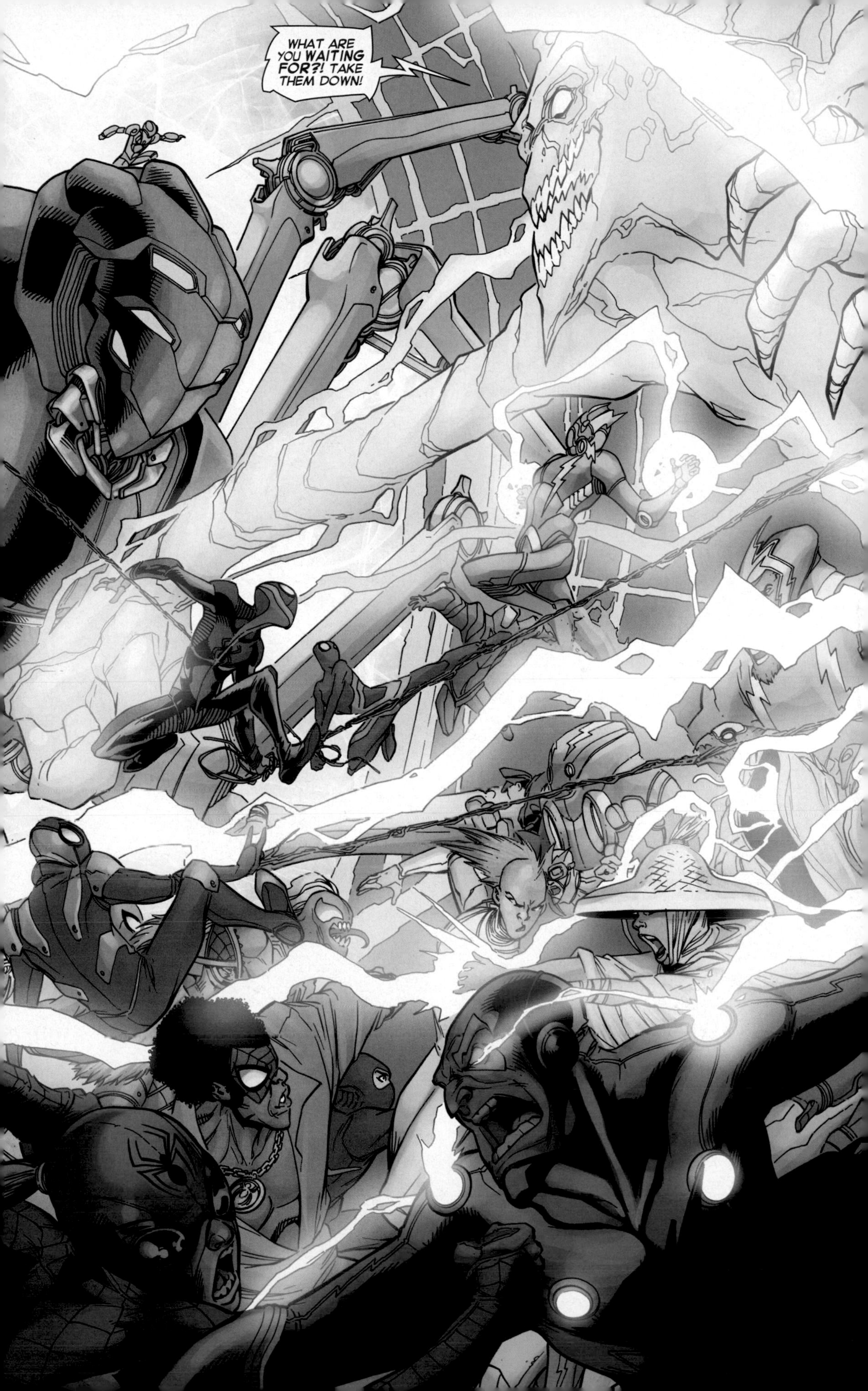
WHAT ARE YOU WAITING FOR?! TAKE THEM DOWN!

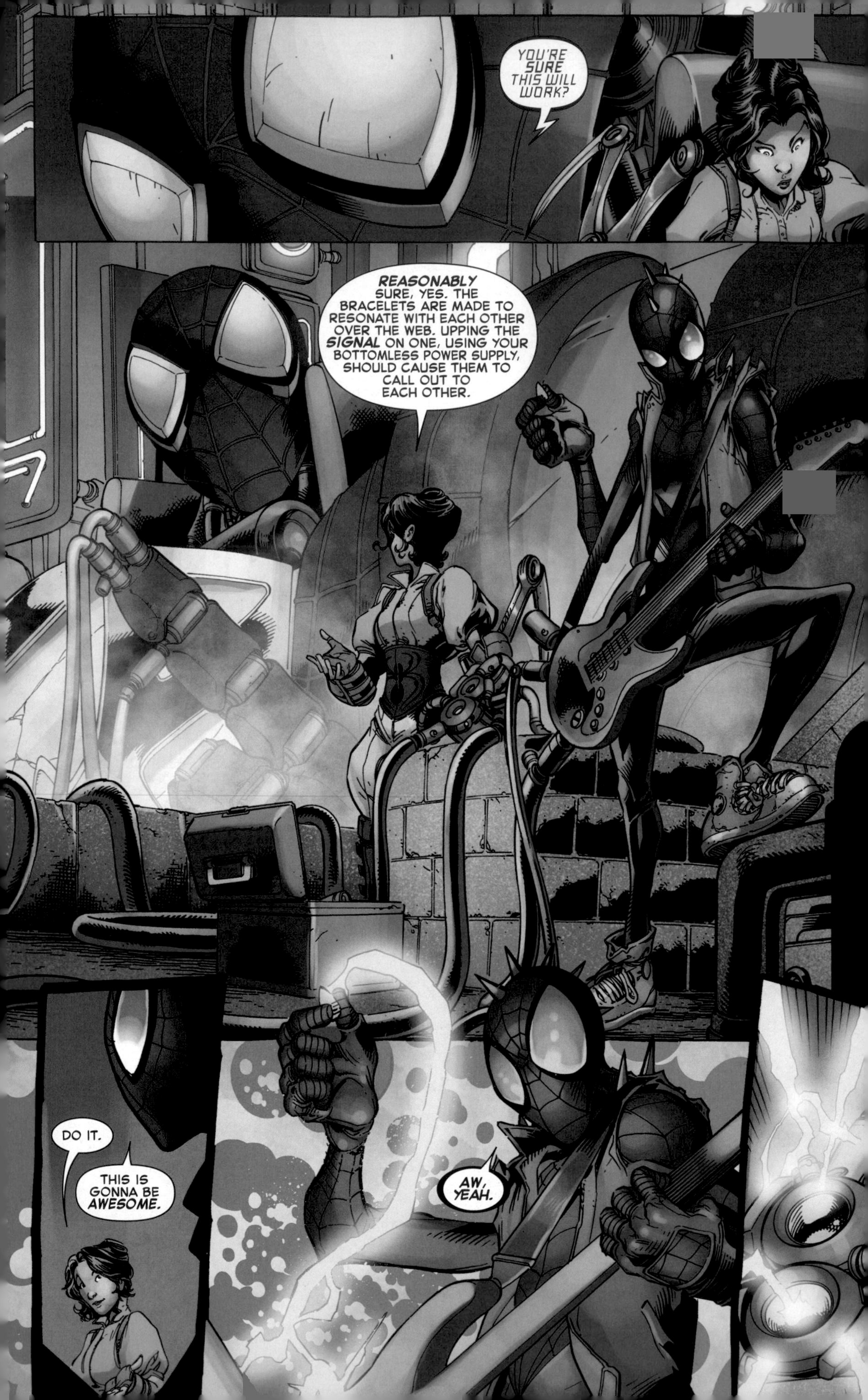
YOU'RE SURE THIS WILL WORK?
REASONABLY SURE, YES. THE BRACELETS ARE MADE TO RESONATE WITH EACH OTHER OVER THE WEB. UPPING THE SIGNAL ON ONE, USING YOUR BOTTOMLESS POWER SUPPLY, SHOULD CAUSE THEM TO CALL OUT TO EACH OTHER.
DO IT.
THIS IS GONNA BE AWESOME.
AW, YEAH.

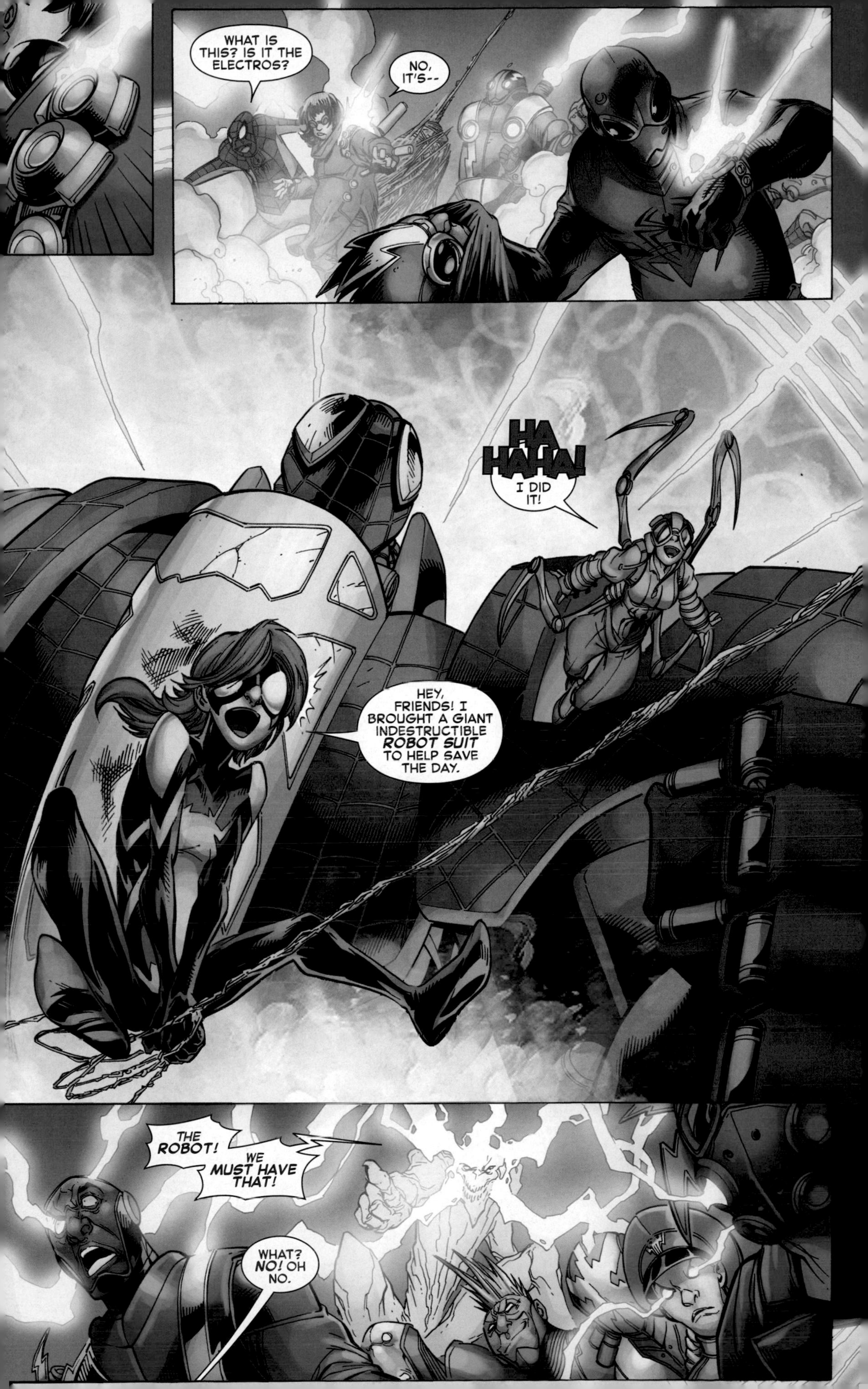
WHAT IS THIS? IS IT THE ELECTROS?
NO, IT'S--
HA HAHA!
I DID IT!
HEY, FRIENDS! I BROUGHT A GIANT INDESTRUCTIBLE ROBOT SUIT TO HELP SAVE THE DAY.
THE ROBOT!
WE MUST HAVE THAT!
WHAT? NO! OH NO.

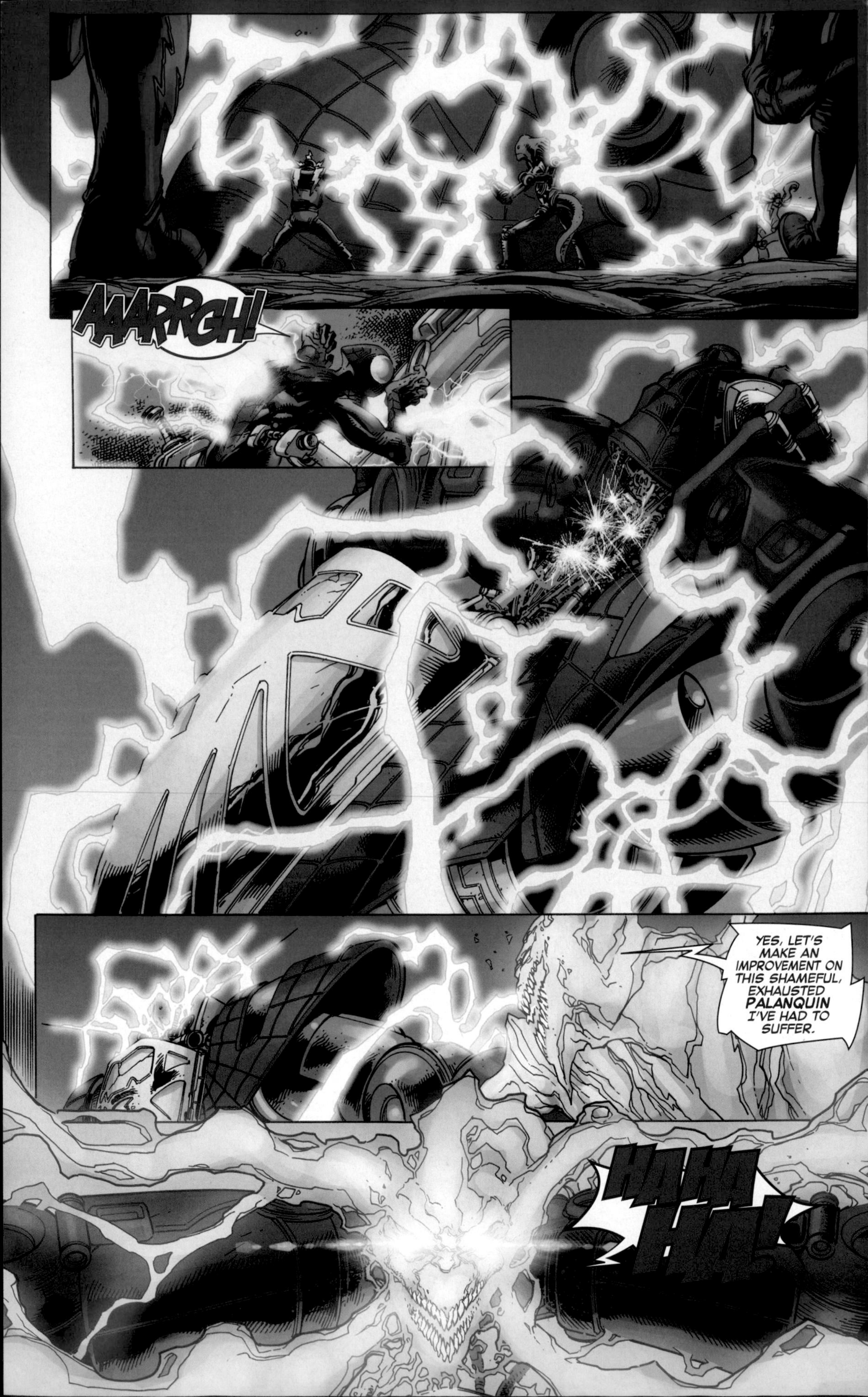
AAARRGH!
YES, LET'S MAKE AN IMPROVEMENT ON THIS SHAMEFUL, EXHAUSTED PALANQUIN I'VE HAD TO SUFFER.
HAHA HA!

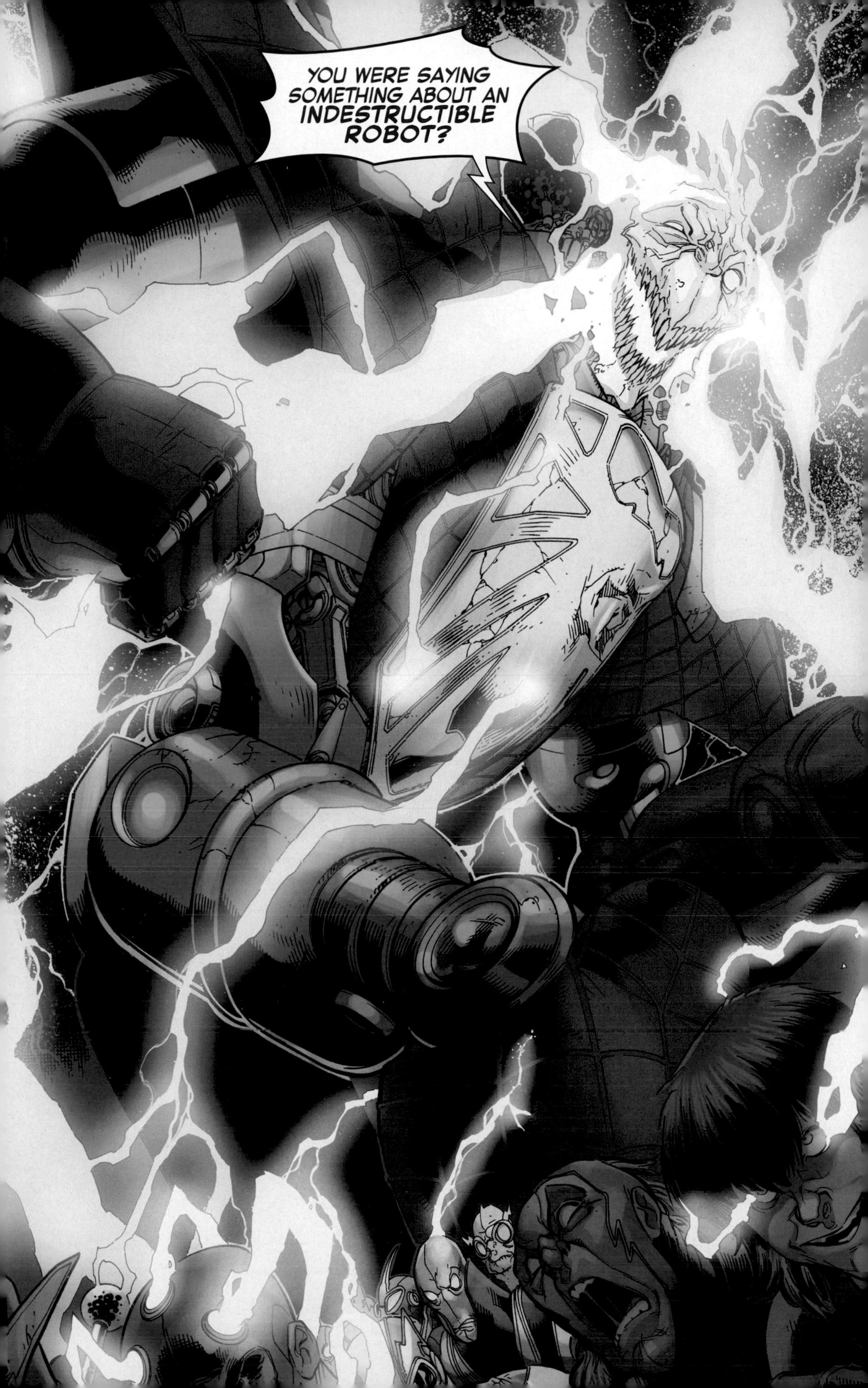
YOU WERE SAYING SOMETHING ABOUT AN INDESTRUCTIBLE ROBOT?

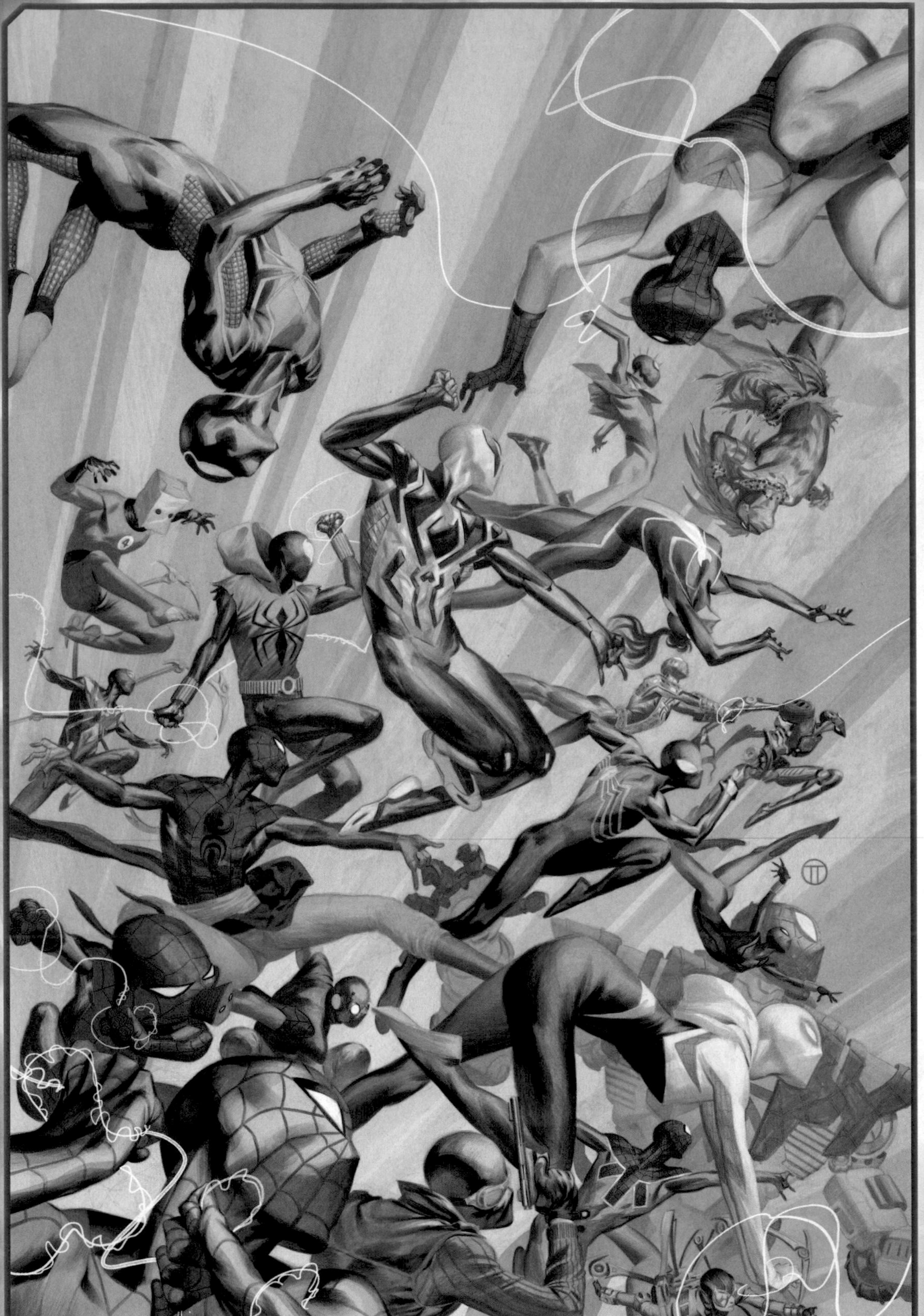

TANGLED STATES PART FIVE : DEMOCRACY

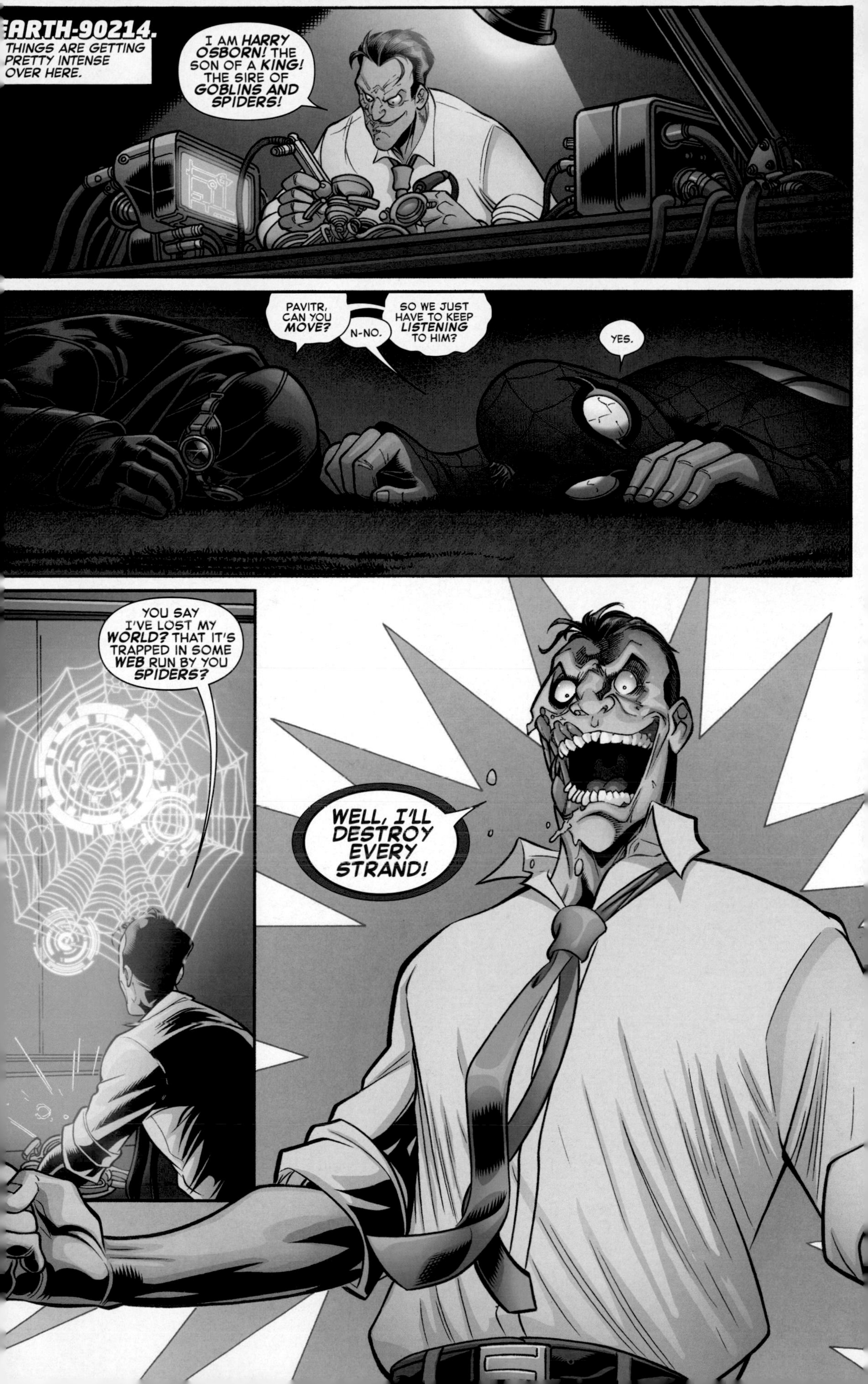
EARTH-90214. THINGS ARE GETTING PRETTY INTENSE OVER HERE.
I AM HARRY OSBORN! THE SON OF A KING! THE SIRE OF GOBLINS AND SPIDERS!
PAVITR, CAN YOU MOVE?
N-NO.
SO WE JUST HAVE TO KEEP LISTENING TO HIM?
YES.
YOU SAY I'VE LOST MY WORLD? THAT IT'S TRAPPED IN SOME WEB RUN BY YOU SPIDERS?
WELL, I'LL DESTROY EVERY STRAND!

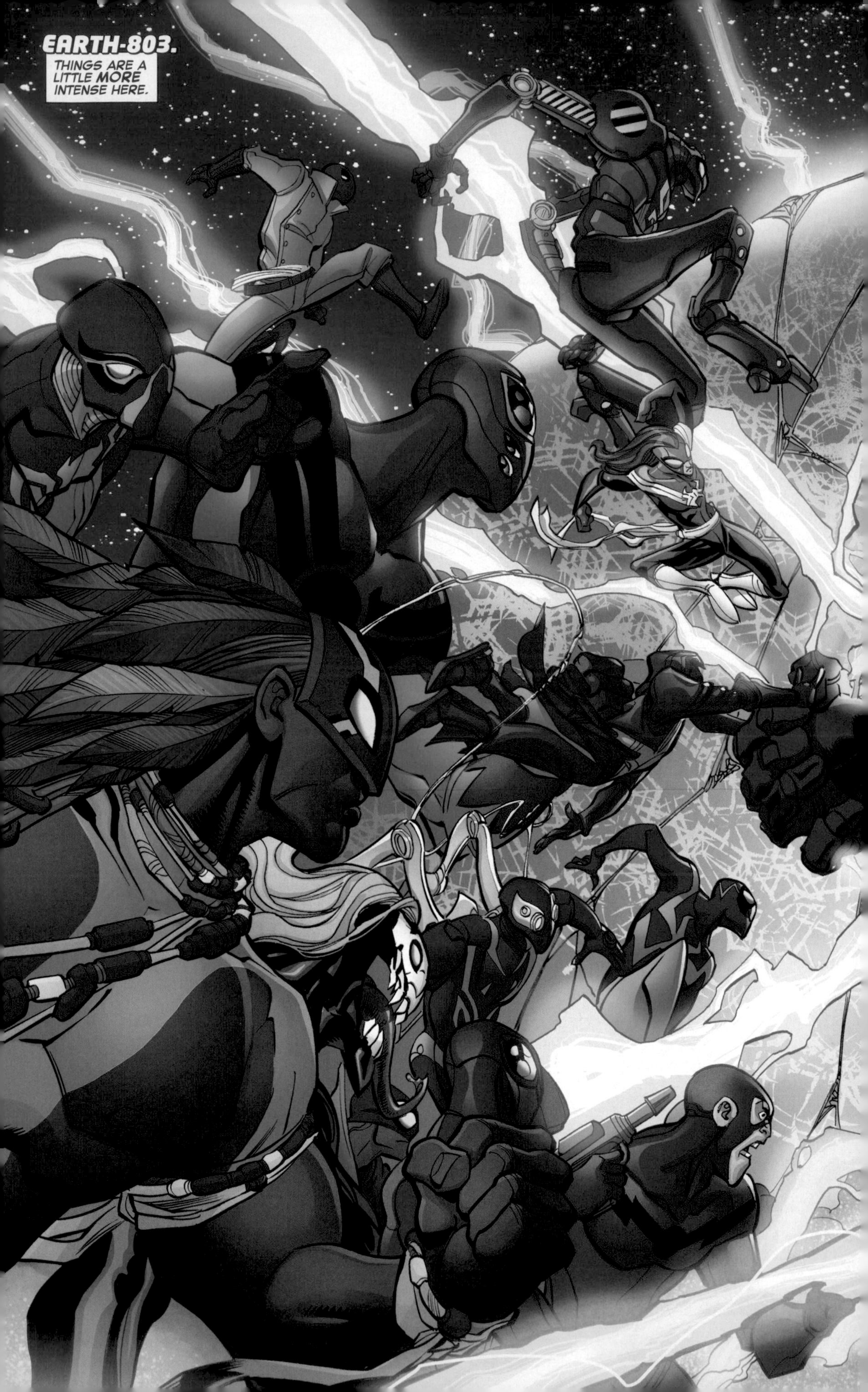
EARTH-803.
THINGS ARE A LITTLE MORE INTENSE HERE.

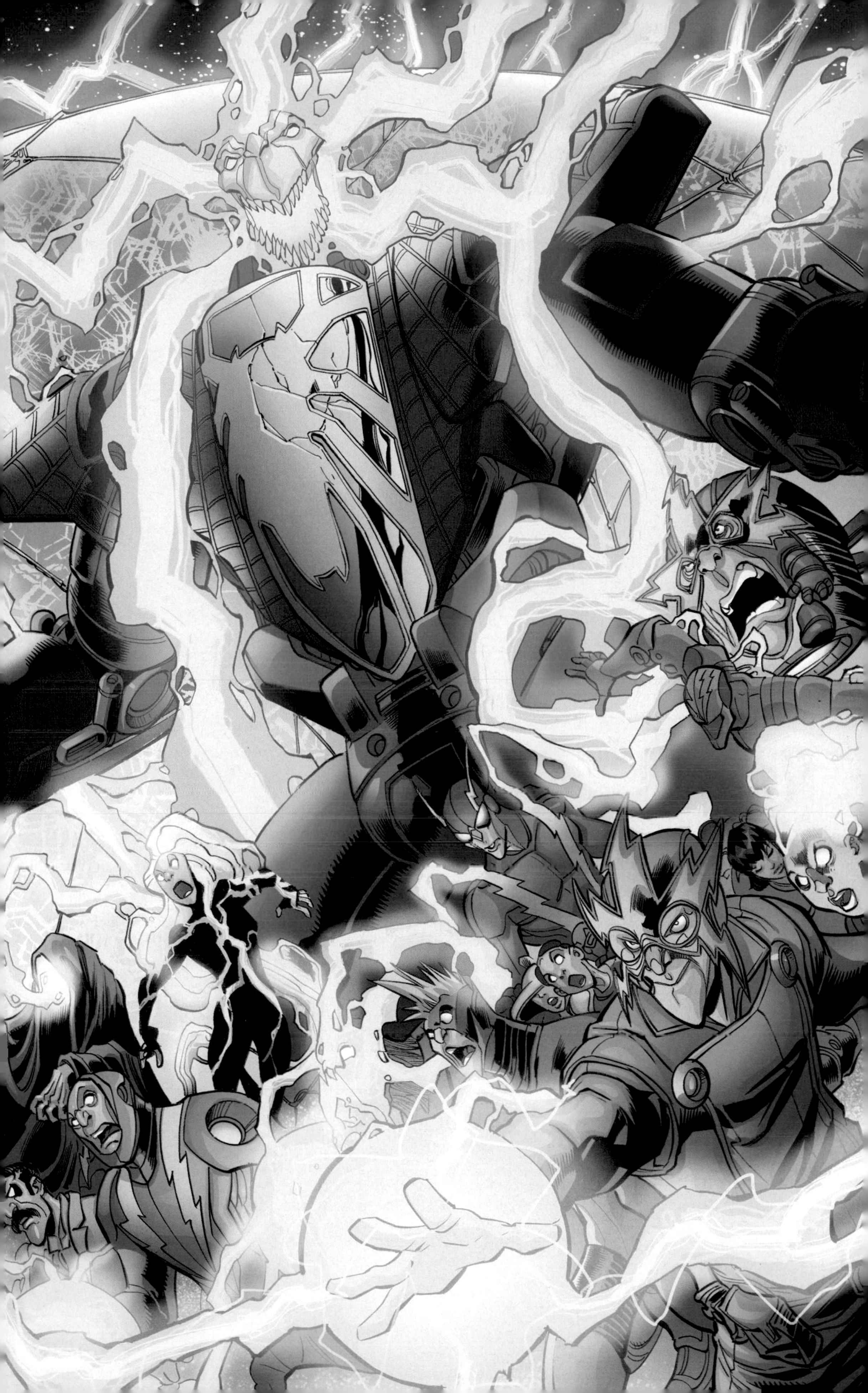

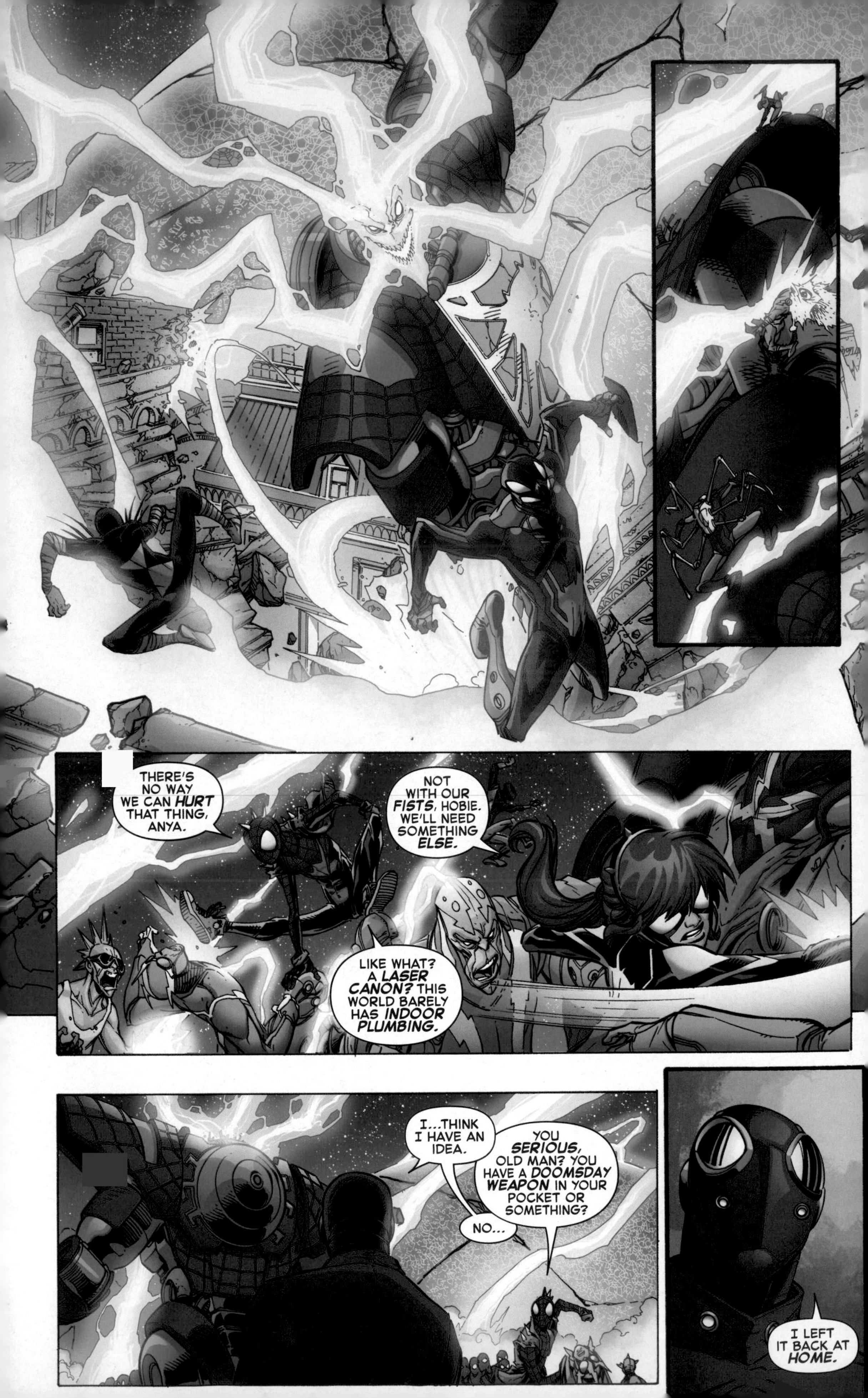
THERE'S NO WAY WE CAN HURT THAT THING, ANYA.
NOT WITH OUR FISTS, HOBIE. WE'LL NEED SOMETHING ELSE.
LIKE WHAT? A LASER CANON? THIS WORLD BARELY HAS INDOOR PLUMBING.
I...THINK I HAVE AN IDEA.
YOU SERIOUS, OLD MAN? YOU HAVE A DOOMSDAY WEAPON IN YOUR POCKET OR SOMETHING?
NO...
I LEFT IT BACK AT HOME.

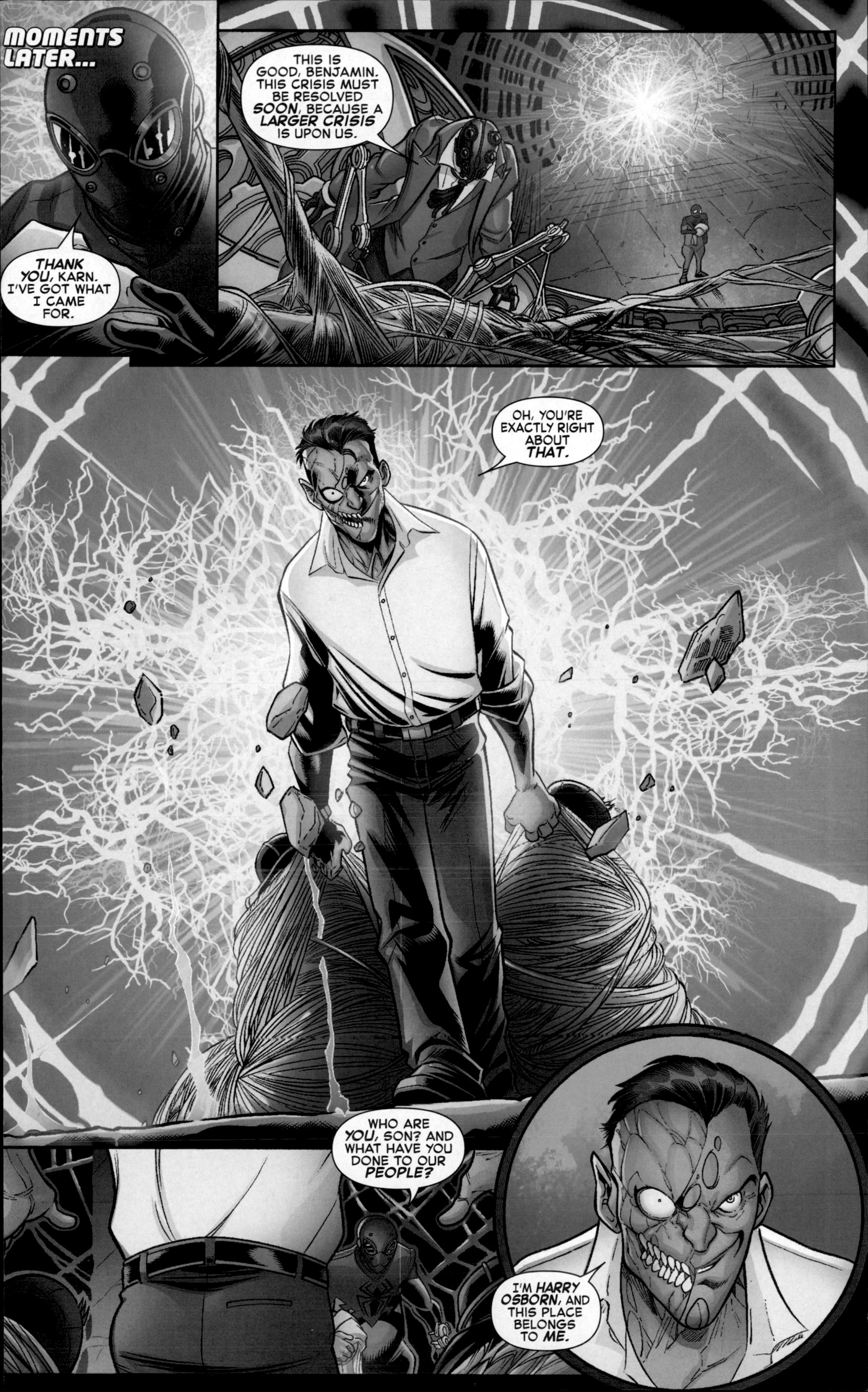
MOMENTS LATER...
THIS IS GOOD, BENJAMIN. THIS CRISIS MUST BE RESOLVED SOON, BECAUSE A LARGER CRISIS IS UPON US.
THANK YOU, KARN. I'VE GOT WHAT I CAME FOR.
OH, YOU'RE EXACTLY RIGHT ABOUT THAT.
WHO ARE YOU, SON? AND WHAT HAVE YOU DONE TO OUR PEOPLE?
I'M HARRY OSBORN, AND THIS PLACE BELONGS TO ME.

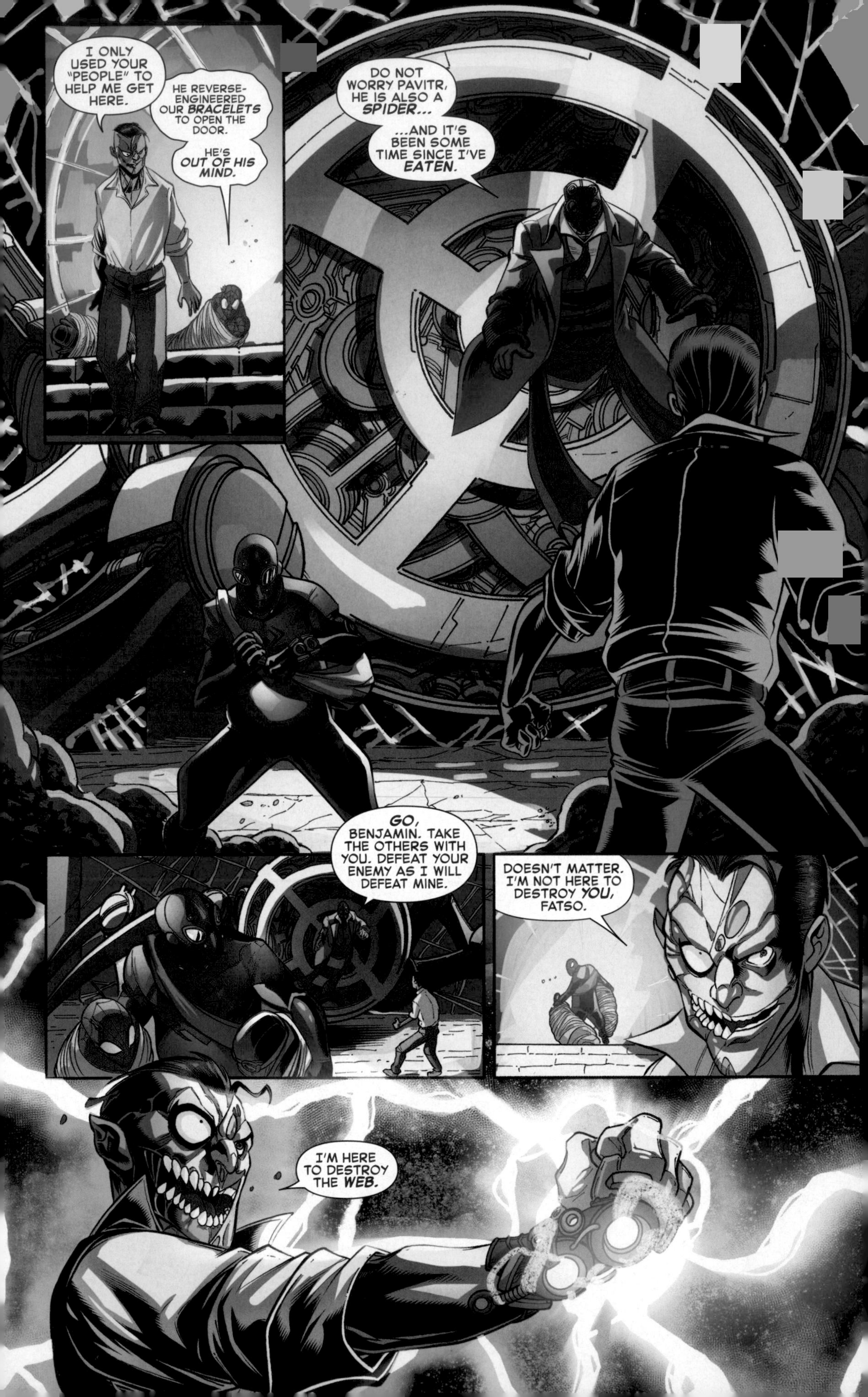
I ONLY USED YOUR "PEOPLE" TO HELP ME GET HERE.
HE REVERSE-ENGINEERED OUR BRACELETS TO OPEN THE DOOR.
HE'S OUT OF HIS MIND.
DO NOT WORRY PAVITR, HE IS ALSO A SPIDER...
...AND IT'S BEEN SOME TIME SINCE I'VE EATEN.
GO, BENJAMIN. TAKE THE OTHERS WITH YOU. DEFEAT YOUR ENEMY AS I WILL DEFEAT MINE.
DOESN'T MATTER. I'M NOT HERE TO DESTROY YOU, FATSO.
...
I'M HERE TO DESTROY THE WEB.

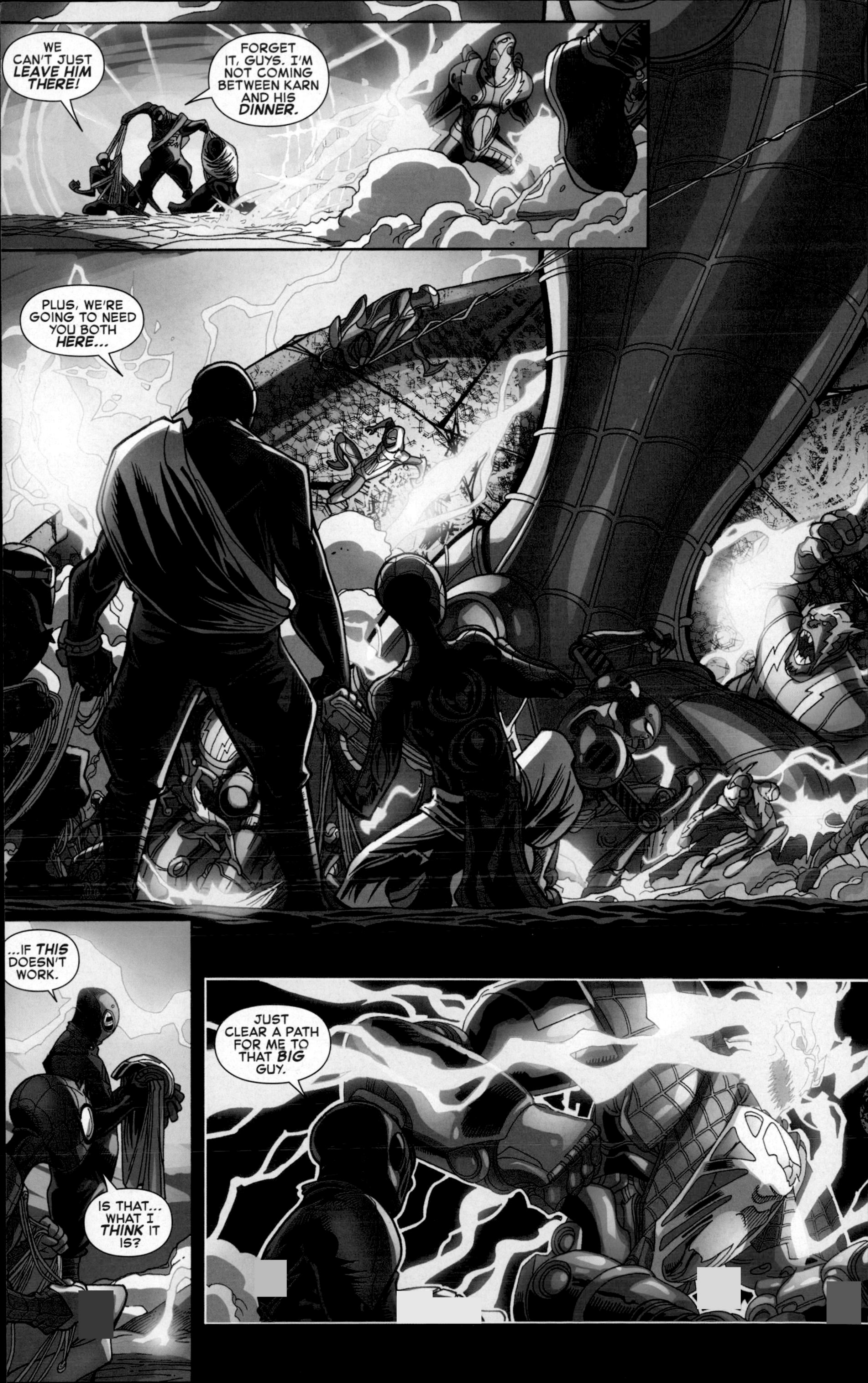
WE CAN'T JUST LEAVE HIM THERE!
FORGET IT, GUYS. I'M NOT COMING BETWEEN KARN AND HIS DINNER.
PLUS, WE'RE GOING TO NEED YOU BOTH HERE...
...IF THIS DOESN'T WORK.
IS THAT... WHAT I THINK IT IS?
JUST CLEAR A PATH FOR ME TO THAT BIG GUY.

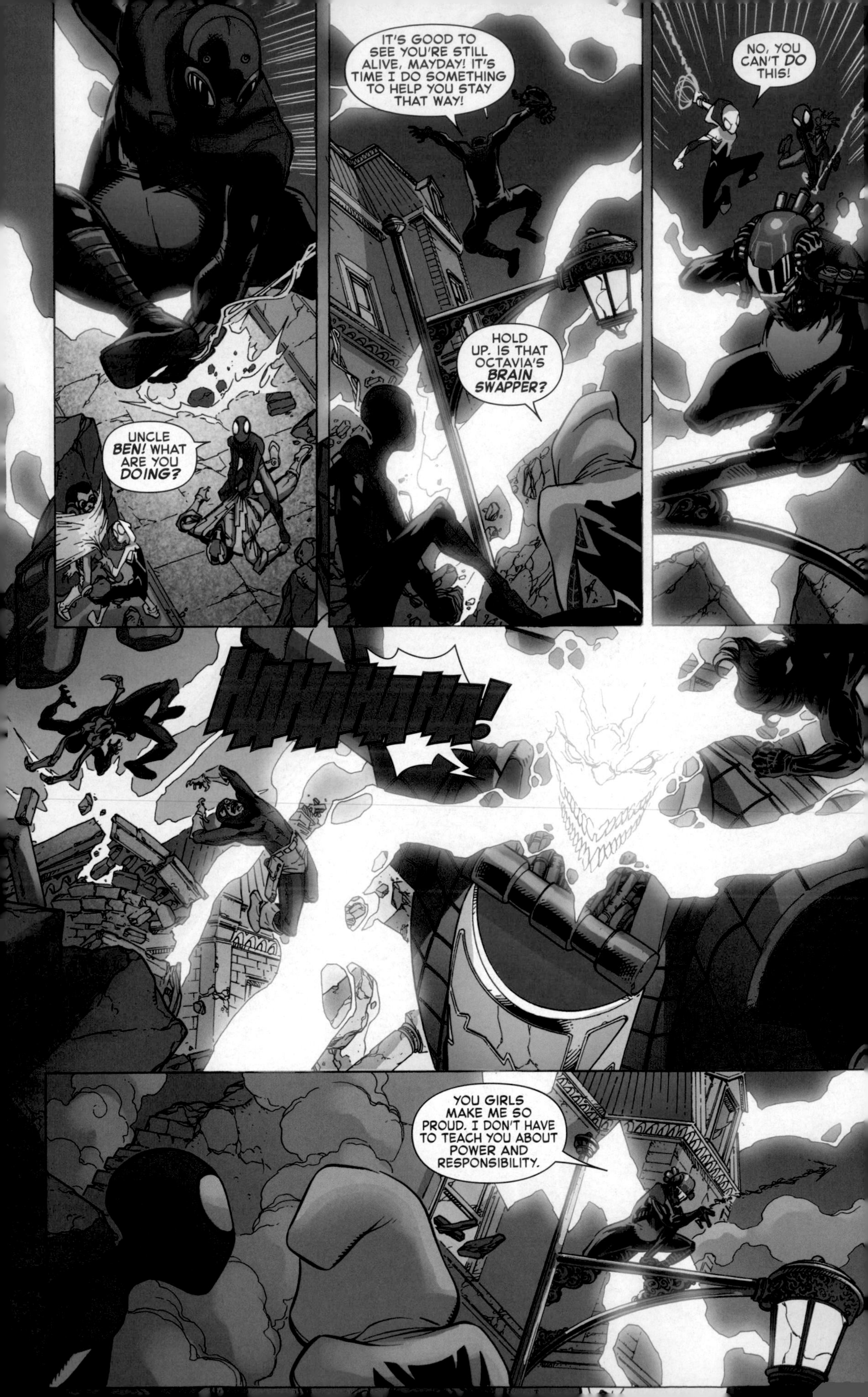
UNCLE BEN! WHAT ARE YOU DOING?
IT'S GOOD TO SEE YOU'RE STILL ALIVE, MAYDAY! IT'S TIME I DO SOMETHING TO HELP YOU STAY THAT WAY!
HOLD UP. IS THAT OCTAVIA'S BRAIN SWAPPER?
NO, YOU CAN'T DO THIS!
HAHAHAHAHA!
YOU GIRLS MAKE ME SO PROUD. I DON'T HAVE TO TEACH YOU ABOUT POWER AND RESPONSIBILITY.

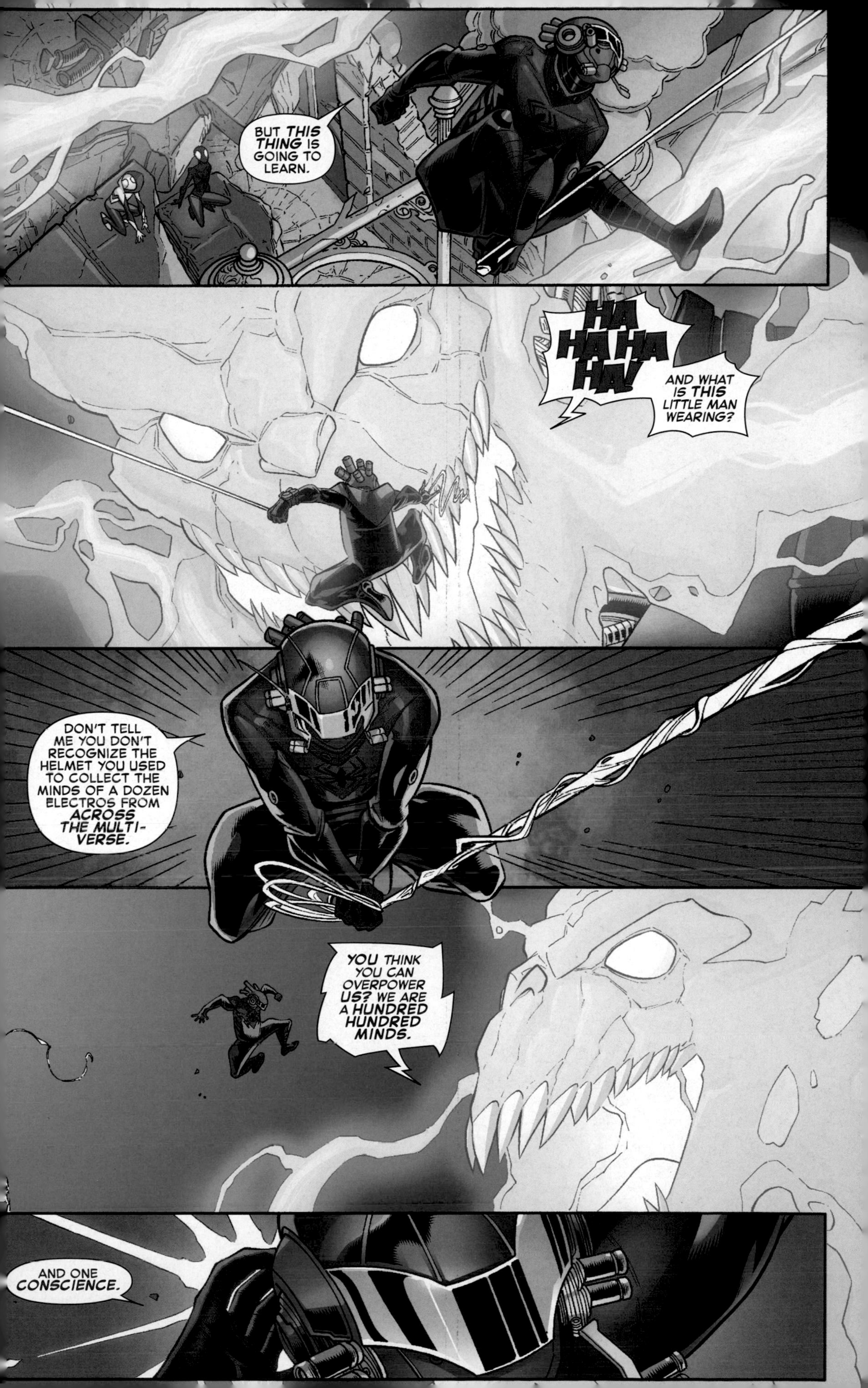
BUT THIS THING IS GOING TO LEARN.
HA HA HA HA HA!
AND WHAT IS THIS LITTLE MAN WEARING?
DON'T TELL ME YOU DON'T RECOGNIZE THE HELMET YOU USED TO COLLECT THE MINDS OF A DOZEN ELECTROS FROM ACROSS THE MULTI-VERSE.
YOU THINK YOU CAN OVERPOWER US? WE ARE A HUNDRED HUNDRED MINDS.
AND ONE CONSCIENCE.

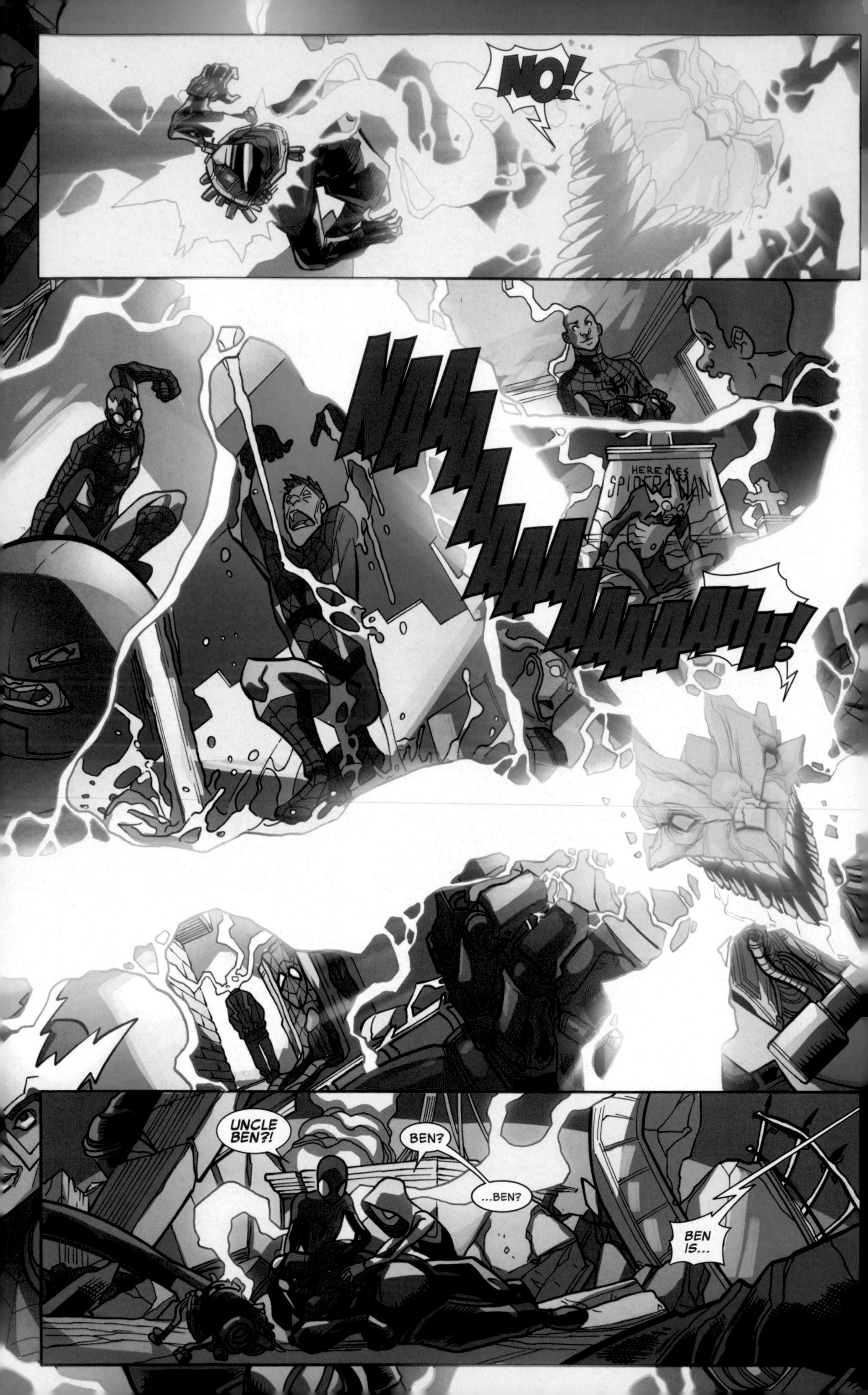
NO!
NAAAAAAAAAAAAAHH!
HERE LIES SPIDER-MAN
UNCLE BEN?!
BEN?
...BEN?
BEN IS...

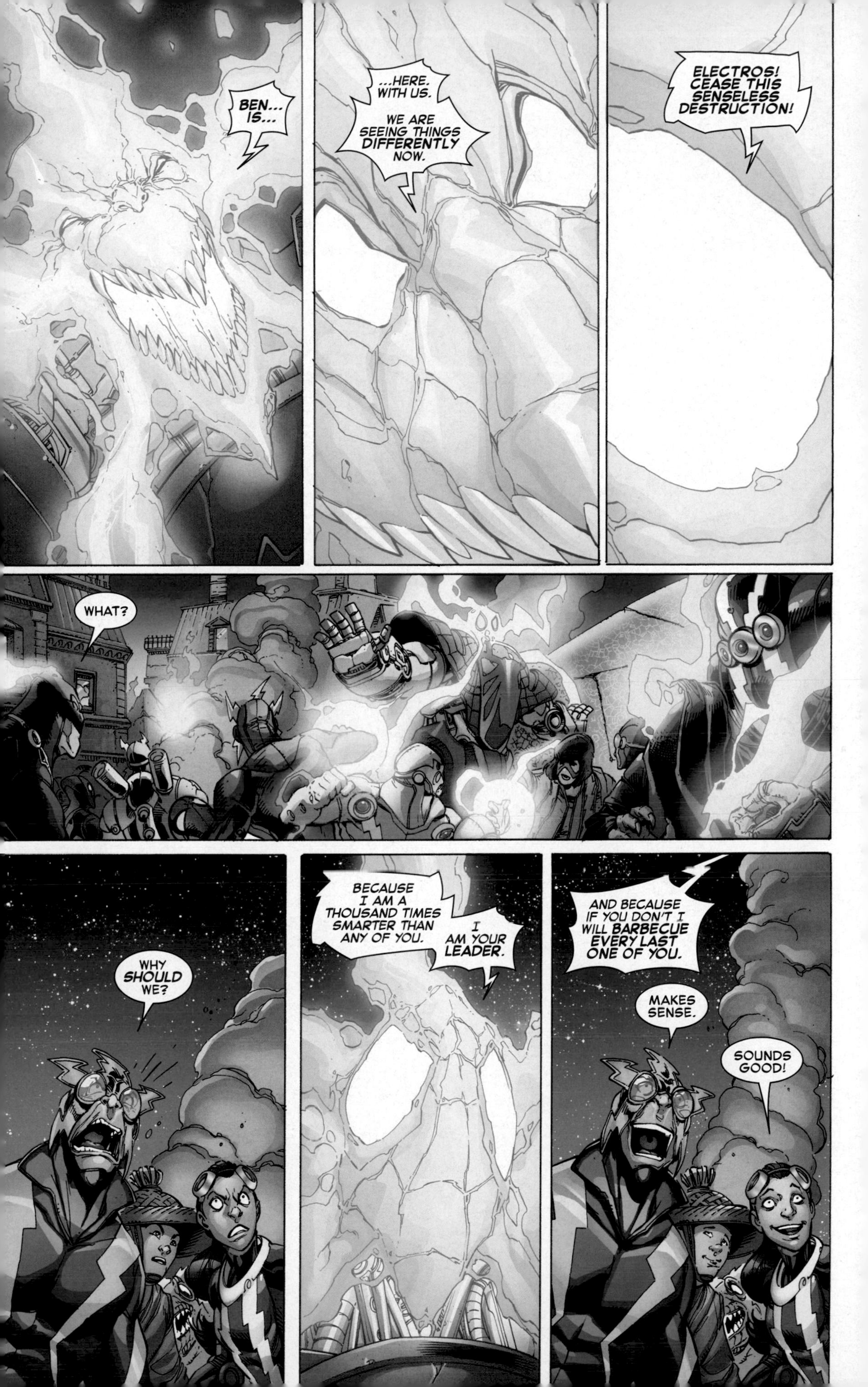
BEN... IS...
...HERE. WITH US.
WE ARE SEEING THINGS DIFFERENTLY NOW.
ELECTROS! CEASE THIS SENSELESS DESTRUCTION!
WHAT?
WHY SHOULD WE?
BECAUSE I AM A THOUSAND TIMES SMARTER THAN ANY OF YOU.
I AM YOUR LEADER.
AND BECAUSE IF YOU DON'T I WILL BARBECUE EVERY LAST ONE OF YOU.
MAKES SENSE.
SOUNDS GOOD!

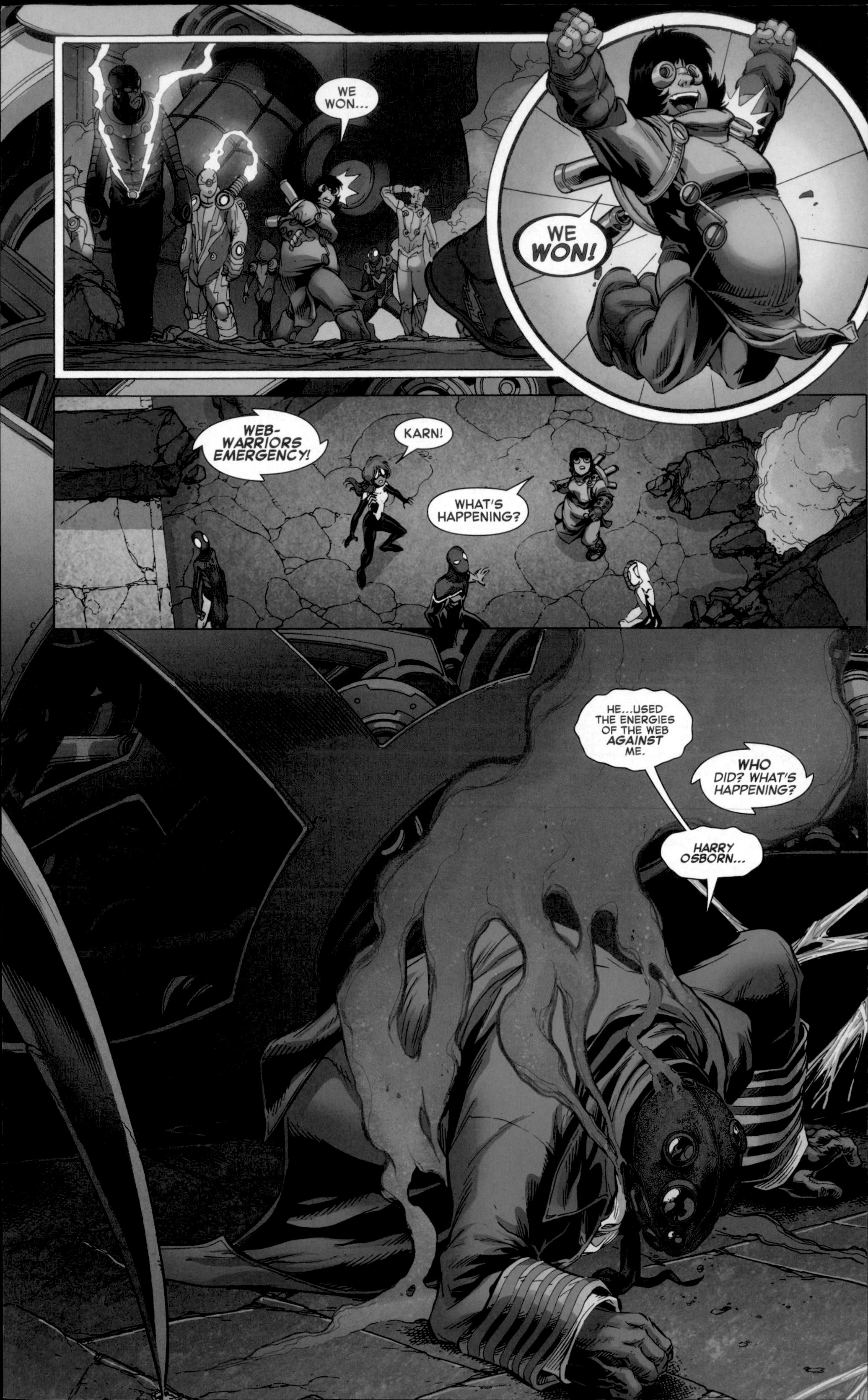
WE WON...
WE WON!
WEB-WARRIORS EMERGENCY!
KARN!
WHAT'S HAPPENING?
HE...USED THE ENERGIES OF THE WEB AGAINST ME.
WHO DID? WHAT'S HAPPENING?
HARRY OSBORN...

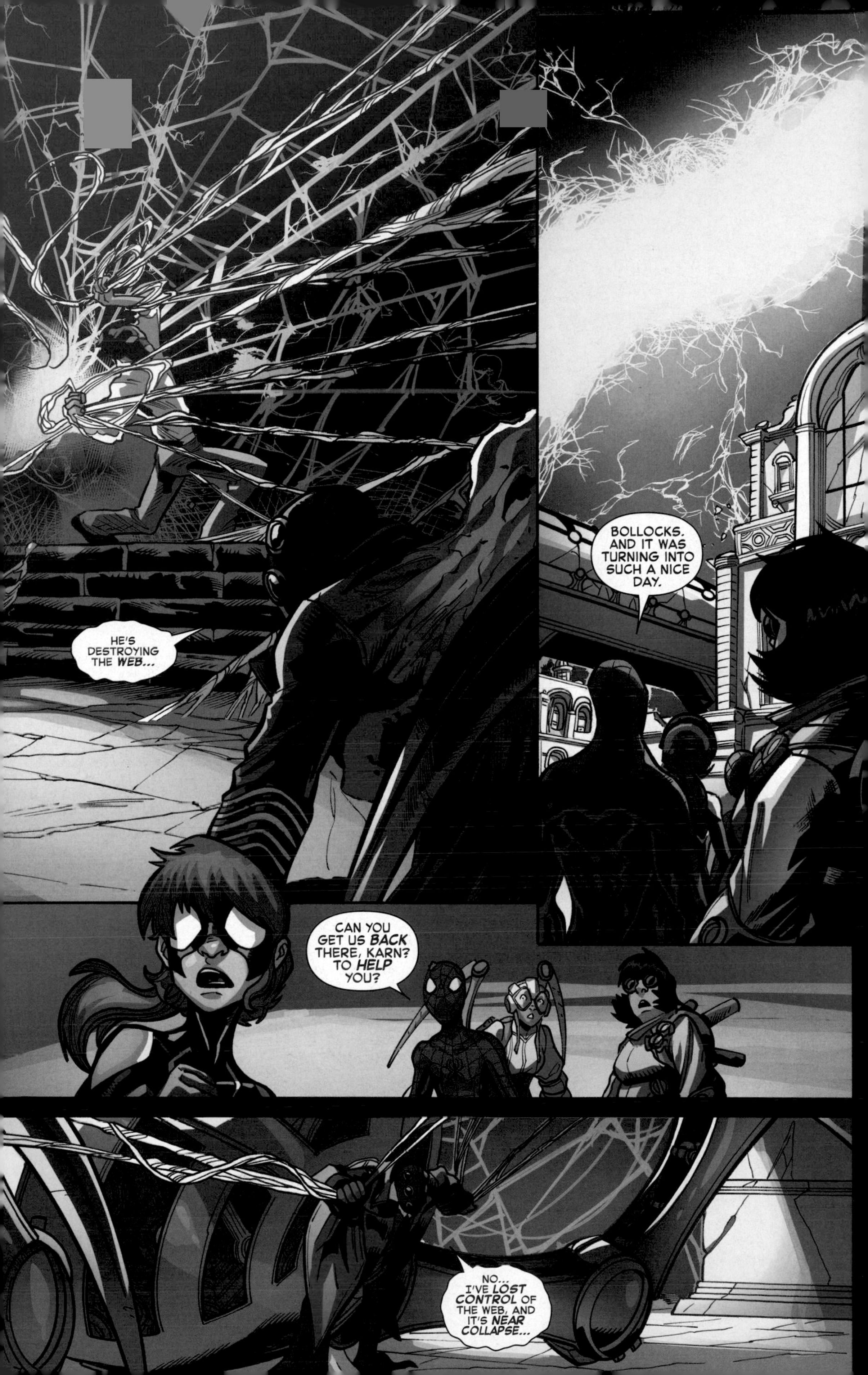
HE'S DESTROYING THE WEB...
BOLLOCKS. AND IT WAS TURNING INTO SUCH A NICE DAY.
CAN YOU GET US BACK THERE, KARN? TO HELP YOU?
NO... I'VE LOST CONTROL OF THE WEB, AND IT'S NEAR COLLAPSE...

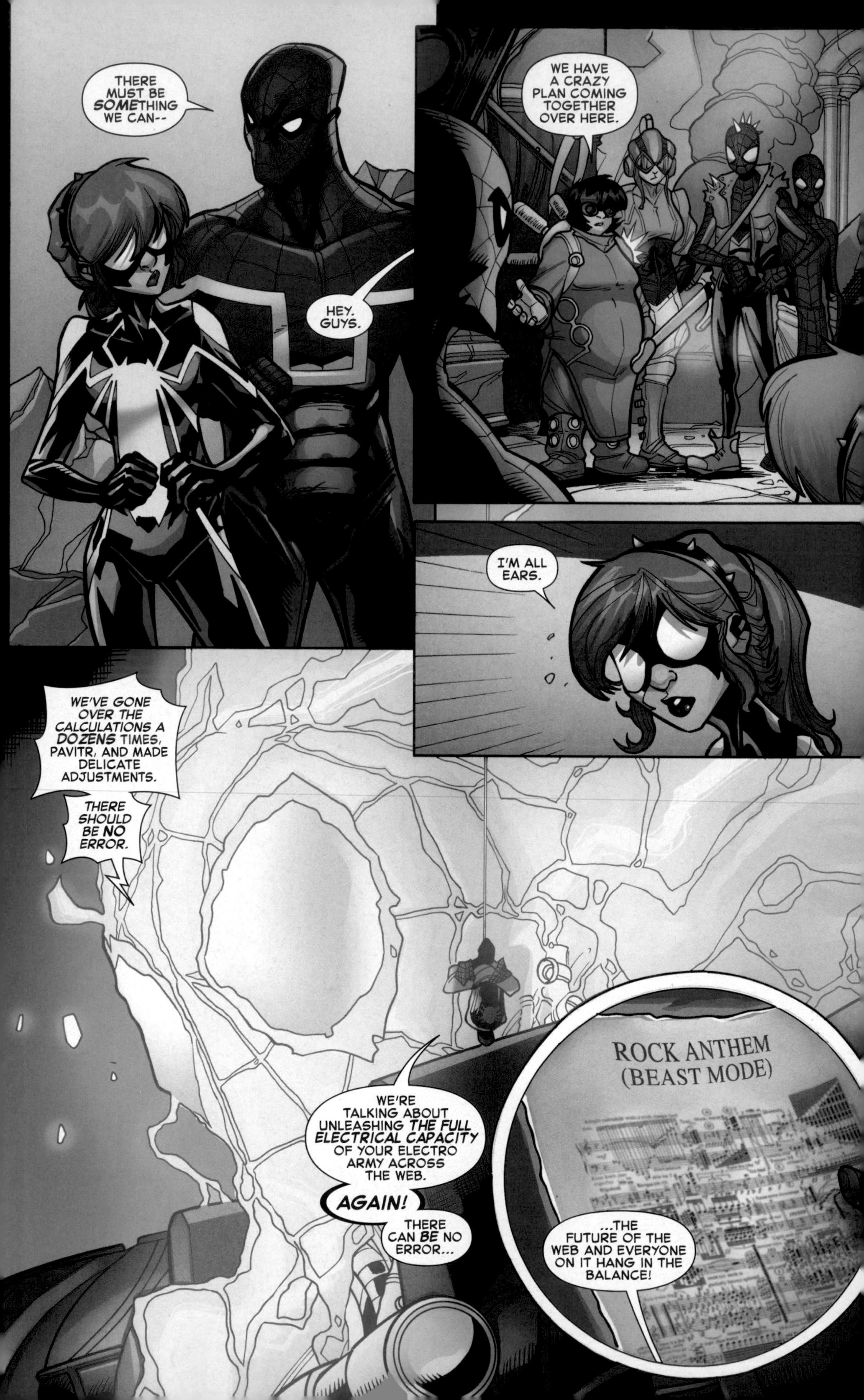
THERE MUST BE SOMETHING WE CAN--
HEY. GUYS.
WE HAVE A CRAZY PLAN COMING TOGETHER OVER HERE.
I'M ALL EARS.
WE'VE GONE OVER THE CALCULATIONS A DOZENS TIMES, PAVITR, AND MADE DELICATE ADJUSTMENTS.
THERE SHOULD BE NO ERROR.
WE'RE TALKING ABOUT UNLEASHING THE FULL ELECTRICAL CAPACITY OF YOUR ELECTRO ARMY ACROSS THE WEB.
AGAIN!
THERE CAN BE NO ERROR...
ROCK ANTHEM
(BEAST MODE)
...THE FUTURE OF THE WEB AND EVERYONE ON IT HANG IN THE BALANCE!

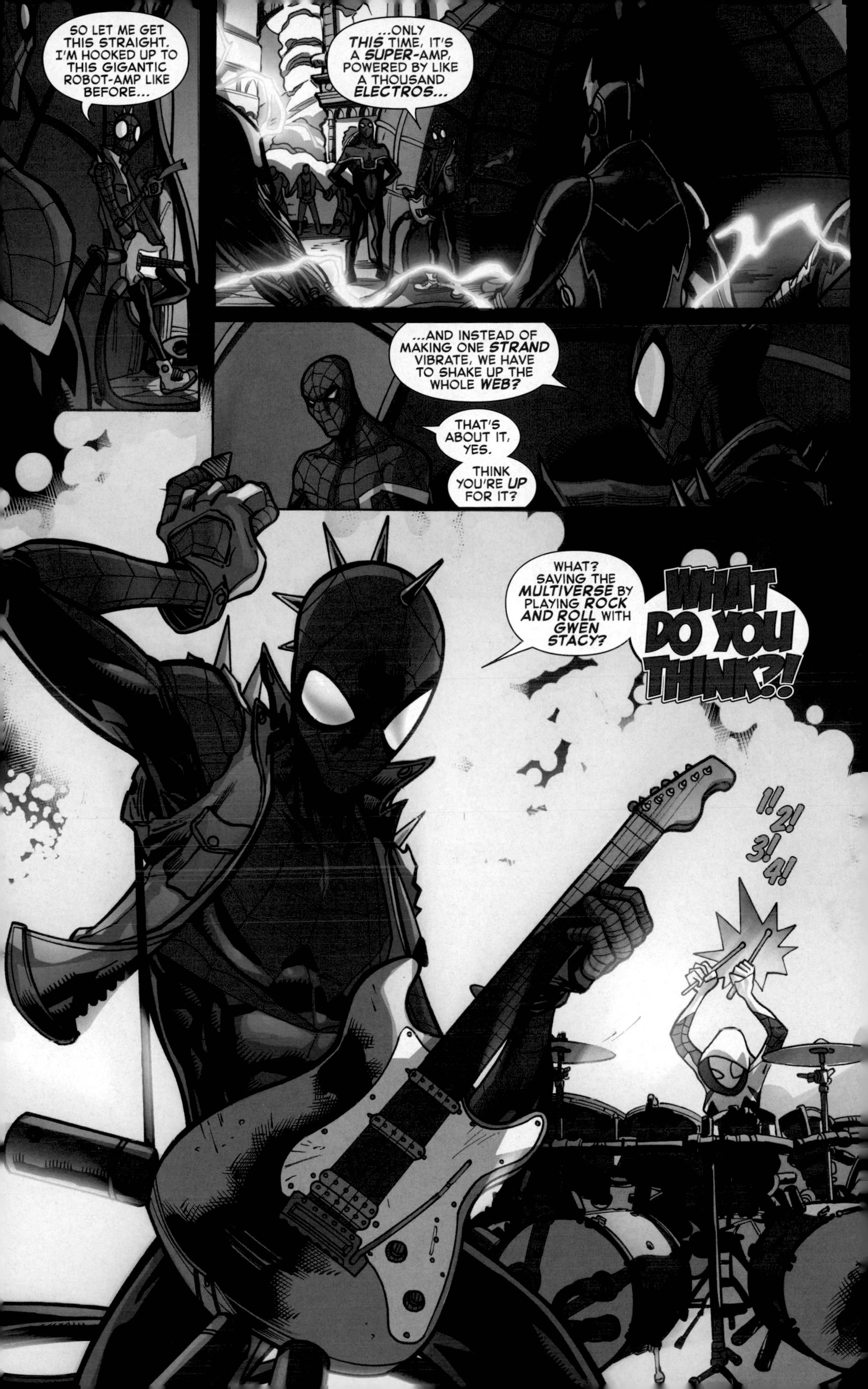
SO LET ME GET THIS STRAIGHT. I'M HOOKED UP TO THIS GIGANTIC ROBOT-AMP LIKE BEFORE...
...ONLY THIS TIME, IT'S A SUPER-AMP, POWERED BY LIKE A THOUSAND ELECTROS...
...AND INSTEAD OF MAKING ONE STRAND VIBRATE, WE HAVE TO SHAKE UP THE WHOLE WEB?
THAT'S ABOUT IT, YES.
THINK YOU'RE UP FOR IT?
WHAT? SAVING THE MULTIVERSE BY PLAYING ROCK AND ROLL WITH GWEN STACY?
WHAT DO YOU THINK?!
1! 2! 3! 4!

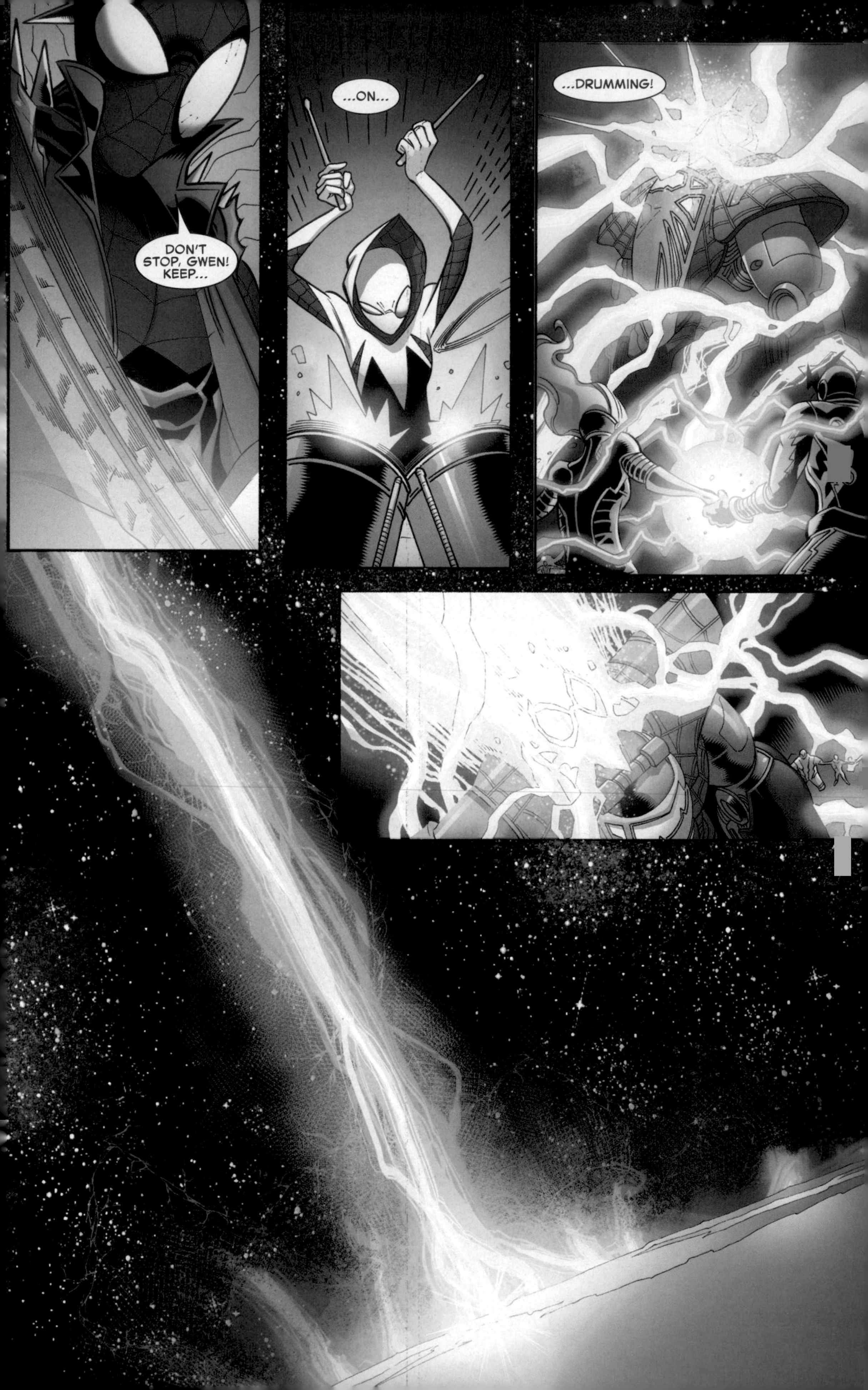
DON'T STOP, GWEN! KEEP...
...ON...
...DRUMMING!

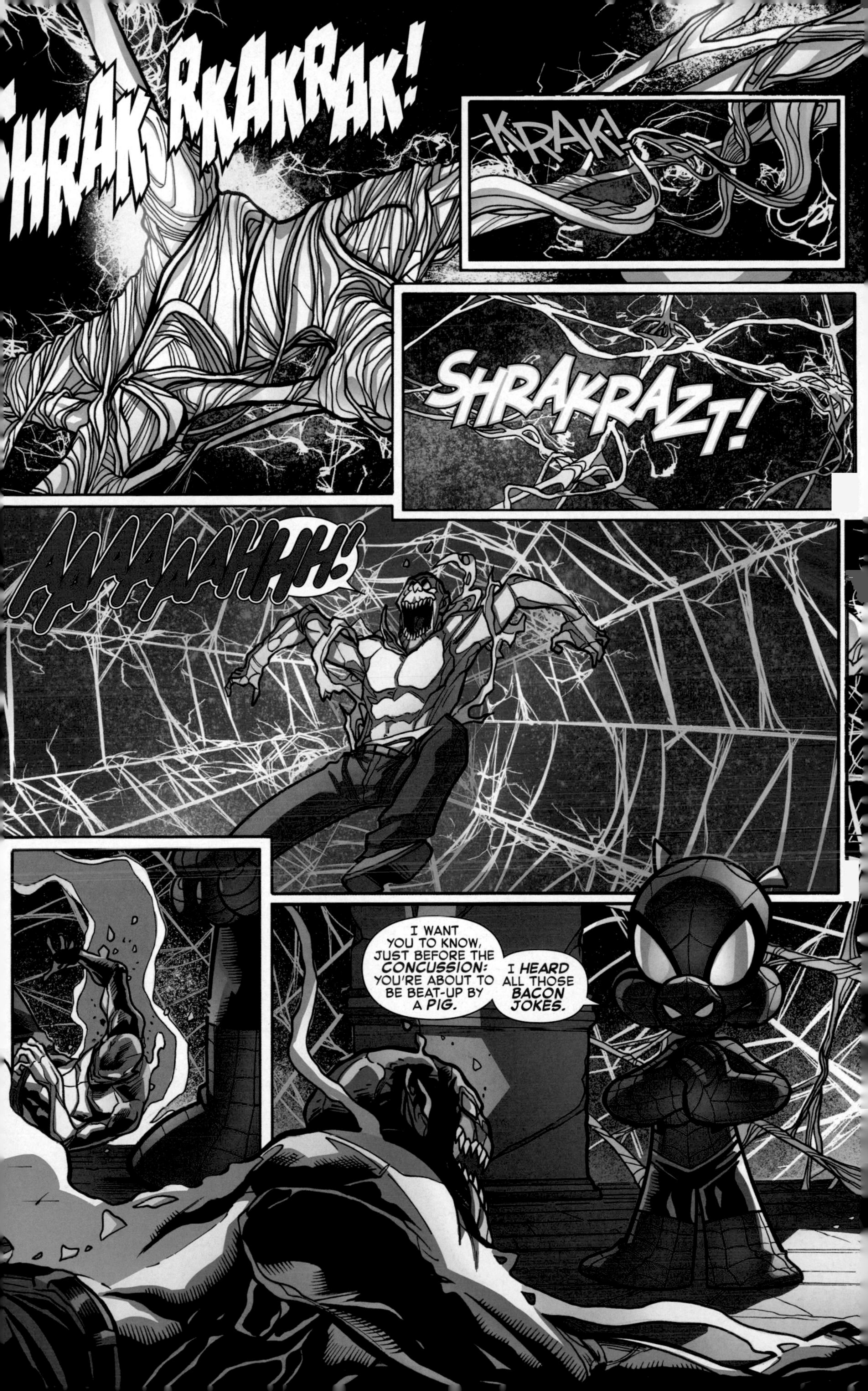
SHRAKRKAKRAK!
KRAK!
SHRAKRAZT!
AAAAAAHHH!
I WANT YOU TO KNOW, JUST BEFORE THE CONCUSSION: YOU'RE ABOUT TO BE BEAT-UP BY A PIG.
I HEARD ALL THOSE BACON JOKES.

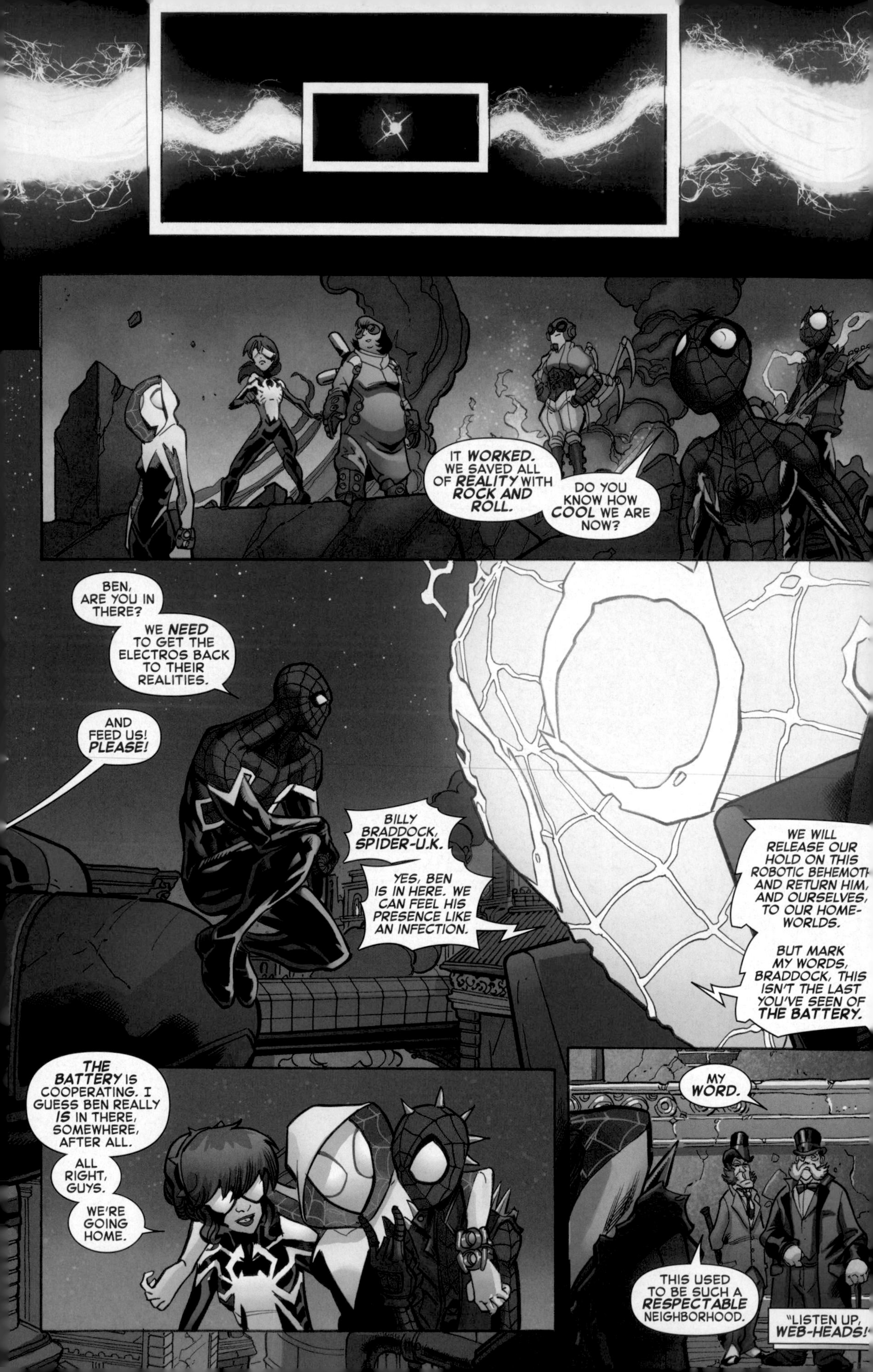
IT WORKED. WE SAVED ALL OF REALITY WITH ROCK AND ROLL.
DO YOU KNOW HOW COOL WE ARE NOW?
BEN, ARE YOU IN THERE?
WE NEED TO GET THE ELECTROS BACK TO THEIR REALITIES.
AND FEED US! PLEASE!
BILLY BRADDOCK, SPIDER-U.K.
YES, BEN IS IN HERE. WE CAN FEEL HIS PRESENCE LIKE AN INFECTION.
WE WILL RELEASE OUR HOLD ON THIS ROBOTIC BEHEMOTH AND RETURN HIM, AND OURSELVES, TO OUR HOME-WORLDS.
BUT MARK MY WORDS, BRADDOCK, THIS ISN'T THE LAST YOU'VE SEEN OF THE BATTERY.
THE BATTERY IS COOPERATING. I GUESS BEN REALLY IS IN THERE, SOMEWHERE, AFTER ALL.
ALL RIGHT, GUYS.
WE'RE GOING HOME.
MY WORD.
THIS USED TO BE SUCH A RESPECTABLE NEIGHBORHOOD.
"LISTEN UP, WEB-HEADS!"

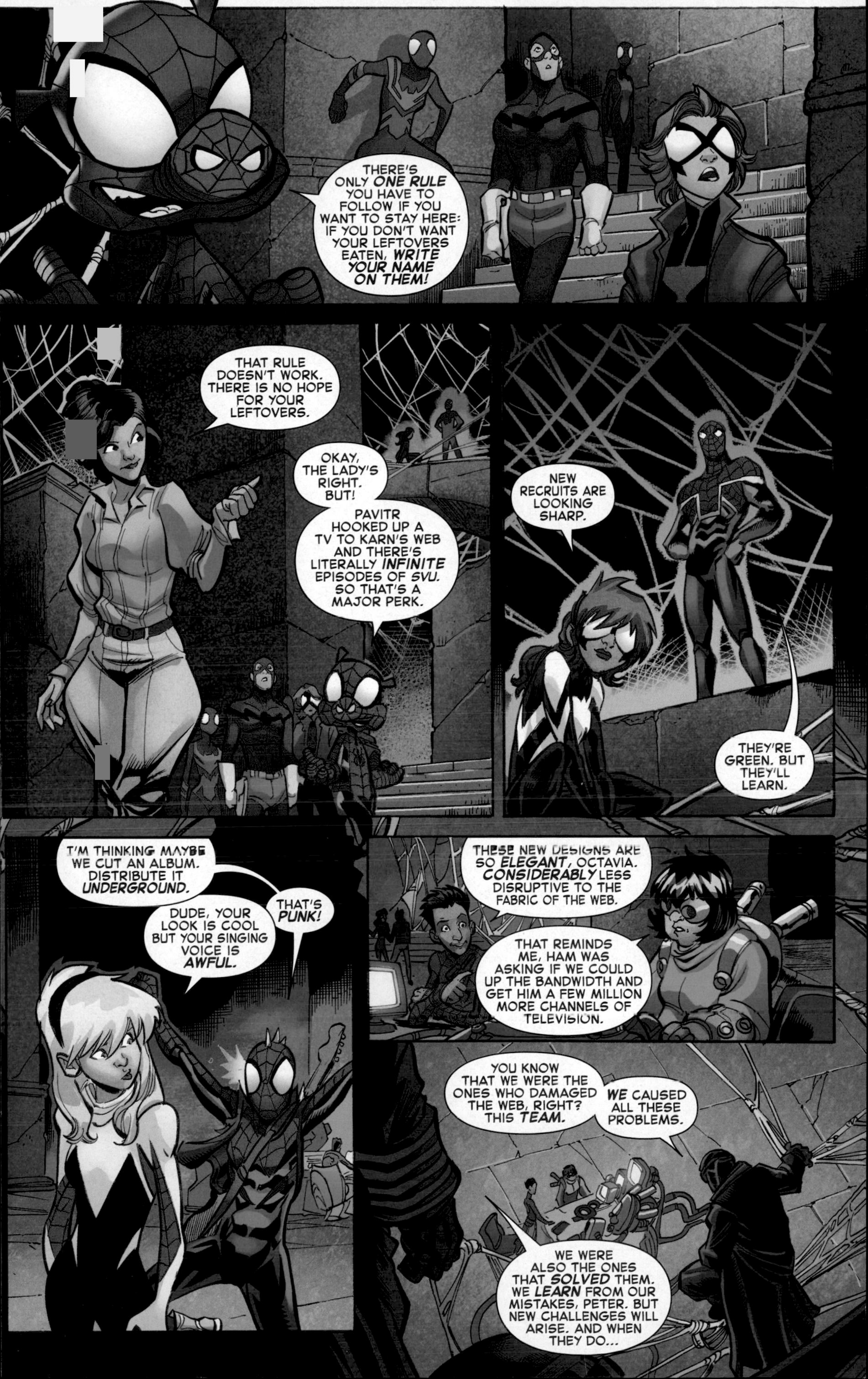
THERE'S ONLY ONE RULE YOU HAVE TO FOLLOW IF YOU WANT TO STAY HERE: IF YOU DON'T WANT YOUR LEFTOVERS EATEN, WRITE YOUR NAME ON THEM!
THAT RULE DOESN'T WORK. THERE IS NO HOPE FOR YOUR LEFTOVERS.
OKAY, THE LADY'S RIGHT. BUT!
PAVITR HOOKED UP A TV TO KARN'S WEB AND THERE'S LITERALLY INFINITE EPISODES OF SVU. SO THAT'S A MAJOR PERK.
NEW RECRUITS ARE LOOKING SHARP.
THEY'RE GREEN. BUT THEY'LL LEARN.
I'M THINKING MAYBE WE CUT AN ALBUM. DISTRIBUTE IT UNDERGROUND.
THAT'S PUNK!
DUDE, YOUR LOOK IS COOL BUT YOUR SINGING VOICE IS AWFUL.
THESE NEW DESIGNS ARE SO ELEGANT, OCTAVIA. CONSIDERABLY LESS DISRUPTIVE TO THE FABRIC OF THE WEB.
THAT REMINDS ME, HAM WAS ASKING IF WE COULD UP THE BANDWIDTH AND GET HIM A FEW MILLION MORE CHANNELS OF TELEVISION.
YOU KNOW THAT WE WERE THE ONES WHO DAMAGED THE WEB, RIGHT? THIS TEAM.
WE CAUSED ALL THESE PROBLEMS.
WE WERE ALSO THE ONES THAT SOLVED THEM. WE LEARN FROM OUR MISTAKES, PETER. BUT NEW CHALLENGES WILL ARISE. AND WHEN THEY DO...

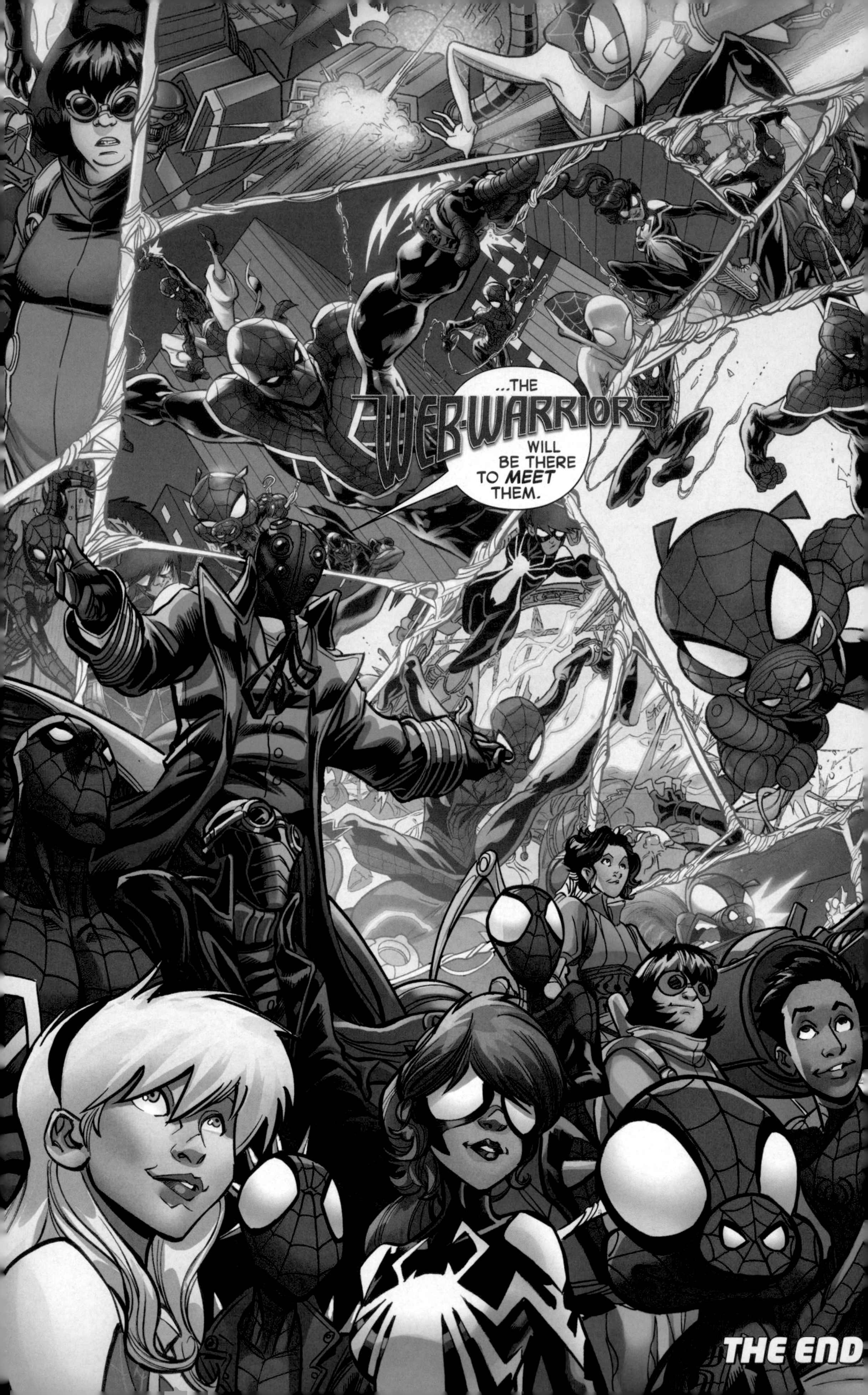
...THE WEB-WARRIORS WILL BE THERE TO MEET THEM.
THE END

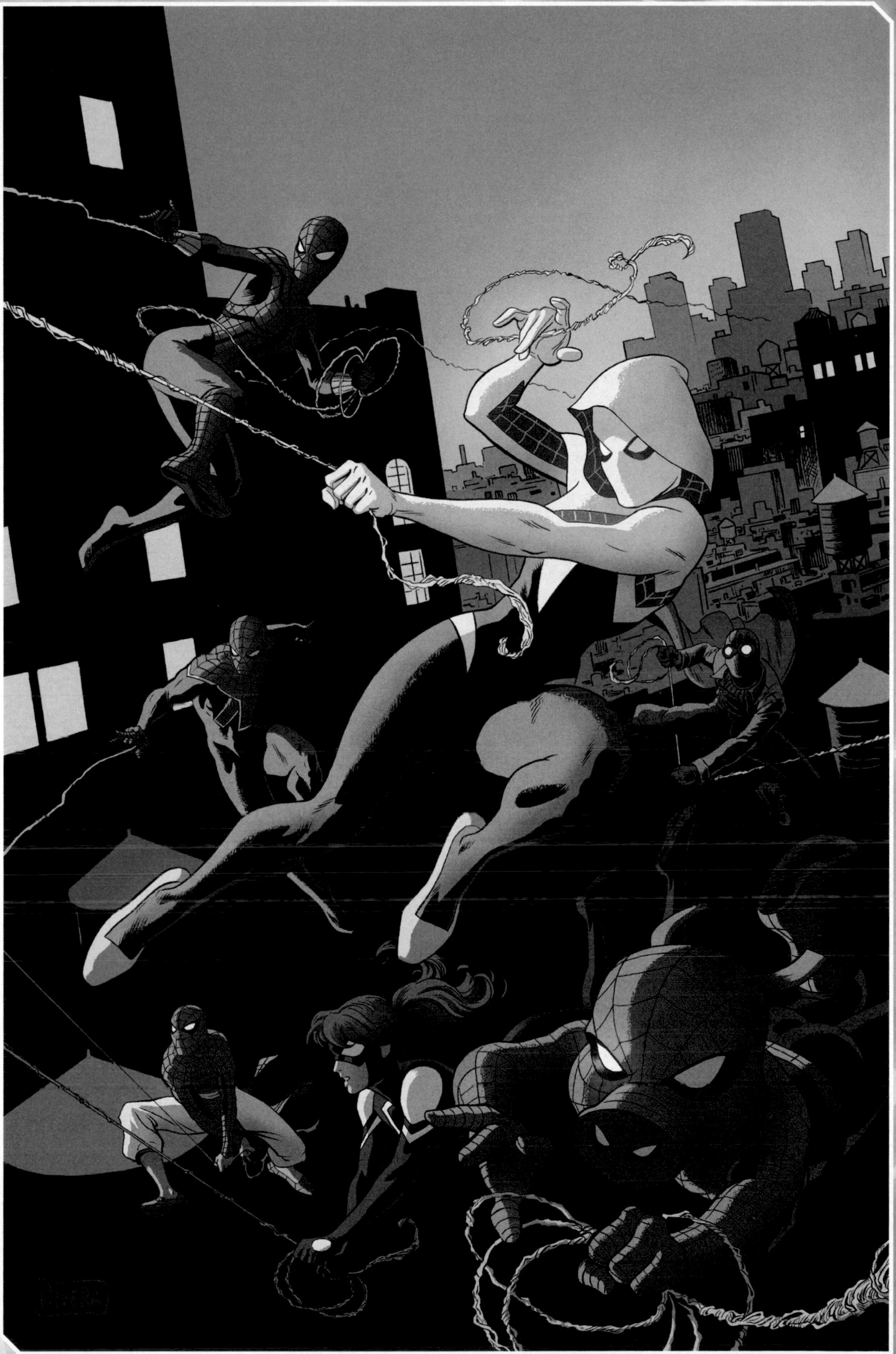

#11 VARIANT BY PAOLO RIVERA

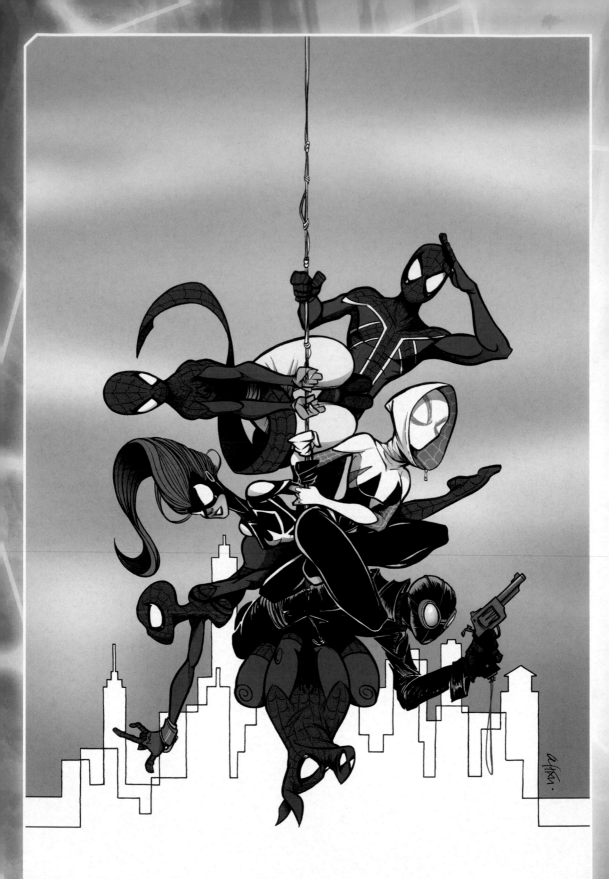

#11 VARIANT BY GUSTAVO DUARTE

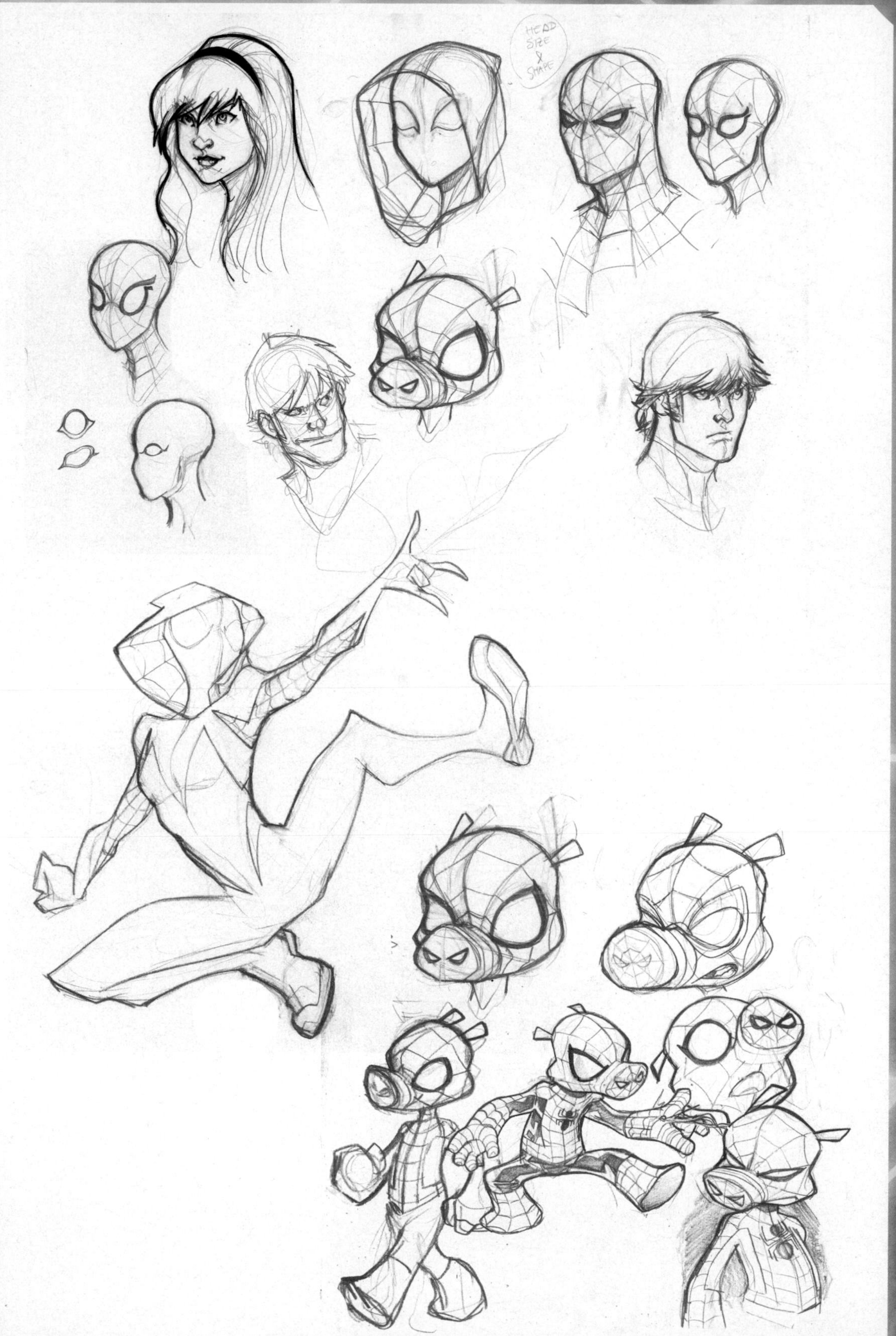
HEAD SIZE & SHAPE

CHARACTER SKETCHES BY DAVID BALDEON

#10, PAGE 1 ART PROCESS BY DAVID BALDEON, WALDEN WONG & MATT YACKEY

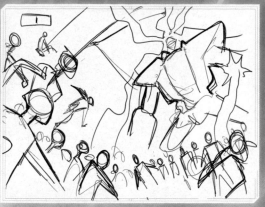

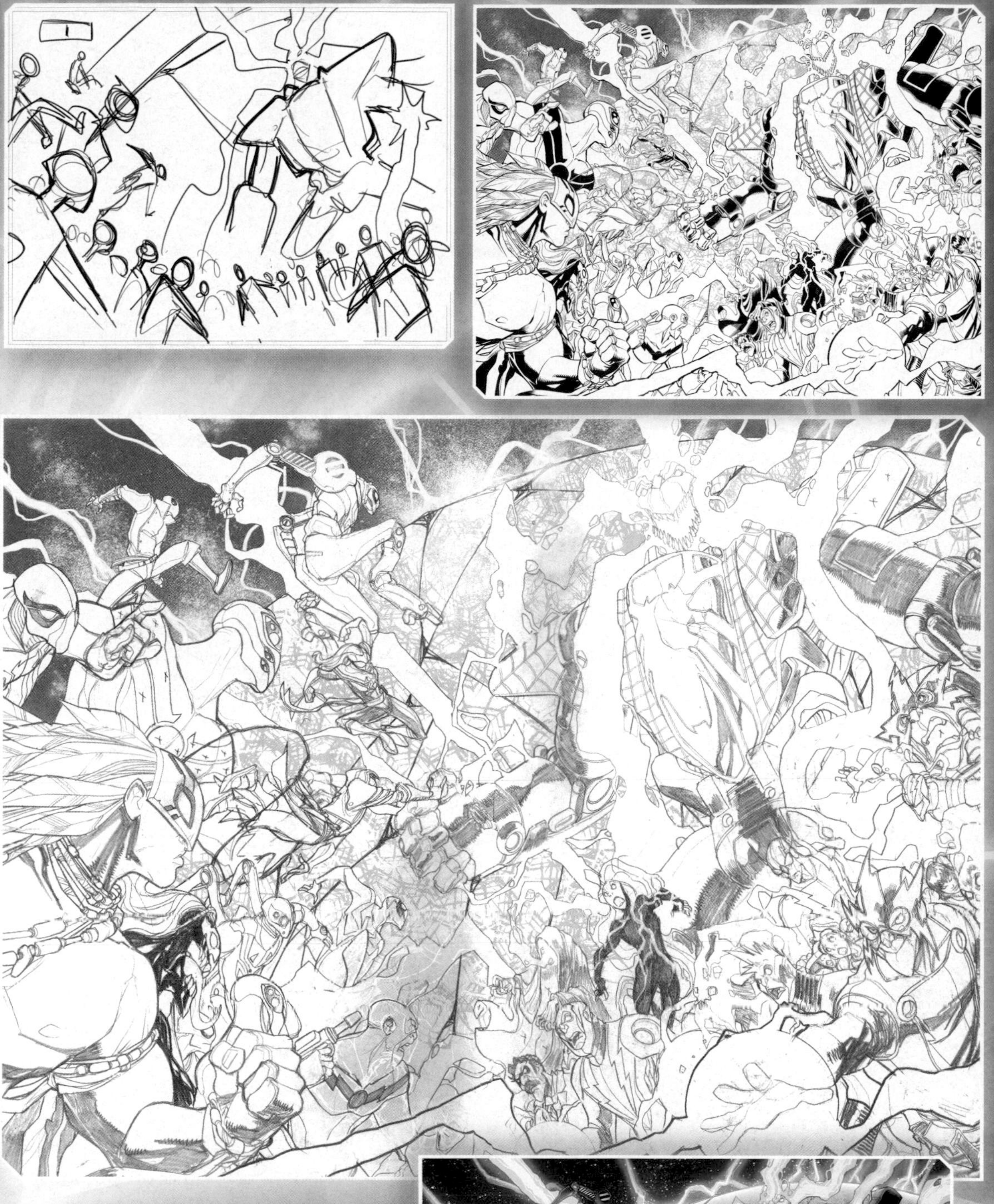

#11, PAGES 2-3 ART BY DAVID BALDEON, SCOTT HANNA & MATT YACKEY

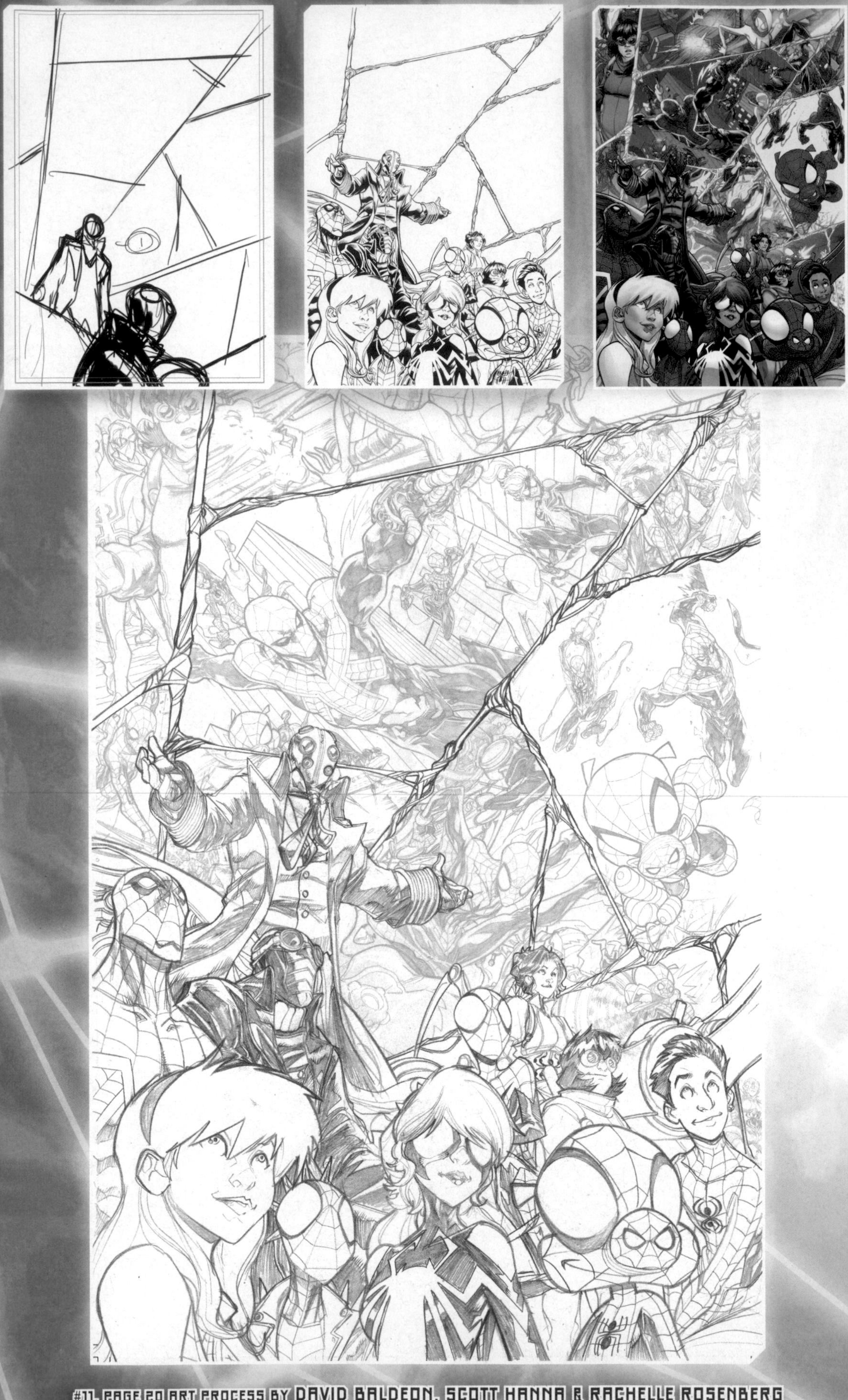

#11, PAGE 20 ART PROCESS BY DAVID BALDEON, SCOTT HANNA & RACHELLE ROSENBERG